Dear America, I'm Still Rooting For You

Commentaries on Race, Politics, & Feminism

Dear America, I'm Still Rooting For You

Commentaries on Race, Politics, & Feminism

HANNAH L. DRAKE

Drake Publishing

Dear America, I'm Still Rooting For You
Commentaries on Race, Politics, & Feminism

Copyright ©2018 by Hannah L. Drake
Published by Drake Publishing
ISBN-13: 978-0997299205
ISBN-10: 0997299207

Printed in the United States of America.

Author Photo: Ebony Campbell

To

Brianna and Cleanna

Because I am trying to leave the world a better place...

Contents

I write for those women who do not speak, for those who do not have a voice because they were so terrified, because we are taught to respect fear more than ourselves. We've been taught that silence would save us, but it won't. – Audre Lorde

To be a Negro in this country and to be relatively conscious is to be in a rage almost all the time."

— James Baldwin

Becky, Uggs Boots and Pink Pussy Cat Hats

While many are celebrating the Women's March On Washington that happened January 21 2017, I sat on my couch staring at the TV feeling more irritated than inspired. I watched crowds of thousands, overjoyed that finally the message of racism, sexism, homophobia, and any other ism was finally being spread to the masses. The rally cry of, "Our rights are under attack", was the theme of the day. I wondered as I turned off the TV, 'where had these women been'? And then this picture came across my social media feed and it summed up everything that I was feeling. A Black woman, Angela Peoples, stood with a sign that shouted the truth, that indeed the majority of White women voted for Trump, as three White women stood behind her, on their phones, taking selfies, as if they were asleep at the wheel. There it was. Everything that I was feeling. A Black woman hard at work to fight injustice and the White women asleep at the wheel or listening to someone give a speech that indeed we had shouted a million times before yet no one heard us.

I was not inspired. I was frustrated. I wanted to scream, WHERE WERE YOU?!

Where were you when we shouted about Sandra Bland dying on a jailhouse floor?
Where were you when we screamed for your husbands to stop fucking us and raping our daughters?
Where were you when Anita Hill was vilified for speaking up against sexual harassment?
Where were you when former officer and convicted rapist, Daniel Holtzclaw, raped Black women?
Where were you when we buried our sons and daughters?
Where were you when Dajerria Becton had a knee on her back and was assaulted by an officer?
Where were you when a young Black girl was thrown across a classroom?
Where were you when Alesia Thomas uttered, "I Can't Breathe", after getting kicked in the throat and groin in the back of a patrol car in 2012, before it became a slogan?
Where were you when we marched for Mike Brown and Trayvon Martin?
Where were you when we demanded that Black women MATTERED in this fight against police brutality?
Where were you when this nation sterilized Black, Native American and Puerto Rican women without their consent?
Where were you when Michelle Obama was called an ape, evil, ugly?
Where were you then?

Similar to the picture of Angela Peoples, you were on your proverbial phone. Resting in your comfort. Sleeping on your bed of privilege. Oblivious to our cries. Turned a deaf ear to our shouts. Until you woke up Wednesday, November 9, 2016 and Trump and his impending policies had stepped on your rose-colored glasses. Until it was your freedoms that were threatened. Until they were coming for your birth control. Until your choice of whether to have a child was in jeopardy. Until it suddenly became inconvenient to just be Becky with the good hair. Until then you were content. You were complacent. It was easy to just appropriate a culture with no connection or concern for the people. It is easy to play the part of Miley Cyrus twerking in your skinny jeans with no regard of the Mapouka dance done in the Ivory Coast of the Dabon. A dance done by our ancestors at religious ceremonies that were culturally respected because they specifically believed that the dance brings them into an encounter with God. It is safe to wear "boxer braids" because Kim Kardashian did with no concern about the origin and the symbolism of a people that were skilled in agriculture. A hair style traced back to warriors, queens and kings. It was easy to dance along to Beyoncé's Formation with no clue or desire to know the underlying message she was trying to get across. And it is easy to march alongside people struggling, staring at your cellphones, in UGG Boots, designer jackets and knitted pink pussy cat hats, taking selfies and curating hashtags for the memories. So, thanks for the memories.

Enjoy your Woodstock euphoria as you go home. Back to your lives. Your sanctuary. And for others the saga and struggle continue. We are here, as we have always been, and if indeed you are about that life, we welcome you for the long haul.

Licking Lollipops On the Way To the Abortion Clinic

Everywhere you look…Black, White, Young, Old they are there. Holding a memory as close to them as their next breath, afraid that if they exhale the secret they have kept will come tumbling out like skeletons from closets. For some, there is no shame, no guilt, for others they try not to think about it but in the stillness of the night, when the house no longer speaks, they remember. Try as they might some stories are just difficult to forget …

Such is my story. The day I found out I was pregnant with my second child I was filled with emotions. It had been just over a week with no signs of my period in sight and my breasts had taken on a life of their own. As a woman, you just know these things so seeing the lines on the pregnancy test were not a shock. Indeed, I had done everything "they" say you should do, just add baby and stir. I was married, had a decent paying job, healthcare, everything a pregnant woman should desire to bring a new life into this world. But I knew that I would be bringing a baby into chaos. My marriage was hanging on by a bent wing and a prayer. Already I was paying all the bills, physically I was tired and emotionally I was exhausted. Also, my daughter was already a teenager and I remembered the struggle of raising her on my own. The late nights, early mornings, never seeming to have enough of anything, the disconnect notices, the eviction, robbing both Peter and Paul to pay John with just a glimmer of hope in the distance. Yet somehow, we managed.

The most difficult days, I felt were behind me and now here I was, about to do it all over again, knowing deep on the inside, I would be alone and the thought of that struggle was insurmountable. Not again. Never again. Babies don't save marriages and even if they did this one was beyond repair. Then the accusations came. He asked me, "How did you end up pregnant after all this time," as if sleeping with his wife every night and his wife becoming pregnant was an enigma to him? I had just returned from being out of town and because of the turmoil in our relationship, he felt that perhaps I had cheated and gotten pregnant. I sat on the bed in shock. This was the nail in the coffin. Baby or not, I knew I would never look at him the same again. I had been faithful my entire marriage, offered more than I was ever given, even now offering his child, our child and that was not enough. His words were a slap in my face.

At that moment I knew our marriage was over. The next day, I made the call to the abortion clinic. They asked me how many weeks I was and I had to think back to when I felt my body changing, attempting to do backward mathematics in my head while a million other thoughts ran through my mind. Was I going to hell? Was I a murderer? Would I be able to forgive myself? Was I selfish? Couldn't I just suck this up and deal with it?

I made my appointment. My arrival time I believe was 7 a.m. My husband knew where I was going. He didn't come with me. Remaining true to how he had been our entire marriage, I was left to make this trip alone. Perhaps some part of me wished he would stop me. Tell me that he loved me and we would make our marriage work. That didn't happen. I climbed in my car, driving through the streets as tears streamed down my face, as I pulled up to the clinic. And that is when I saw them. The people, faces in odd contortions, screaming as they held grotesque pictures of aborted fetuses and signs scribbled on cardboard that I was going to hell. I was a religious woman, I loved God yet I never knew there were so many scriptures in the Bible to condemn me. I didn't need to read their signs. There was no need to tell me that I was going to hell, the inside of my car felt like an inferno. I pulled around the corner and heard the chants all jumbled together, I couldn't make out what they were saying. I could hardly see through the tears that spilled from my eyes and down my cheeks. I saw young ladies fighting through the crowd, racing to the arms of women with yellow vests on, escorting them inside the building. An escort banged on my window and shouted, "Do you need to be escorted inside?" My fingers gripped the steering wheel. It was all too much—the pictures, the shouting, the crowd screaming. I drove away quickly, crying as I raced through the streets. I called my friend and she met me at a restaurant for breakfast. I needed to talk to someone. Let someone remind me that I was human again even though I felt like I was in this vacuum of confusion. I couldn't eat. Couldn't think. Could hardly breathe. The pictures of those babies kept flashing in my mind.

"I guess you are having a baby," she said trying to be encouraging.

"I guess," I managed to say in a whisper.

I wasn't happy with my decision. While ultimately it was my choice, I felt as if I was robbed of a fair choice. A choice without interruption. I felt forced into the decision. I didn't make a choice based on what was best for my family and me. I made a choice based on intimidation and fear. Life however is not without its irony. Less than a week later, in a bathroom at work, I miscarried. There I was, once again alone as my child left my body and I went home to call my doctor with panties filled with blood and unrecognizable fetal tissue.

When I see what is happening across this nation when it comes to women and their right to choose, I remember that lonely drive on my way to make a decision that would alter the course of my life. There was no celebration, no high-five's, no joy. The way men write, rewrite and disregard the laws already on the books concerning abortion make it appear as if women are licking lollipops, skipping to the abortion clinic. Believe me, abortion is not something a woman takes lightly. This is my body, my uterus, my womb, my life and my choice! There are days that go by and I do not think of the child I lost. But on some days, I still remember because forgetting is not an option. The memory is there, embedded in my being along with the memory of those contorted faces shouting outside an abortion clinic telling me that I was going to hell for my choice! When will women be allowed to make decisions for their bodies, their wombs without men in suits sitting in rooms to tell them how to feel, how to be, when to become a mother?

This story was the skeleton in my closet. Invisible baby bones that rattle and remind me why I fight for women to have a choice. Their choice.

Don't Show Me Your Pink Pussy Cat Hat, Just Let Me Cry

Hearing the loud announcements of gate changes in the JFK, New York airport made my heart beat, thump, almost explode in my chest. I was home. Back in America. The land of the free. So why did I feel like I was in shackles? The entire trip I had longed for a Big Mac, hot, crispy fries with salt and a large Coke with ice. Yet walking slowly through the airport I found my tastebuds and my soul yearning for Poulet Yassa, a traditional chicken dish from the Casamance region of Senegal.

Senegal, where I had spent the last two weeks. Finally placing my feet on African soil, my land, my home, the place that I intimately yearned for. The place where everything made sense. I found myself there, pieces of my heritage scattered among the shores of the Atlantic Ocean. Senegal, where I felt free, liberated. Free to be me for two weeks—336 hours, 20,160 minutes, 1,209,600 seconds that I could just breathe. I didn't think about being Black. My skin no longer a barrier and at times in America a shield. I wasn't concerned about people following me in stores to determine if I was stealing. I didn't think about my hair, my vernacular, my style of dress. I didn't wonder if people understood me, even with the language barrier there was an undercurrent of understanding. Mutuality. "I see you, Sister." And then, as I left Goree Island, after standing in the doorway of The Door of No Return, running my fingertips along the rough concrete of the rooms where my people were held, weeping as I imagined the horrors that took place there, I made my way back to the boat to return to the mainland of Dakar. A man, dressed in full African garb said four words that I will never forget. "Welcome Back Home, Sister." I turned in shock, "What did you say?" I asked as I fought back the tears. "Welcome Back Home, Sister," he repeated. "Thank you," I managed to spill out of my mouth as I hugged him tightly. This was my home and I had made it back. I was born in America but Africa, indeed was my home.

Returning to America was not an easy feat. I felt like a stranger in a foreign land. The week I returned I didn't want to leave my house. I kept my blinds turned down, my curtains closed. I didn't want to walk back into my reality. A world where just 24 hours before I boarded a plane Philando Castile was murdered by a police officer and bled out on Facebook Live in front of the mother of his child and his daughter. A world where a young Black woman was tossed across a classroom like a rag doll. A world where Sandra Bland could be moving to a new state and end up dead on the floor of a jailhouse cell. A world where being Black just seemed to be criminalistic. I dreaded the thought of coming back.

Yet here I was and life is life so I had to return. On the day I came back to the office, Chris Strub was waiting to interview me about Smoketown- a predominately Black neighborhood in Louisville, Kentucky that is deep in the throes of gentrification. Sitting with Chris was everything I wanted to avoid. The reason I locked myself in my house reveling in my solitude. He was a White male and although I did not know his economic status, I ascertained he came from a life of comfort, perhaps not privilege but indeed comfort. Not today my mind was screaming. Quite frankly the last thing I wanted to do was spend my first day back in the office talking to a White male about Smoketown and the challenges of Smoketown. How could he even begin to understand systematic oppression? I was tired, discouraged and overwhelmed. Must every day be a fight when you are just trying to exist?

Chris and I sat at a table and he asked me about Smoketown and then he asked about the shootings that were taking place in America. I felt a lump in my throat. Not now. No. And I said, " Chris look, America has a problem with admitting its atrocities. There is no harm in saying, "This happened and I'm sorry." We can never begin to heal until we acknowledge what happened. It was not so long ago. This entire system is based on racism. It is based on oppression. It is based on them versus us. It is based on the have and the have-nots. It was built on our backs to keep us on our backs.

And I started crying. And I kept crying. Cried for all the police shootings and buried children. I cried for Sandra, and Aiyana. I cried for Trayvon and Mike. I cried for the blood running in the streets. I cried for my ancestors in Africa that was stuffed onto slaveships and brought to this land to endure a life of hell. I cried for those that hung from trees, that were killed senselessly. I cried for 4 little girls in Birmingham. I cried for all the suffering and hurt and pain. I cried for everything we lost. Everything that was stolen. I cried for what could have been. I cried wondering why we just couldn't have been left alone? It all came out, poured out in waves of tears and I said, "Sometimes people just need to hear, 'I'm sorry'". And he looked at me and said, "I don't know if this will help but I'm sorry." He didn't say anything else. We let the air, heavy with years of pain marinate between us. He didn't tell me that slavery was so long ago, get over it. He didn't attempt to tell me how his ancestors were enslaved too. He didn't attempt to justify the bullshit. He didn't tell me he would be marching at the next Black Lives Matter rally. He didn't tell me he made catchy signs for a march on Washington. He didn't ask me what do you want me to do? He didn't say, "Well I have Black friends." He didn't say, "Well that wasn't me that was them."

He didn't say anything.

He remained silent.

He just allowed me the space to cry.

And sometimes that is what we need.

Just let us cry. In peace.

Dear America, You Should Have Listened. Sincerely, A Black Woman

Everything you need to save this nation can be found in a Black woman. The mother of all civilization and creation. Black women are the epitome of grace under pressure, resilience, power, love and strength. Black women have always been at the forefront of a movement, under-girding a movement for liberation.

It was Harriet Tubman that reminded us how to deal with oppressors, "Never wound a snake, Kill it."

It was Ellen Craft, a slave, that used her privilege to pass to free herself and her husband and declared, "I have never had the slightest inclination whatever of returning to bondage."

It was Mamie Till, who allowed the world to see the horror of racism by allowing an open casket funeral for her son, Emmett Till.

It was Coretta Scott King that displayed silent strength as she sat veiled at her husband's funeral, poised and stoic as her daughter rested her head in her lap and knew that she would have to continue the fight for Civil Rights even though being in the fight made her a widow.

It was Betty Shabazz that showed the love of a mother as she grabbed her children and pushed them to the floor beneath a bench shielding them with her body as her husband Malcolm was assassinated.

It was Sojourner Truth that was a one-woman feminist movement declaring, "If the first woman God ever made was strong enough to turn the world upside down all alone, these women together ought to be able to turn it back, and get it right side up again!"

It was Phillis Wheatley that reminded us, "In every human beast, God has implanted a principle, which we call love of freedom; it is impatient of oppression, and pants for deliverance."

It was Fannie Lou Hamer that told us, "Nobody is free until everybody is free." She stood boldly in the face of injustice and said, "I guess if I'd had any sense, I'd have been a little scared - but what was the point of being scared? The only thing they could do was kill me, and it kinda seemed like they'd been trying to do that a little bit at a time since I could remember."

It was Diane Nash that reminded us that we are the leaders that we have been searching for. "Freedom, by definition, is people realizing that they are their own leaders."

It was Jo-Ann Robinson that was social media before social media was social media who created flyers to organize support for the Montgomery Bus Boycotts in 1955.

It was Assata Shakur that reminded us, "It is our duty to fight for our freedom. It is our duty to win. We much love each other and support each other. We have nothing to lose but our chains!"

Black women have always stood on the front lines and the sidelines. We have endured humiliation and embarrassment. We have stood naked on auction blocks and watched the world pick our bodies apart and put them on display. We were shamed for our appearance as this world made White women the standard for beauty, yet White men snuck into our quarters to rape us. We were humiliated for our skin color, lips and hip size yet this world built an empire trying to imitate what we were given naturally. We were subjected to playing wet nurse to your babies when we couldn't even be there for our own. We were the conductor on the railroad to freedom. We fried the chicken, made the cornbread and packed the lunches for marches so our people could have nourishment. We ironed the shirts and pressed the pants, kept a clean home and cooked dinner in between fighting off the KKK. We made the signs and provided slogans that would change the world. We sat at the counters all while they spit in our faces and poured milkshakes over our heads. We endured the bites of dogs and hits from billy clubs. We assisted this nation in exploring the universe yet couldn't even use the restroom in the very building we worked. We started movements that shook a nation. We stood backstage as the world demanded a man be center stage garnering credit for a movement. We buried our sons and our daughters too soon. We endured medical malpractice as the medical community used our bodies for Frankenstein research. We became the face of a movement fueled by our children's blood. We were pioneers for freedom. We stood up to the system. We organized. We prayed. We fought. We resisted. We sang songs that encouraged our people to rise up, to speak out, to stand up. We warned you, America that this day would indeed be coming because chickens always come home to roost.

Do not ask us to console you during this time. We are no longer your wet nurse, your mammy, your maid. Your head will no longer rest in our bosom. For years we have listened to the cries of our ancestors from just beneath the soil, we have watched our husbands swaying in the trees, we have buried our daughters and wept as our sons were gunned down in the street. Daily, in this world, we rest on a bed of despair, we awaken to false hope. We screamed for justice and you turned a deaf ear and blind eye to our plight. Do not call us because you now wonder about your sense of security, something we have never known. We do not have the time or the inclination to be concerned about your tears. Because even as we wept, no one was ever concerned about ours. This time, you must weep alone. We resign ourselves from being the shoulder that you need to cry on. Find your own hope. Search for it deeply. I suggest, looking in the mirror first. Perhaps there you will find the reason that you now weep. And when you see your reflection, look beyond yourself and see the pain, suffering, and acts of horror that have been inflicted on people that did you no harm, that wanted NOTHING from you, that just wanted the basic right to simply be human and to be left alone.

So perhaps where America should start is making right everything that it has done wrong. Until then, I stand on the words of Ms Celie, who said, "Until you do right by me, everything you even think about gonna fail!"

Sincerely,
A BLACK WOMAN

Dear Becky, Being Kinda Racist Is Like Being Kinda Pregnant

I awoke one morning to check my Facebook page and was greeted by Laura who took issue with my blog post, Dear America: You Should Have Listened. Sincerely, A Black Woman.

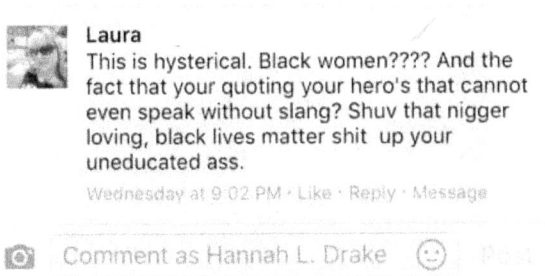

Laura
This is hysterical. Black women???? And the fact that your quoting your hero's that cannot even speak without slang? Shuv that nigger loving, black lives matter shit up your uneducated ass.
Wednesday at 9:02 PM · Like · Reply · Message

Comment as Hannah L. Drake

I am not above people disliking my blog posts. I am simply a Black woman with a pen, a notepad, a computer and an opinion. Not everyone has to agree with my opinion and in fact, I write with the inherent belief that many people will not. So to wake up and see her comments on my Facebook page, was intriguing. I was confused because the title of my blog was very clear, yet still she read it and was so moved to leave a racist comment.

And then the hits just kept on coming. Laura at this point is clearly big mad.

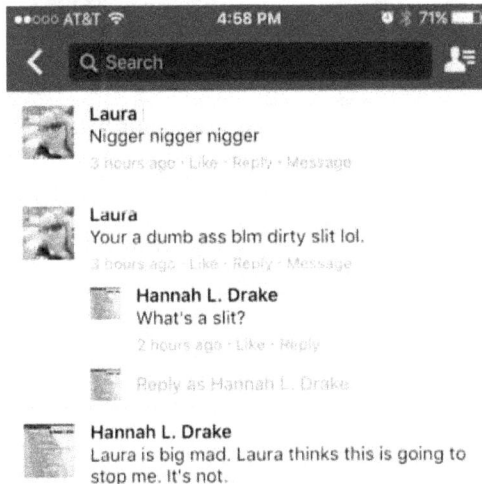

●●○○○ AT&T 🔗   4:58 PM   🔋 ⚡ 71% 🔋▶
‹   Q Search

Laura
Nigger nigger nigger
3 hours ago · Like · Reply · Message

Laura
Your a dumb ass blm dirty slit lol.
3 hours ago · Like · Reply · Message

Hannah L. Drake
What's a slit?
2 hours ago · Like · Reply

Reply as Hannah L. Drake

Hannah L. Drake
Laura is big mad. Laura thinks this is going to stop me. It's not.

I wanted to know who ~~Becky~~ Laura was and how our paths happened to intersect, so I viewed her Facebook page. She appeared to be a woman stuck in between two worlds. One, compassionate and understanding the other racist and xenophobic.

I understand the difficulty she finds herself in. It is hard to deny the truth. It is difficult for some to recognize genius, magnificence, Black in all its splendor. It is hard to set aside delusions you have about a people whose resilience and power are unstoppable. Every horror that could be done to Black people has been done and yet here we stand. Perhaps that is why Laura and many others are torn with their emotions and decide to drudge up the N word as if that is Kryptonite to Black people.

On the one hand, you hate us for simply being Black, yet on the other you celebrate Storm- an African American X-Men character. Storm, the daughter of a tribal princess from Kenya, born with superhuman abilities, fighting for peace and equality.

Indeed, Becky, today is the day that you have met your Storm, live and in color.

I understand the duality you must be facing. It is difficult to want to be racist yet still admire, cherish, covet, love, long for and benefit from so many things that are not of your race and culture.

You want to be racist but you love dancing to Single Ladies.

You want to be racist but you think Kevin Hart is hilarious.

You want to be racist but you love the full lips so many Black people possess.

You want to be racist but you want to tan to have darker skin.

You want to be racist but there is something that collard greens do for you that just doesn't cut it with a wedge salad.

You want to be racist but you can't help but notice how delectably fine Idris Elba is.
You want to be racist but you just can't understand how to kinda hate Black people yet kinda love everything about them.

Newsflash, Becky, there is no Racist Lite. "Give me a side of a Black person that passes the brown bag test, hold the darkies and I will take a side of their inventions and culture to go." Life does not work that way. Being kinda racist is like being kinda pregnant, you either are or you are not. Being racist is not something you can place in a box. Racism is like cancer, it invades your thoughts, your decisions, your very being.

Should you decide, Becky, that you would like to give up everything Black by all means, please do, and in doing so, revoke your privilege to peanut butter, the fold out bed, potato chips, riding on a train, shoes, the light bulb, blood transfusions, receiving your mail, the telephone, pacemakers, video games, cataract removal, any movie with 3-D special effects, super-soaker water guns, the refrigerator, birth control, the elevator, the microphone, the traffic signal, sugar, the cell phone, scooping ice cream, the dustpan, the squeeze mop, the clothes dryer, the ironing board, diamonds, paper, home security systems…The list of our contributions is endless.

We were here before time was time and we have minds that have changed the very course of your modern-day existence, Becky. Thank you, would have been sufficient. However, you were right in your photo assessment. We are superheroes. And every day we fight to bring the STORM! Consider this the rain!

Dear Ashley Judd, Every Time A Black Person Plays Sports It Is Political

Dear Ashly Judd,

I recently read your Facebook Post concerning you attending a University of Kentucky Basketball game and being confronted by a Trump supporter that told you, "We like Trump". As I read further you indicated that this exchange made you sad and frankly scared. You went on to suggest that college basketball should be a "no politics here" space. And that is where you lost me. There are two issues that you combine- sports and safe spaces- that must be addressed, especially the undertone of privilege.

I appreciate your feminist views and I appreciate that you stand up for those that are marginalized but this view is one written from an angle of pure White privilege. While I can understand you being sad and a little scared that someone told you, "We like Trump", many Black and Muslim people are being physically assaulted and killed simply based on the color of their skin or what people assume is their religion. My daughter attends the University of Kentucky, the very school for which you cheer and support. While she was protesting on campus, and being called the n-word, had things thrown at her, called a monkey and spat it, there was no safe space. After the election, she called me concerned and fearful about walking to class. There was no safe space. There is no hashtag that I can create that will make my daughter feel safe on campus in a Trump America.

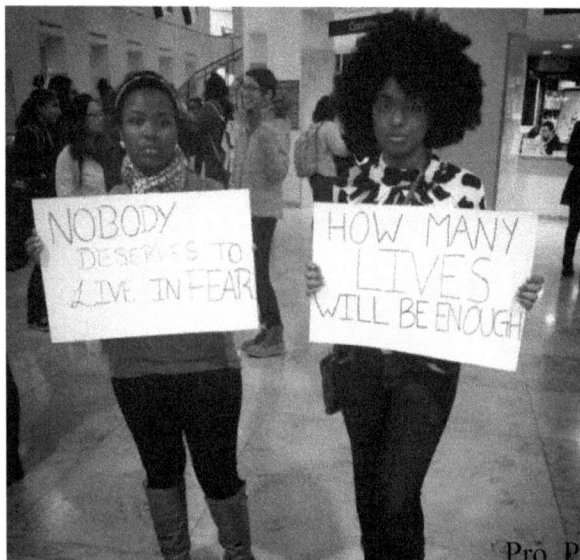

Photo 1 Diane Ishimwe & Brianna Wright University of Kentucky, BLM Protest

There is nowhere in this country that I can go and turn off my color. There is no hashtag I can create that will make Trump supporters not scream, "Go back to your country", before shooting and killing an innocent man in a bar. Tell me outside of college sports, what other areas do you suggest should be no politics spaces? The grocery store? The mall? The post office? There is nowhere that I can go that a hashtag will provide a safe space. Even my home is not safe as I wonder what my White neighbors with their Make America Great Again signs are wondering about me. Every day I come home wondering, "Is this the day, like so many others in America, I will find racial slurs spray painted across my home?"

Also, any time a Black person plays a sport, it will always be political. It seems the only time some White people can support a Black person is if they are playing a sport. It is a privilege to be able to simply watch a sports game and as you say, "root for the underdog, wait for the upsets, and believe our team can go all the way." However, when I watch sports I look beyond what is happening just within the game.

I recall Jesse Owens, who showed the world that Hitler's claim that White people were the dominant race was futile as he sprinted past ignorance and into history.

Let us not forget Tommie Smith and John Carlos, who raised the Black Power fist at the Olympics and stood on the podium as gold and bronze medalists, in solidarity with Black people around the world that were suffering under the weight of oppression.

Even our own Kentucky native Muhammad Ali, who defiantly tossed his Olympic gold medal in the Ohio River, after he was refused service in a White only restaurant.

Let's remember the backlash the greatest tennis player in the world, Serena Williams, received after defeating Maria Sharapova to win the Olympic Gold and breaking out into the Crip Walk. The world saw a dance. We saw us. We saw Serena dancing all over injustice in a sport that says she shouldn't be there.

Let us not forget the backlash some Black New England Patriots players faced for not agreeing to attend the White House meet and greet after their 2017 Super Bowl victory yet, for the most part White America was silent when the captain and quarterback, Tom Brady, did not visit when former President, Barack Obama was in office.

And of course, we cannot forget San Francisco 49er Colin Kaepernick, who boldly took a knee during the National Anthem for NFL games. Even as he was being vilified and ridiculed, Colin said, "I am not going to stand up to show pride in a flag for a country that oppresses black people and people of color. To me, this is bigger than football and it would be selfish on my part to look the other way. There are bodies in the street and people getting paid leave and getting away with murder."

The list is endless of Black sports players that have used their platform to bring awareness to the suffering, injustice and oppression of Black people. You may see a sport. We see beyond the sport. We see Black athletes that stand with us as we fight against injustice. We see Black athletes showing their prowess beating the system at their own game. We were delighted to see a Black man named Tiger Woods dominating in a sport that has been predominately White. We rejoiced for Dominique Dawes and Gabby Douglas because the world told them, "Some sports just ain't for your kind." We stood on our feet and clapped when Surya Bonaly did a backflip on the ice, even at the expense of being disqualified, because she was showing the world not only can I do this, I am better than you while I do this!

So, no, Ashley, sports will never be a "no politics space" for Black people. It will never be a safe space for Black people. Consider this world a gigantic sports arena and know that Black people will always be fighting for justice on and off the court.

Black...Female...Missing & White America Doesn't Give A Damn

My daughter was born in Boulder, Colorado the year that JonBenet Ramsey was found murdered in her Boulder home. I will never forget the energy in Colorado surrounding her mysterious death. It was almost palatable. News outlets were descending on Boulder with wide-eyed reporters and armchair detectives attempting to break the case. It was the perfect scene for the media. A wealthy White family with a missing child in a picturesque college town. JonBenet was a competitor in beauty pageants and the media made sure we would never forget this fact. Pictures and videos of this young girl with Goldilocks hair and couture miniature evening gowns filled the airwaves, newspapers, and magazines. Lifetime made a movie about JonBenet and just last year CBS did a two part docu-series. Even over 20 years later Netflix is set to release a documentary entitled Casting JonBenet April 28, 2017.

America seems as if it is enraptured when a person is missing. As it should be. Indeed, we should demand the world pays attention when someone preys on, kidnaps and murders someone. However, it appears America only has selective outrage and concern, when it is a White woman that is missing.

For days and months sometimes even years we were inundated with images of White women that have been kidnapped and some subsequently murdered. The names Laci Peterson, Natalee Holloway, Chandra Levy and Elizabeth Smart have become household names. Their stories were shown daily, we met their families through interviews, their stories were made into movies and their images became emblazoned into the American conscience.

However, the names of Anjel Burel, Relisha Rudd, Dashann Wallace are unknown.

Missing Teen Girls from Metro Washington DC   March 1, 2017 - March 17, 2017

The Washington DC Metropolitan Police Department is now making an effort to publicize critically missing persons in their area by utilizing social media and press releases. All of the children shown went missing during a two week period during March 2017. #DCmissing   Please help spread the word and bring these children home!   #DCmissing

Anonymous tips call 202-727-9099 or text 50411

I suggest that you, White America are co-conspirators in their disappearances. Because you don't care. You never cared. White America is the biggest perpetrator of Black girls coming up missing. You have set this lackadaisical attitude towards the safety and humanity of Black women into motion. You have laid the foundation. You have set the scene. You have designed and developed the environment to be one in which no one would care that Black women are missing. There will be no national TV coverage not when you own and control the information that is dispersed. Their disappearances will not make the rounds on magazine covers because it is believed that only pretty, blond women on a cover can sell magazines. The families of Black missing women will not be shown on Dateline NBC with strategic lighting and intriguing Breaking News intros. Because you don't give a fuck. Let's just be honest. Because you never saw Black women as human. You can't wrap your mind around the knowledge that Black women are women. That Black women deserve the same outcry, support, and resources when they are missing. Where are our Amber Alerts? White America has essentially said, "Finding a jersey is more important that finding a Black girl that is missing."

When the community hosted a town hall meeting, there was not one White face in the picture. This is just three months after White women stormed the streets of Washington DC to shout about justice, freedom, and equality for all women. However, your lack of standing with these Black families and standing in the gap for those missing speaks volumes.

You continue to say you want to stand with all women however your actions show otherwise. You paint the picture and scribe a narrative of the strong, militant, loud and angry Black woman which lends itself to the underlying theme, that Black women do not need help, cannot be victims, do not need support, do not the world to pause when our candles lose their flames. That is only reserved for you.

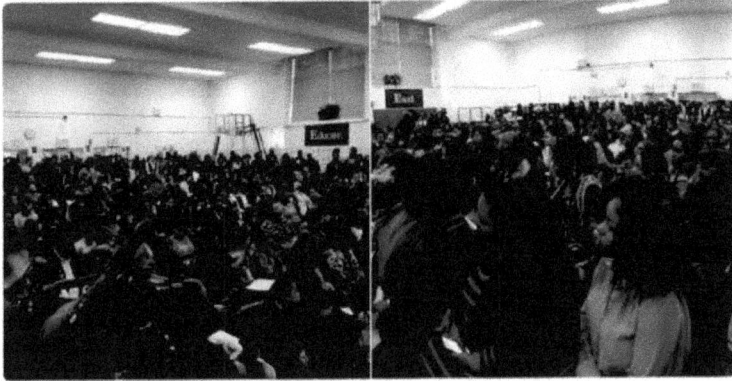

#BlackBoyJoy
@TheThurgood_

Follow

Photos from the D.C. Town Hall meeting about the missing girls; a room full of African Americans....but #AllLivesMatter right?

Photo 2Photo Credit: @TheThurgood/Twitter

No one cares when Black women are missing because Black women do not fit the stereotypical White damsel in distress that America is so in love with. White women are allowed the space for sympathy, compassion, and understanding. White women are allowed not to just play the victim but to be the victim, to be the martyr. Even when a White woman lies about being victimized by Black men, the world still grants her grace to be seen as innocent and demure. When Breana Talbott was found to be a liar and charged with a misdemeanor after falsely stating she was kidnapped and gang raped by 3 Black men, some media outlets chose to run her Facebook photo (first picture below) instead of her mugshot. Even in her lies, the media still wanted to paint her as innocent.

This is the White damsel in distress narrative that America supports because it has been the same story for years. We witnessed this with the narrative that White America clung to for decades about Emmett Till only to find out that his accuser Carolyn Bryant Donham falsified her story that led to his murder.

Photo 3 Emmett Till and Carolyn Byrant Donham

Even writing this blog as I was doing my research and searching Black Women Missing, MSN News has posted that a White woman has gone missing in New Zealand right underneath the search for Black women in Washington DC. I wasn't even searching for White women that were missing but internet algorithms made sure that I would be reminded that while I was searching for Black women, a White woman is missing in New Zealand.

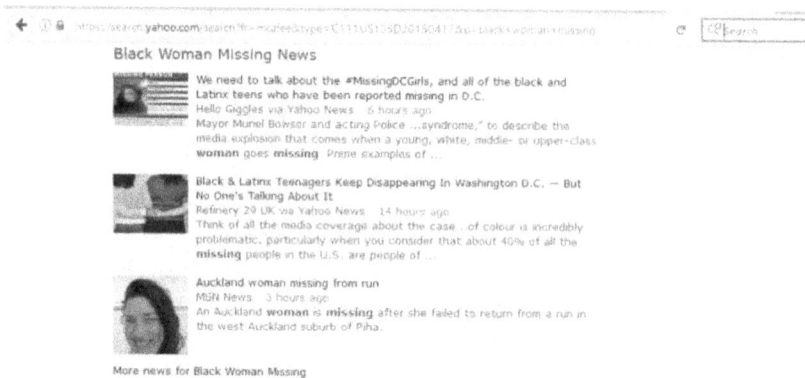

Photo 4 Google search for Missing Black Women

When Black women disappear, if the media does focus on them, their disappearances will be couched in between their socioeconomic status, relationships and any baggage the victim may have and they are often labeled as troubled runaways. The media does everything within its power to make a Black victim the criminal, to make it somehow her fault that she has been kidnapped.

We as Black women are always told that we are too much of everything. Too loud, too strong, too there. And now this is yet another reminder that for some people, we are even too Black to be missing. But we see you, Black women and it our responsibility to see you even if the world doesn't. We know how this is world is designed so we must work to be vigilant about finding our girls, bringing our girls back home. We must take on this responsibility because it is obvious until we care, no one will care. Post an article, tweet a missing person flyer, contact your legislators, city officials and law enforcement officials and ask them what is being done in your community as it pertains to Black women that are missing. Whatever you do, do not turn your head in the other direction. We have the power to rewrite this narrative. We have the power to make the safety and well-being of Black women a priority.

If you have any information concerning the disappearance of these Black women, please contact the anonymous tip line at 202-727-9099.

You're Damn Right Mitch: Nevertheless, She Persisted!

I never imagined as a resident of Louisville, Kentucky that I would ever have anything to thank Majority Leader, Mitch McConnell for however I have been proven wrong. Mitch McConnell has, in the way of trying to reprimand Senator Elizabeth Warren, gave women one of the most powerful slogans in decades.

"She had appeared to violate the rule. She was warned. She was given an explanation. Nevertheless, she persisted."

These were the words Mitch spoke as he attempted to explain why he had used a little-known rule to silence Senator Warren as he interrupted her speech concerning Jeff Sessions's impending nomination. Mitch said that Senator Warren had breached Senate rules by reading a letter with statements against now confirmed and celebrated by ~~racist, anti-Semitic, a scourge to the face of humanity~~ David Duke, Attorney General, Jeff Sessions, from Coretta Scott King.

In Mitch's attempt to put Senator Warren "in her place," he opened a can of Feminist Whup Ass! CAN YOU SMELL WHAT SENATOR WARREN IS COOKING?! I can! And it smells like thousands of women, violating the rules, shrugging off your warnings, saying fuck your explanations and persisting by any means necessary. It smells like Molly Shah, leading a group of protestors to Mitch's doorstep to read Coretta Scott King's letter. It seems like Mitch's attempt to be a world class chauvinist failed. His failed attempt to silence Senator Warren only amplified our voices.

I am thankful for the women that violate the rules. That shrug off warnings. That disregard futile explanations. That persist. Even as some men are telling us to quit. Even as some men attempt to silence us. Once a lioness begins to roar, you cannot shut her jaws.

I am thankful for all the women throughout history that persisted!

It was Alice Walker that reminded me, "The most common way people give up their power is by thinking they don't have any." So, every day I awake I remind myself that I am powerful beyond measure.

It was Audre Lorde that reminded me, "When we speak we are afraid our words will not be heard or welcomed. But when we are silent, we are still afraid. So it is better to speak." So, every day I awake I remember my voice and that I was born to stand in the gap and be a shout for others that life has silenced.

It was Laurel Thatcher Ulrich that reminded me that, "Well-behaved women seldom make history." So, I am not afraid to misbehave, to break the rules, to stand when you say I should sit, to shout when you say I should whisper.

It was Anais Nin that reminded me, "How wrong is it for a woman to expect the man to build the world she wants, rather than to create it herself?" I am master and creator of what I want to see in this world and I do not need a man's approval to be innovative and creative.

It was Angela Davis that reminded me, "We have to talk about liberating minds as well as liberating society." So, with everything that I write I attempt to loose shackles on someone's enslaved mentality.

It was Margaret Thatcher that reminded me "In politics, If you want anything said, ask a man. If you want anything done, ask a woman." So, I will not be silent for the next four years as those in power simply tweet, but I will work with women that are fighting for justice and equality for all people.

Photo 4 Hannah Drake and Angela Davis

It was Harriet Tubman that reminded me, "Every great dream begins with a dreamer. Always remember, you have within you the strength, the patience, and the passion to reach for the stars to change the world." So every day I wake up with the belief that something I do, can and will change the world for the better, for the next generation, for those coming behind me ready to grasp the baton for justice.

You see, Mitch, your problem, among many of your problems, is that you underestimate the power of women. Especially women that are pissed off and sick of your shit. Never attempt to paint us into a corner, because baby was NEVER meant to be put in a corner. My life cannot be defined by coloring in lines! I am three hundred and sixty degrees of pure femininity and as Madonna said, "I'm tough, I'm ambitious, and I know exactly what I want. If that makes me a bitch, okay."

Call me whatever you want and still I will persist!

I have locked hands with time before time was time. I walked alongside the Pyramids. Painted my fingertips in gold. Dipped my soul in pink waters. Twirled cotton in between my fingers.I have cut down strange fruit from oak trees. Jumped over weathered broomsticks. Did pirouettes with angels on clouds. Tap danced on flames with the devil. I swallowed the Nile. Long jumped over the Himalayas. Carried babies against my breasts, buried heartbeats too soon. Balanced water pots on my head. I laid down in a king size bed as a whore and rose as a queen. I have tasted blood and sweat. Sipped tears from crystal flutes. Choked down bitterness and regurgitated hope. I have been to the four corners of the earth. Rested my back against the equator. Tiptoed through galaxies. Wore clouds as couture. Dripped myself in stars as jewels. Allowed sunlight to bask in my spotlight.

AS A WOMAN, I HAVE BECOME ALL THINGS SO THAT ONE DAY ALL PEOPLE COULD TASTE FREEDOM!

Why Beyoncé's Loss Was a Reminder, Stay In Your Place, Blackgirl

Beyoncé's Lemonade album was simply flawless. Beyoncé allowed us to into an area of her life like she has never before with songs that spoke about love and heartbreak, the challenges of marriage, the empowerment of women and for me, most importantly Black Power. The visual album was stunning, laced with poetry written by Warsan Shire, remarkable imagery that took the viewer on a life journey of an artist finding her way through loss, hate, redemption, love and ultimately freedom.

While only 3 Black women have won album of the year, Natalie Cole, Whitney Houston and Lauryn Hill in the history of the Grammy's, surely last night was Beyoncé's time to shine. And just like that, the moment was gone when it was announced that Adele had won Album of the Year.

While theoretically I understand awards are just awards, and this takes nothing away from the Lemonade album, there was something in that moment that reinforced what I already believe. That Black women will always have to run faster, jump higher, work harder, get up earlier, go to bed later, to get half of anything in this world.

When Beyoncé didn't win Album of the Year it wasn't just a loss to me. It was a reminder to stay in your place Black girl, don't make waves Black girl, be invisible, Black girl, don't challenge the system, Black girl, don't walk in your authority, Black girl, don't empower Black women, Black girl. Who do you think you are, Black girl?

"The most disrespected person in America is the black woman." Malcolm X

It was a reminder that for many people our Black will always be too loud, too greasy, too bold, too messy, too sexy. We as Black women have always been told that we are just too much of everything.

Hearing Adele's speech, while I understand what she was attempting to do, was yet another slap in the face for me. I love Adele and believe that she is a phenomenal singer. Her last album 21 was on constant rotation in my car. Still, in that moment I felt shock, embarrassment and sadness as she gave her acceptance speech. Standing on that Grammy stage she was a White woman reminding a Black woman, you were better, but still I won. How many Black women throughout history have been better? Have excelled more? Have done more and still never won? Never got the recognition they deserved? Never earned the money they should have? Never got the credit they so rightly deserved? And then to add insult to injury, Adele told Beyoncé, "The way you make my Black friends feel is empowering." And "I want you to be my

---

mommy." That is when I lost it. A White woman telling a fully pregnant, glowing woman that just embodied Oshun, (a Yoruba deity from West Africa that is the goddess of fertility and love), that she would like her to be her mommy. We have stopped playing mommy to children that aren't ours years ago. We are no longer the mammy or the wet nurse. Those days are over.

I woke up today, knowing as I always do, that in this world, I will always have to work harder to get half as much. Still I am determined to do it like Beyoncé, FLAWLESSLY!

There Will Be No White Saviour

This week, House Bill 14 was introduced into Kentucky legislation. House Bill 14, also known as the Blue Lives Matter Bill, is a direct response and slap in the face to the Black Lives Matter movement. The Blue Lives Matter Bill would make it a hate crime to target first responders simply because of the position of their job. Killing a police officer or firefighter is already a capital offense in Kentucky, punishable by the death penalty or life imprisonment, often without the possibly of release or an inmate needing to serve 85% of their sentence. House Bill 14 covers attacking a police officer, firefighter or first responder and I wonder how "attacking" will be defined? Nevertheless, with all the pushback and questions, the bill floated through the House Judiciary Committee and will find itself in the House to be voted on.

I was not surprised in the least bit. Indeed, Kentucky always manages to show it true, bluegrass when it comes to any issues that center around oppression. However, what was surprising to me is that many Black people seemed shocked that Democratic State Representative, McKenzie Cantrell voted in favor of House Bill 14.

Really? Really?

I was actually stunned that we are still at this point in our fight for justice. I am never surprised when water is wet, fire is hot and ice is cold. Similarly, I am not surprised when a White politician votes for laws that serve to further oppress and victimize People of Color.

Was 53% of White women voting for Trump not enough to convince you?

Some of my fellow fighters in the league of justice must have drunk the Kool-Aid.

Look, anytime someone's Facebook cover picture is a picture of them surrounded by children of color as if they have just finished a backpacking tour for world peace through Ghana, red flags should go up.

Newsflash, there will be no White Savior.

I know we have been conditioned to believe that some White person, typically with blond hair and blue eyes will come riding in on a horse to somehow relieve us of our oppression, this will not be happening.

There will be no John Smith

There will be no Jack Sully.

There will be no Kahlessi.

There will be no Katniss Everdeen finding renewed strength in the murder of Rue to avenge The West End, District 11.

If we are going to liberate OURSELVES, the solution must be found IN US! It resides in us. While we can have many allies, there will be no White person to lead this movement.

This movement calls for White people to stand with us, not dominate us. Not swoop in on their white horses, donning a cape and whitewash our causes. This liberation movement is not about photo ops, cute slogans scribbled on cardboard, and tax write-offs. This liberation movement is not so you can say, "Look what I did for 'those people'". This liberation movement is not about garnering votes for your political power only to turn your backs on the very people who helped place you in office. This liberation movement is not for Facebook, Twitter and Instagram likes.

No, my dear. This liberation movement is pain and sweat and tears. It is using your privilege to benefit others. It is using your political power to fight policies that seek to oppress People of Color. It is using your resources. It is leveraging your power for the least of those. It means lessening so others can be greater. It means listening instead of talking. It means ugly and oftentimes uncomfortable conversations. It means confronting friends, family and loved ones that say racist jokes at the dining room table. It calls for you to stand with us. To be a follower when People of Color lead, find their voices and speak their truths. Giving space for People of Color to voice their hurts and frustrations. To agonize in the face of defeat yet find the strength to get back up again and fight another day.

This liberation movement is not your whitewashed movement. This liberation movement will be Black, fingersnaps, collard greens, afros and multicultural. It will be hijabs, cornrows and pico de gallo. It will be queer, sagging jeans, durags and shea butter. It will be for la raza. It will be David's psalms, Africa's drumbeat, Eric Garner's last words. It will be Nina Simone's blackbird, Paul Dunbar's mask. It will be Maya's knowledge of why the caged bird sings at last and Langston's raisin in the sun. And when it's all done, it will be us that stood finding freedom that looks like us and taste like us and smells like us and feels like us!

So, continue to fight my people! Buck up! Stand up! And stop being dismayed and surprised when water is wet! What else did you expect?

Dear (Some) White People: Why Do You Want To Be Oppressed So Badly?

On most days, I enjoy scrolling through my Twitter feed trying to determine how much water and can food I need to stock up on since it is inevitable that Trump is determined to be the leader of World War 3 before 2018. Truthfully, I find some petty pleasure in watching ~~the girl from The Ring~~ Kellyanne Conway sell her soul to ~~Steven Bannon~~ the devil daily in her video clips and trying to determine if I can actually tell Sean Spicer apart from Melissa McCarthy. I can't. In fact, I think she is a better Sean Spicer than Sean Spicer is Sean Spicer. I try to keep an open mind and breathe, count to ten, meditate, down a bottle of vodka as I read just how ~~full of shit~~ hypocritical this entire administration actually is. There is not a day that goes by that I cannot call a flag on the play.

But yesterday took the cake when a picture appeared on my feed by cartoonist, Glenn McCoy that compared Betsy Devos to the iconic painting of Ruby Bridges, The Problem We All Live With, by Norman Rockwell.

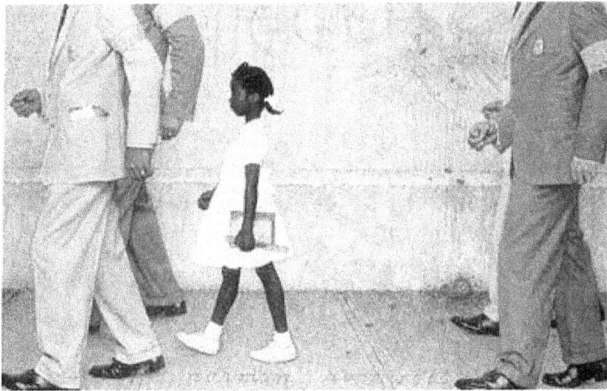

Photo 5 The Problem We All Live With/Norman Rockwell

Let me get this straight. This cartoonist is trying to make some twisted comparison between BILLIONAIRE Betsy Devos being blocked by a handful of protestors as she attempted to enter Jefferson Middle School in her plaid designer suit, leather bag, and is escorted back to a chauffeured Black suburban, only to be allowed into the school later?

Really? Really? This incident is what is being compared to Ruby Bridges daring journey just to attend school, under a court order, November 14, 1960? Ruby Bridges, a little six-year-old girl, walking into William Frantz Elementary, in her Mary Jane shoes, showing unwavering courage as she walked by a large crowd of people that gathered, throwing things at her as she passed. Every morning Ruby went to school a woman would threaten to poison her and that made President Dwight Eisenhower dispatch US Marshals to accompany her. The fear that she would be poisoned was so great that Ruby was only allowed to eat food brought from home. Ruby was taught alone, by Barbara Henry as all other teachers refused to teach a Black student.

And it didn't stop there because oppression and racism tend to spread like a virus. Ruby's father lost his job, the grocery story would no longer allow her family to shop there, and her grandparents, who were sharecroppers, were turned away from the land that they used to make a living and survive. Indeed, Ruby was warned. Nevertheless, she persisted.

That is oppression. That is what racism looks like. Going to school as a six-year-old girl and trying to learn under the threat of death.

Oppression, my dear Betsy Devos is not your designer suits, cushy pay to play government position and riding chauffeured in a suburban. Oppression looks like a six-year-old girl, finding every ounce of strength within her to stand tall, endure the chants and death threats because she had a right to learn. And being Black while learning shouldn't be a crime. You, Billionaire Betsy, have no clue what oppression looks like. It looks like a 12 year old Black boy shot dead on a playground in under 2 minutes by the police. You do not know what oppression smells like. It smells like rotting Black flesh hanging from trees. You don't know what oppression tastes like. It tastes like eating defeat and trying to regurgitate an ounce of hope daily.

I do not understand why some White people have this desire to be oppressed so badly!

Why isn't there a White Entertainment TV channel? Because pretty much EVERY other channel caters to White people.

Why isn't there a White History Month? Because every day, every month, every year WE are taught about White people. Ask your children the last time they learned something about Black leaders that was not during Black History Month and then ask them did they learn about anyone else other than Martin Luther King Jr. and Rosa Parks.

Why can't All Lives Matter? If All Lives Mattered there wouldn't have been slavery, there wouldn't have been Jim Crow, Black people wouldn't be imprisoned at an alarming rate for the same offenses the justice system allows some White people to skip through the lilies for. Where was this All Lives Matters crew during slavery? Where was this All Lives Matters crew during Jim Crow? Where was this All Lives Matters Crew during the War on Drugs which was really a war on Black people? Where was this All Lives Matters Crew when Black people were being gunned down in the street before the invention of the camera phone?

Why must we have affirmative action? Because this nation is built on a system that has had its foot on the necks and backs of Black people for hundreds of years and it is right to offer Black people a chance that inevitably we know we will have to work twice as hard for anyways. We can do it this way or give us reparations with interest. I'll wait...

Why did Beyoncé have to be soooo Black on her Lemonade album? Because Beyoncé is Black! It was a celebration of sisterhood and Blackness in all its splendor! Everything isn't about you!

Why is Netflix streaming a show called Dear White People? Because it is a clever comedic commentary that opens up a dialogue across sectors and may actually bring awareness to some of the racism that many Black people experience that many White people claim to be oblivious to. If you don't want to watch it, stream The Office.

Why can't we have White Girl Magic? Because this entire world celebrates and holds White women as the standard and it is important that we recognize and be vocal about our ability as Black women to shine.

Why can't I sit out in the sun? Melanin. Take it up with God.

There is no beauty in creating oppression that does not exist. It is an insult to those who are fighting daily just to breathe. It is any insult to our history. It is an insult to those who are truly oppressed and are fighting for freedom. It is an insult to our struggle and what we are attempting to build.

The next time you feel you are systematically oppressed, I suggest grabbing a Kleenex, wiping your tears and discovering a way that you can fight with people that are truly fighting against oppression. Until then, save your fake oppression for someone else.

Dear Trump: All Black People Do Not Know Each Other

I half-heartedly watched the Trump press conference today as it was more of the same and reminded me of listening to Charlie Brown's teacher. Wah wah wah, "It's gonna be bigly." Wah wah wah, "Wall." Wah wah wah, " Law and Order in Chicago." Wah wah wah, "It's gonna be huge. I'm fantastic. Big crowds. Big hands." Wah wah wah, " Repeal Obamacare." Wah wah wah.

I was just about to throw in the towel and then Trump in all his Trumpness gave me gold during his exchange with reporter April Ryan which went   like   this: "When you say the inner cities, are you going to include the CBC (Congressional Black Caucus), Mr. President, in your conversations with your urban agenda, your inner city agenda—" American Urban Radio Networks reporter April Ryan asked.

Am I going to include who?" Trump said. YOU MEAN THERE ARE BLACK PEOPLE INVOLVED IN GOVERNMENT BESIDES BEN AND OMAROSA? SHE NEVER INFORMED ME. DAMNIT! NOTE TO SELF, INVITE CONGRESSIONAL BLACK CAUCUS TO EAT DINNER AT WHITE HOUSE.

"Well, I would. I tell you what, do you want to set up the meeting?" Trump said. "Do you want to set up the meeting?" HUH? So you want the reporter to set up your meetings?

PLEASE, SOMEONE TELL ME THIS IS THE TWILIGHT ZONE!

"Are they friends of yours? No, go ahead," Trump continued. "Set up the meeting."

I tried not to laugh when I heard him ask April Ryan, "Are they friends of yours?"

God help me! ARE THEY FRIENDS OF YOURS?

I am certain, that April knows ALL 45 members of the Congressional Black Caucus and they get together and have sleepovers, braid each other's hair all while chowing down on fried chicken, hot water cornbread, and watermelon in between sipping red Kool-Aid and listening to NWA.

Although, perhaps I can laugh at this exchange, I only laugh because it is so ridiculous and you would expect that someone like the President of the United States would know not to ask this question to an African-American reporter. But why would I believe that Trump would ever say anything when it comes to Black people that has a modicum of respect?

This is a common question that many Black people are often asked. It is assumed because we are Black that we know every Black person in the world.

Why just the other day I was going through the 6 Degrees of Black Separation to see how I could meet Oprah. Surely someone Black that I know, knows someone that knows someone since we are all besties.

Digging beyond the surface, while I jest, it is an affront to a Black woman that has the education, the skills, the credentials, the references, the authority to stand and ask questions like any other reporter. Something tells me he wouldn't have asked this question had she not been Black. Do not attempt to paint April or any other Black person into a box. We don't like boxes. Maybe it's because claustrophobia is embedded into our DNA from our ancestors being kept like sardines on slave ships. While Trump may want to only meet with Black rappers and entertainers, we do possess other jobs.

Who we are transcends anything that Trump believes we are supposed to be. We reject limitations. We defy stereotypes. Don't get it twisted. The same way I can chug a Colt 45, I can sip Dom Perignon from a crystal flute, eat a Big Mac or filet mignon, speak in Ebonics or change my lexicon to suit the hour and color of the day. As a Black woman, I have mastered the art of being a chameleon. I can be all things, because in this world I am required to be all things, impeccably.

How Many More Documentaries Will It Take, White America? My Thoughts and Reflections on I Am Not Your Negro

As I drove home from the Speed Museum after a viewing of I Am Not Your Negro, a documentary on race in America brought to life through the impeccable words of James Baldwin, I felt tears welling up in my eyes. Somehow, I managed to make it through the viewing without crying, fighting back the tears as I saw the faces of Trayvon, Tamir and Ayiana. I put my head down and closed my eyes, refusing to watch the beating of Rodney King. Some images just never leave you. I was only 15 years old when the grainy video made its way across this nation on TV screens. Who knew years later we would watch the death of Black men on cell phones and computers around the world. I watched buildings burn to the ground and even at that age, I understood the fires, the broken windows, even the looting. This nation pretended to be oblivious to the riot that was bubbling up inside of Black people. An internal volcano simply waiting to erupt.

I Am Not Your Negro was a phenomenal documentary, jarring, piercing, raw, sad, and honest. Baldwin does not mince words. His eloquence and dominance of speech are tremendous. By far he is one of the most powerful orators I have ever heard.

However, in general, there was nothing in this documentary that was new information to me as a Black person in this world. As a writer, I am a fan and reader of James Baldwin. I was always amazed by the way he spoke, each word deliberate, delivered with a surgeon's precision as he spoke truth to power. The agony behind many of his speeches was palatable. The words jumped off the screen, drawing the viewer in, demanding attention. The images of Black injustice gave life to his words. Images we have seen before. Images that are burned into our psyche. Images as a Black person I have vowed always to remember and to tell the story.

I sat in my seat angered and disenchanted. This is the day to day life of so many Black people. Not much had changed. Outside of the clothing and things that would date era, it looked like 2017. Just another day being Black in America.

After the movie had ended there was a talk back with Sadiqa Reynolds President of the Urban League. I know Sadiqa personally and professionally and I knew if anyone could stand in that space after that movie, she could. Her summary indeed spoke what I knew many of us were feeling.

And then it was time for the audience to give comments. I sat through a few comments and questions and I felt like my head was going to explode. I had to leave. As I walked back to my car, I wondered, how much more?

How much more do you want us to take?

How long are we going to keep playing this game?

How many documentaries will it take, White America?

How many showings does the Speed Museum need to do? Ten? Fifteen? What will be the right number?

How enlightened are you now?

Does hearing about the plight of oppression from Baldwin sound different than when a Black male is shouting I Can't Breathe?

Help me understand!

What is different now from what Baldwin was saying over FIFTY years ago?

And still, here we are. Still fighting for basic rights! Just base level civil rights. Still. Fighting.

How much longer is it going to take for you to get it?

How much longer do you want us to wait for you to get it?

Don't stand up and ask me what you need to do! I do not have the desire or inclination to hold your hand through this fight because I am too busy using both my hands to fight for freedom. Just, look around you! The world is on fire! Grab some damn water and help put it out!

Forgive me if I sound upset. But my faith is waning. My patience is wearing thin. I'm tired. You pretend as if you haven't seen injustice all around you. You pretend as if we haven't been shouting. You pretend as you didn't see Philando Castile shot by an officer bleed out on Facebook Live. You pretend as if Mike Brown's body didn't stay in the street for 4 hours. You pretend as if Trayvon wasn't just a young boy going home after buying Skittles and tea. You pretend as if Rekia Boyd was just at the wrong place at the wrong time. You pretend as if our rage is not justified. Stop pretending! You are not fooling anyone!

Just admit you were asleep at the wheel. Admit you turned a blind eye! Admit you didn't care because it didn't affect you! Admit that you are racist. Admit that you agree with the policies that make it almost impossible for Black people to rise. Admit that you and your lineage benefited from our oppression! Look in the mirror and admit something!

I can deal with an admission but I cannot deal with pretending as if you didn't see. If you didn't see it is because you made a conscious decision NOT to see. TAKE THE BLINDERS OFF! Take a look America. This blood is not on our hands. This one we will not take responsibility for. We were never guilty. It is you, that shoulders the blame. And you must own it!

You ask me what you can do? OWN WHAT YOU DID! OWN WHAT YOU ALLOWED! OWN YOUR SILENCE! OWN YOUR NEGLECT! OWN YOUR COLLECTIVE HISTORY! OWN YOUR SHAME and then VOW TO DO SOME SHIT TO CHANGE IT!

Stop Going in The Backwoods with White People-Get Out Movie Review

When I was younger, I loved horror movies. From Jason, Nightmare On Elm Street, Halloween, I watched them all. Back then the bogeyman was someone that we could see- Jason, Freddy Kreuger, and Michael Myers. To this day if I hear the theme music to Halloween, I can feel the hairs on the back of my neck stand up.

In Get Out, written and directed by Jordan Peele, evil takes on a more sinister form – racism. This is much scarier than the monsters that we can see because this form of evil is pervasive, can shapeshift, can jump from person to person, is stealth, cloaked and often, people never see it coming.

It is almost as if Get Out is the 2017 Invasion of the Racist Body Snatchers. This was a theme that resonated with me because after the 2016 election, I felt that I was living in a real life horror movie. And unfortunately, I had no idea who was the bogeyman. I didn't know who voted for this monster, who supported his evil rhetoric and who was living among me. Everywhere I went, I looked at people wondering if they were who they said they were or had they been concealing what they truly felt this entire time.

(Before I go any further, let me shut this down real quick. In Get Out, the racist White people are the villains. While I have heard rumblings about this making some White people upset, the movie industry has built an empire off the backs of Black people and Muslims being portrayed as the usual suspect. This time it is simply your turn so get in line.)

The movie opens in the apartment of Chris, an established African-American photographer, with all the accoutrements of a millennial on the rise, exposed brick and pipe in the living room, plants on the kitchen counter that take minimal care and the ever-cute dog that has been diagnosed with IBS. To complete this picture of "I have arrived", Chris is soon greeted by his White girlfriend Rose, coming to bring coffee and breakfast muffins, before they begin their trip to visit Rose's parents. Funny how success can make you forget that indeed, you are Black too.

Although they have been dating for five months, Chris finally decides to ask Rose if she has told her parents that he is Black. If you have ever dated outside of your race, and I have, we all know that question. While you and your significant other are cool, you want to know just how many generations that "coolness" goes back. Like are you the generation that is cool and your parents are still stuck in Jim Crow cool and your grandparents think I should be out tending to their land cool? What level of "I am not racist", has been achieved in your family? Let me know. Rose assures Chris, her family is "I-would-vote-for-Obama-a-third-term-if-I-could" cool. I love how voting for Obama is now the measuring stick for how NOT racist someone is. I believe that has almost surpassed my best friend is Black.

They embark on a trip to visit her parents and this is where my spidey senses start to go up. There were just a few things I noted in this movie:

1. Don't EVER go on a road trip with any White person in the backwoods of ANY town. EVER! I don't care where we are going I am NOT riding in the backwoods of some random town with White people and I am the ONLY Black person. I am always thinking where are we going and who the hell do you know back here? If something pops off I already know The Children of the Corn aint gonna let me go. We have heard enough stories about Black people coming up missing in the backwoods of some town. Nope. If we are going to visit your parents they better live in a city, right off a highway exit or I can't come!

2. When Black people are "the help"…RUN! I don't care how you slice it, I will always look at White people with a raised eyebrow that has Black people serving them grits, doing their laundry and ironing their clothes. In this day and age, White people clean houses too. Hire them.

3. When the parents ask you, "How long has 'this thang' been going on", PACK YOUR DAMN BAGS! This thang? I am leery of White people that feel the need to put on a 'blackcent' when they are around Black people. Nope. Be who you are. If you can't, I wonder what you are concealing.

4. When EVERYONE is WHITE, look for the exits. I have been in many situations where I am the only Black person and trust and believe I have scoped out the exits 20 times over. I know how to get out, how long it's gonna take to get out, who I might need to drop a 2 piece and a biscuit on to get out.

5. STOP trusting EVERY White person that says they aren't racist! There are many people that think they aren't racist because they voted for Obama, have 2.5 Black friends, or listen to Beyoncé and John Legend.

They can still be racist! Listen and observe EVERYTHING! People can only pretend for so long. Eventually a racist joke, story, assumption will come out.

6. Tell your Black friends where you are going. Look I get it, you are grown but everyone needs a friend like Rodney. In Get Out, Rodney knew something wasn't right with Rose and sometimes you need your Black friend to talk to you down. I know we are growing, this is 2017 and we are all trying to unite but there is just some shit I am not going to allow my Black friends to do. Bungee jumping, skydiving, real camping, deep sea diving, eating White people's potato salad, you just aint gonna be allowed to do it. LISTEN TO YOUR BLACK FRIENDS! We love you and we have your back!

Get Out was an ingenious movie that utilized a very real subject matter that many Black people are dealing with today to create a horror movie that spoke to racism, police relations, the history of Black people and medicine, interracial relationships and a host of other issues. While in a Hollywood setting, these are issues that Black people face daily and Jordan Peele utilized a medium that can create a pathway for conversations. I am always intrigued by those that use art in a way that can open a door for social critique. Get Out pulls from real life situations and places them in a setting that can allow the viewer to chew the reality of what Peele is getting at in bite sized pieces. For Black people, this is not just a movie. Google Henrietta Lacks, or the Tuskegee Experiment if you want to understand how White people have utilized medicine to victimize and take advantage of Black people. Google James Byrd Jr., if you want to know how the story ends when a Black man went off with White people that pretended they were his friends. Getting questioned by the police is not just something that happens in the movies. Accounts of Black men and women unlawfully stopped are countless with many of these stops ending in death.

This is reality. Even as scared as I may have been watching Jason, Freddie Krueger or Michael Myers, I knew I could turn the TV off and the movie was over. In Get Out, I walked out of the theater knowing the bogeyman was indeed real and although the credits were rolling, art simply blended with real life. I looked over my shoulder as I walked to my car, wondering how long I would have to live this nightmare...

Were We Not Enough?

In recent weeks with the tragic and unfortunate murder of Heather Heyers, it seems the world has turned its eye to the United States of America, wagging its finger in shame. The blatant acts of racism that ascended upon Charlottesville, Virginia have been rebuked by actors, comedians, senators, congressmen, congresswomen, reporters, CEOs, restaurant owners, even some law enforcement, and everyday people in the world. The funeral of Heather Heyers was attended by hundreds and the events of that tragic day many have said impacted the very course of the presidency. Heather's last Facebook quote, "If you are not outraged, you are not paying attention," has been shared countless times on social media.

Indeed, either America was not paying attention or simply did not care because the people screaming for justice were Black. The recent events that have shaken this nation for many Black people and me are not new.

Let me be clear before I go any further; this is not an indictment on Heather, the life she led and the life she sacrificed for justice. Heather did Heather's part. And Heather lived her life in a way according to her mother, that was always about standing up for others. I believe that Heather, with her last quote, would share my sentiments in this blog.

Recently in Kentucky, residents were asked to fill out a form about statues that "can be interpreted to be honoring bigotry, racism, and slavery." I posted the link on my social media accounts and encouraged people to complete the form, but as I was filling it out, I thought, "Why must I complete a form to speak to my humanity? Why do I need to complete a form for people to review it to decide if a statue erected in honor of someone that stood for racism should be taken down? Why is my humanity regulated to an online form?"

In the wake of this recent uprising for justice, I cannot help but ask as a Black woman, mother, poet, and activist, were we, as Black people, not enough?

When we took to the streets, we were labeled as thugs and degenerates, but now people taking to the streets are labeled the resistance, were we not enough?

When we stood in the streets screaming for justice after the murder of Mike Brown, were we not enough?

When we took over the streets of Ferguson, Missouri fighting for justice, were   we   not   enough?
When we watched in horror as Philando Castile bled out on Facebook Live, were we not enough?

When we screamed, "Wrong!" as we watched Eric Garner choked by an NYPD officer, were we not enough?

When we screamed for justice after Trayvon Martin was killed simply walking home after buying Skittles and tea, were we not enough?

When we yelled for justice after Sandra Bland was found dead on a jailhouse floor, WERE WE NOT ENOUGH?

When we openly mourned after watching Rodney King beaten on a grainy video, were we not enough?

When we wept watching 7-year-old Aiyana Stanley-Jones (killed by the police) grandmother testify in open court, were we not enough?

When we watched in horror as a young Black girl was thrown across her class room by an officer, were we not enough?

When we stood in disbelief as no one was found guilty after the death of Rekia Boyd, were we not enough?

When we expressed outraged that countless police officers were found not guilty after senseless killings, were we not enough?

When we stood up against monuments erected to uphold the mentality of a slave nation, were we not enough?

When we fought to bring down monuments built in honor of those that supported the institution of slavery, and no one heard us, were we not enough?

When we took to Twitter with the #NoConfederate hashtag and David Benioff, Dan Weiss and HBO turned a blind eye to our concerns, yet now the world sees pretending slavery never ended is not wise, were we not enough?

When we watched the world spit in the face of Black America, were we not enough?

When we buried our Black sons and daughters too soon, were we not enough?

When we told you that you should be outraged, were we not enough?

It seems Black pain, suffering and injustice can only be understood by this world if it is viewed and encapsulated through the eyes of a White world.

I stand puzzled why so many White people are now surprised that America is not ice-cold lemonade and apple pie? Have Black people not been screaming this truth?

What did you think we meant when we told you Trump upheld a racist agenda? What do you think we meant when we told you Trump's slogan, Make

America Great Again, really meant, Make America White Again? What did you think we meant when we said electing Barack Obama into office did not mean we entered a post-racial America? What do you think we meant when we said our reproductive rights were being stripped away daily? What did you think we meant when we told you that your healthcare would be impacted? What did you think we meant when we were protesting police brutality? What did you think we meant when we were on Twitter for weeks practically begging David Benioff, Dan Weiss and HBO not to promote a show about slavery never ending? What did you think we meant when we told you voting for Trump was a vote for racism and hatred? What do you think we meant when we were yelling for righteousness?

What I believe is that you thought it would never affect you. I believe you thought those are just some Black people making noise that you didn't want to hear. I believe you thought this hate, racism, and intolerance would never step on your front porch. But now you know, chickens always come home to roost. As Martin Luther King Jr, said, "We are caught in an inescapable network of mutuality, tied in a single garment of destiny. Whatever affects one directly, affects all indirectly."

There is no getting around us. We are not going anywhere. What we speak today and what my people have spoken about for years, is cold, hard, reality. The plane is now on fire.

One day I pray this world can take the truth of what Black people say straight with no a chaser. It is my hope that one day this world will listen when Black people speak. It is my hope that our cries against injustice won't need to be autotuned, laced over a trap beat to catch the frequency of White America. It is my hope that the truth that Black people speak will be taken at face value. It is my hope that White people will not continue to profit by studying what Black people have already told White America was true. It is my hope that Black people's cries for justice will not need to be White-splained. It is my hope that the struggles of being a Black woman in this world doesn't need to be decorated in pink pussy cat hats before it is considered truth. It is my hope that a White person will not write an op-ed about racial inequities and it gets more views, publicity and credibility than a Black person that has said the very same thing for years. It is my hope that no blood, neither White or Black needs to be shed before White America realizes the error of its ways. It is my hope that one day, White America will hear, listen and act when Black America speaks, and it will not need the filter of a White person to react to Black truth.

Dear America: Chickens Always Come Home To Roost

It is difficult as a Black woman to type this blog and not feel some sense of "I told you so" as White America is reeling from the untimely death of Justine Damond, an Australian native murdered by the police. (Let me first say, I am against ALL police brutality and racism.) My site is filled with blogs about the deaths of Black men, women, and children that seemingly were off the radar for White America. However, there is nothing more shocking to White America than when chickens come home to roost.

When Colin Kaepernick posted a tweet about the police being an offshoot of the slave patrols- to White America, it was laughable. When Tamir Rice was killed on a playground in under two minutes, White America wanted to speak about his height. When Mike Brown was murdered in Ferguson with his hands in the air, White America wanted to paint him as a thug. When Rekia Boyd was shot in the head by police, White America said she was in the wrong place at the wrong time. When Sandra Bland was murdered in her jail cell, White America said, "If only she would have complied." When Eric Garner was suffocated in a chokehold, White America said, "He should have listened to the police." When Philando Castile was murdered, and we watched him bleed out on Facebook Live, White America said, "Well, he was getting his wallet."

And now here we are, White America, with Justine Damond, dead. Murdered by the police.

From all media accounts, which made sure to point out she was blond, saved ducks, was a future bride, seemingly a good person that was simply calling the police to report an alleged assault and she is dead. Killed by Somali Officer Mohamed Noor. We only have the account of the officers because there is no dashcam footage and the body cameras were turned off. Such a familiar story.

The problem, White America, is that police brutality, unjustified police shootings and murders are like cancer often rooted in racism. It is of no concern to me that this time the officer is Black and the victim White. He operates within a system with a foundation built on racism. I have repeated this time and time yet it appears White America is not hearing me.

WAKE UP WHITE AMERICA! LISTEN!

Racism in a way is like cancer. Without immediate intervention, you cannot contain or destroy cancerous cells. Similarly, you cannot contain racism that is built within system. (Why do you think they try to stop cancer before it spreads to the lymphatic system?) Racism spreads and goes where it wants to go until it invades your entire being. If you go to the doctor and the doctor says, "I am sorry. You have cancer." You don't say, "Well, that's fine. If we don't talk about it, it will go away." You don't say, "Well, it's just kinda cancer, not really cancer. I have friends with cancer, so I'm cool." Or how about, "Well, cancer happens to those people not me so I should be okay." Or how about, "Well, let's just keep the cancer in its spot and pray it doesn't spread anywhere else." If you said that about cancer, we would think you were insane.

The same goes for racism. You cannot contain racism. Racism will not be confined. It will not be held in a neat little box. It will not be hidden among the leaves on your family tree. Racism is a poison that always goes down to the roots. Infecting everything it comes into contact with. Racism is pervasive. It spreads into policies, legislation, and systems. And similarly, to cancer, the only way to combat racism, is to eradicate the cells. And we cannot begin to eradicate racism by pretending and portraying the death of Justine Damond differently than the death of Philando Castile. The ONLY reason this police shooting is NOW an issue is that Justine was WHITE. Period. The family's attorney called her, "The most innocent victim in police shootings." REALLY? REALLY? What about Rekia Boyd, walking? Jordan Edwards, getting in a car to ride home. Aiyana Stanley-Jones, seven years old sleeping on her couch MURDERED by the police. Who is more innocent than a 7-year-old sleeping? The only difference is THEY ARE BLACK!! Does that make them less innocent?

And while I do not agree with the Blue Lives Matter agenda, where are they? Where is Blue Lives Matter? SILENT! If Blue Lives REALLY mattered, they would stand behind him. This is what we have repeated time and time. Blue Lives Matter is a White agenda to uphold and defend White police officers. What Blue Lives Matter REALLY means is White Police Lives Matter if you kill a Person of Color. If you kill a Black or Brown person, they will rally behind you, create an online campaign for funds, bring your family casseroles and defend you relentlessly on social media but now it is different because a Black officer killed a White woman. Suddenly, running up on a police car, in the dark with a cell phone in your hand means NOTHING! Yet when every time a Black man reaches for his wallet, holds a cell phone, or breathes in broad daylight and is murdered by the police, anything in their hands magically appears like a gun, and that's okay with White America. The, "I felt threatened" excuse seems to work ANY OTHER TIME. Yet surprisingly officers and White America as a whole do not stand behind this "Blue Life". I wonder why? What's different this time?

White America you have some explaining to do. Your hypocrisy is showing! From police brutality to drug addiction to healthcare you are a hypocrite.

States are bending over backwards to prove that White people strung out on opioids and heroin are now a health crisis. Really? Because White middle-class kids are now strung out, it is now a public health crisis? White America is demanding rehabilitation clinics, and lesser jail sentences and the media is painting White drug addiction in pretty words. Yet during the crack epidemic, which hit and wiped out a huge portion of Black mothers, fathers, sons and daughters, no one cared. No one gave a damn about investigating the governments roll in introducing crack to the Black community. Crack addiction was not a health crisis. Calling mothers addicted to crack wasn't met with nice words from the media. They were crack hoes and crack bitches. And their children weren't considered suffering and the state finding a way to make them well; they were just cast off as crack babies. Crack offenses were dealt harsh sentences in the legal system. And now, White America wants to care, because drug addiction has come home to roost. It doesn't feel good when drugs hit Johnny and Becky, does it? It doesn't feel good when you've built an empire off the backs of Black people, and Johnny and Becky are too high and strung out to sustain your legacy does it?

Now reality has hit Middle America, and now it's a tragedy. How does that feel?

The same goes for healthcare. When a Black President was trying to give you health care, masses of White America hated the idea! Hated "Obamacare"! White America rallied around Trump to repeal Obamacare because they didn't have Obamacare, they had the leprechaun, magical Affordable Health Care not realizing they had been duped. When Trump was talking about taking healthcare away from people, White America was fine. Great! Take it away! However once White America saw, Trump meant them too, now magically, they don't have a problem with "Obamacare". An article recently came out and someone said, "I don't know why I had a problem with it before." Really? NOTHING CHANGED! So if you had a problem before but not now, it leads me to believe you had a problem because a Black man came up with the idea! And you allowed your racism to override your health! IDIOT!

White America, you can continue to pretend if you want. But your dirty laundry is showing. My mother always told me, "What doesn't come out in the wash, will always come out in the rinse." And your dirty laundry is on display. Dirty laundry that we have told the world about since time was time.

White America this blog is a chin check to your bullshit and hypocrisy. White America you are fooling no one but yourselves. And now you cannot lie any longer. There is a well-known quote by Martin Niemöller that says:

"First, they came for the Socialists, and I did not speak out—Because I was not a Socialist. Then they came for the Trade Unionists, and I did not speak out—Because I was not a Trade Unionist. Then they came for the Jews, and I did not speak out—Because I was not a Jew. Then they came for me—and there was no one left to speak for me."

I changed this quote to say, "First they came for BLACK PEOPLE and White America said, 'Who cares?'" Perhaps if White America would have cared about Black people we wouldn't be here now. We tried to tell you. Now here we are. Make room in the coop. More chickens will be coming home.

Dear Trump: On Behalf of Many Black People Everywhere, Do NOT Include Us In Your Bullshit

On the last day of Black History Month, Trump took his position giving his address to Congress. Just when I thought Beyoncé losing Album of the Year to Adele and the Oscars ruining Moonlight's Best Picture of the Year thunder, was all I could take, Trump, ~~bic rhetoric~~ decided to open his ~~shit show~~ speech, with comments on Black History Month. Really? Really? Black History Month.

On behalf of the spirit of Frederick Douglass (yes, Trump, Brother Frederick has gone on to glory), Martin, Malcolm, Huey, Harriet, Rosa, Nat, Trayvon, Eric, Sandra, DO NOT INCLUDE US IN YOUR BULLSHIT!

We want no part of it. If I may quote a wise sage, Sweet Brown, "Ain't Nobody Got Time For That!" Please leave us out of your bullshit!

While I know you want to attempt to blame former President Obama because the White House is leaking information like air in a Tom Brady football, please refrain from blaming "The Black Guy".

Have you seen Obama out here living his best life ever? Does he look like a man that is thinking about you? Really? REALLY?

This is a man that is kite surfing with a billionaire. He is not thinking about you. Hell, I wonder if he is thinking about me?! I feel like Mary J. Blige. I WAS YOUR LOVER AND YOUR SECRETARY, WORKING EVERY DAY OF THE WEEK…(Call me Barack! PLEASE!)

I have had to face the fact that Obama has broken up with me. For a moment I was foolish enough to believe that we were in that awkward stage where we might get back together but once I saw him getting in a suburban with his top collar unbuttoned, I knew it was over. You cannot blame "The Black Guy" anymore. You shoulder the outcome of America for the next four years.

I was moved by the resounding applause for those that have lost loved ones to the hands of violence. I was looking for Parvatha Vardhini, the mother of Srinivas Kuchibhotla, who was killed in a racially motivated shooting by Adam Purinton in Kansas, as he yelled, "Get out of my country." She was nowhere to be found in the stands. Who stands to applaud for her?

As a matter of fact, throughout your speech, I wondered who would stand and applaud for the least of those? It is nice to exist inside of a bubble with the majority of people supporting your policies and beliefs. Be mindful Trump of believing your own press, even the press that you and your minions create through alternative facts.

The world that I live in, that I know, that I support, consists of people that exist outside of the bubble. People that wonder about their healthcare, their preexisting conditions. People that wonder about their employment, people that know you will not be bringing back coal jobs. People that fight to worship the way that they choose. People that just want to go pee, freely, in a bathroom-ANY bathroom. People that wonder about education. People that wonder about police relations. People that see though your Kellyanne Conway Veil of bullshit.

Tonight, you may have fooled America. But what more can I expect? You fooled enough people that live in the backwoods of humanity to vote against their own interests so that you are now the President. And so here we are. Spinning in a web of your lies, alternative facts and bullshit.

Please do us a favor, keep Black folks out of it. We didn't vote for you.

Funny, after all this time, we still don't go along with the slave master.

P.S. As a viewer, Mike Pence is just waiting to take your job. Know that.

This Shit Has Really Got To Stop! Rachel Dolezal You Are Nothing But A Low Budget Kardashian!

Rachel Dolezal, I was over your fake tan and tacky hair weave foolishness a few years back until I awoke this morning to your Anglo-Saxon bullshit, fuckery and shenanigans. You in your "I wanna be Black so desperately" ignorance just TAKING a West African name. You don't just TAKE an African name. How are you just going to take something that is NOT YOURS? Typical White people bullshit. Our history is NOT your history! Just Stop! Try as you might, you will never be a Black woman.

When I returned to Senegal with Roots and Wings I immediately felt at home. The moment I placed my feet on African soil I knew this is where I came from. It was as if something in me connected with the air, the soil, the spirit of Africa. Finally, there was a place where I belonged. Where I was not an outsider. Where my face looked like other faces. Where my actions, my mannerisms made sense. Even the food I ate all my life, the jewelry I wore made sense. It was like I found something I had been searching for my entire life.

Photo 6 Roots and Wings Naming Ceremony in Dakar Senegal/Josh Miller

A few days into our trip we were told that we would be given our Senegalese names. I remember the deep emotion that we all felt. Our names. Not names passed down to us through slavery but names from our people, our home, our culture. Selecting a name in Senegal is not just randomly picking something that you think SOUNDS BLACK Rachel!

Names in Senegal are based on your characteristics. We didn't choose our names. The elders chose for us. Our names were selected based on who they saw us to be and who we could grow into. Our names were placed on us like a cloak and we were partnered with our namesake. The name given to me is Binta which means seeer, spiritual healer, leader. We stood with our namesakes and gained a new family. We gained a sense of purpose. We became grounded in our history that was STOLEN from us by people that look just like you! We cried tears of joy because we finally were connected and we cried tears of pain for everything that we lost.

Photo 7 My Senegalese Namesake Binta and Family

You are a liar and a pretender! All you have ever done is steal and pretend to be something that you are not. It is a disgrace for you to take something that means so much to Black people and co-opt it as your own. I don't care how much you tan, you will never be Black. I don't care how many cornrows you toss in your hair, you will never be Black! I don't care what vernacular you attempt to speak, you will never be Black! What you have done is not Black! It simply proves you to stand in line with people that have done nothing but stolen and taken from Black people when they saw fit! It proves you are everything I believe you to be. You are a White woman that has simply stolen something from Black women. Trust me, you are not the first. You are nothing but a low budget Kardashian and I am hardly impressed, Rachel.

We Are Complicit in the Murders of Each of These Women

A friend once told me, "When you don't know something, it is okay to say that you don't know something." I do not write these words because I am a guru on transgender issues. I don't know how it feels to wonder about my gender identity. I do not know how it feels to wonder where and if you will be allowed to go to the bathroom in a public space. I do not know what it feels like emotionally and physically to go through a personal transition. I don't know how it is to battle systems to be able to change your name. I don't know how it feels to be called the wrong pronoun. I don't know how it feels to wonder when it is the right time to discuss your gender with your family, friends and loved ones. I don't even know all the correct terminology.

There is a lot about being transgender that I will never know. So, I respectfully ask you to love me through my learning, love me through this writing and know that I do not stand here as someone with all the answers. As a matter of fact, I don't know if I have any answers. We are all in this sea of racial, sexual, and gender discord fighting just to stay afloat. However, please know that I am open and willing to learn. To stand alongside you. To add my voice to yours when the world demands that we should whisper. I can readily admit when I do not know something but as Black woman I do know how it feels to be overlooked, counted out, disregarded and erased from history.

I do know how it feels to be screaming and no one can hear you!

I do know how it feels to watch White celebrities and White women march for a movement that doesn't include you.

I do know how it feels to be discriminated against simply because of the way that you look.

I do know how it feels to have your issues debated all around you by people that have no understanding of what you face in your day to day life.

I do know how it feels to have White men that sit in ivory towers decide what you can do with your body.

I do know how it feels for an entire movement to overlook you because of who you are.

I do know how it feels to have male names synonymous with a movement and for Black women to be forgotten.

I do know how it feels to suffer in silence. To wonder about your healthcare, your finances and your future.

I do know how it feels to stand alongside White people that say they understand your issues but never once acknowledges their privilege.

You see, there are some things that I do know. And what I do know is that 6 Black transgender women and 1 Indigenous transgender woman, were murdered this year and for the most part the world was silent, turned its head, looked the other way. Because they were not us. But Angela Davis reminds us, "If the come for them in the morning, they will come for us in the night." So now is not the time for us to pick and choose who gets to taste the sweet nectar of justice. Now is not the time to hand out justice to who we think is deserving like we are on a civil rights assembly line. Justice is not served on a buffet table. Freedom, Equality and Basic Civil Rights are NOT Transgender Issues. These are my issues and your issues. THESE ARE ALL HUMAN RIGHTS ISSUES!

Six Black transgender women are dead. One Indigenous transgender woman is dead. Who shouts their names? Jaquarrius Holland, Ciara McEvleen, Jojo Striker, Keke Collier Mesha Caldwell, Jamie Lee Wounded Arrow and Chyna Dupree. Would it have mattered if they were men? Would it have mattered if they were White? Would it have mattered if their last name were Jenner? Would it have mattered if it was your child lying dead in the street?

So, my question is who will cry out for them? Who will remember them? Who marches for them? Who knits the pink pussy cat hats for them? Who organizes a national day off work for them? Who makes the protest signs for them? We bear a responsibility in our fight for justice to remember that it is not justice unless it is justice for everyone. Until everyone is free then no one is truly free. So today is the day to align yourself on the side of righteousness and remind yourself that these transgender women, were human beings! And it is our job to write their names in history alongside Oscar and Trayvon and Mike and Eric.

I was stunned as I stood in a circle at the vigil as the names and biographies of each woman were read. The ages of the each of them varied but many were very young. Just starting to live. Some didn't even make it to the age of my own daughter. With each name, I wondered, "What are we doing as people? Who have we become that someone can be viciously murdered simply because of their race, sexuality and/or gender?" I grew up in the age of Brandon Teena and Gwen Amber Rose Araujo. Crimes against transgender people sadly were not new to me. But hearing those names and standing in solidarity with those that attended the vigil, I felt a sense of guilt. We were in collusion with the perpetrators of these crimes. While we may not have held the weapon in our hands, we indeed were complicit. Because we were silent when we should have been a shout. We vilified people for their differences and demonized people with our doctrine. We hid in our own closets, shut our doors and closed our blinds allowing those that may want to love who they love to act out in fear, anger and hate rather than face our judgment. We created an environment for the perfect storm. And for that I am sorry.

These were women who took a stand in all their splendor to simply be and that in itself, is an act of justice! We remember each of them; Jaquarrius Holland, Ciara McEvleen, Jojo Striker, Keke Collier Mesha Caldwell, Jamie Lee Wounded Arrow and Chyna Dupree. They lost their lives living their truth and for that, we stand and vow to carry the torch on for everyone to live in freedom.

Photo 8 Jaquarrius Holland, Ciara McEvleen, Jojo Striker, Keke Collier Mesha Caldwell, Jamie Lee Wounded Arrow, Chyna Dupree/Photos courtesy of Facebook, Twitter and GoFundMe

(SPEECH GIVEN AT RALLY FOR JUSTICE FOR TRANS WOMEN OF COLOR - MARCH 5, 2017)

And The Negro Please Award for 2017 Goes to Ben Carson

By now you have read the news. Not six damn days out of Black History Month, Housing and Urban Development secretary, Ben Carson, decided to add to the complete idiocy of this administration by making the following statement, "That's what America is about. A land of dreams and opportunity. There were other immigrants who came here in the bottom of slave ships, worked even longer, even harder for less."

What in the almighty ancestorly fuck is he talking about?

Slaves were immigrants that worked for less? Where do I even begin? Let's start with the word immigrants. I'm gonna take, 'Are You A Natural Born Idiot for a 100, Alex?' Immigrant is defined as a person who migrates to another country, usually for permanent residence. The definition implies that a person has made a CHOICE to come to another country. Africans were not allowed the CHOICE to come to America. Are you insane? What did you think slavery was? Leonardo DiCaprio trying to hitch a ride on the Titanic? Slavery is not something to trivialize or romanticize. This was not a ride on a Carnival Cruise ship to America.

Then to add insult to injury Ben Carson said they "worked for less". Less than what? Minimum wage? Why I can hear the slaves now. "Gee, master we sure would enjoy getting paid nothing. I mean it is less than nothing. But I guess nothing is something." Are you insane?

I have read that Ben Carson is a neurosurgeon. I am starting to doubt that. Seriously. Has anyone checked his credentials? For all we know he got his degree from Trump University. Better yet, someone needs to make sure he didn't attend ACME University because he is certainly a cartoon. How does someone who was respected in his field subject himself to becoming a caricature?

According to Wikipedia, Ben Carson was Director of Pediatric Neurosurgery at Johns Hopkins Hospital in Maryland from 1984 until his retirement in 2013. Ben Carson was a pioneer in neurosurgery, performing the only successful separation of conjoined twins joined at the back of the head. He pioneered the first successful neurosurgical procedure on a fetus inside the womb, performed the first completely successful separation of type-2 vertical craniopagus twins, developed new methods to treat brain-stem tumors, and revived hemispherectomy techniques for

Negro *Please* AWARD

FOR ADDING TO THE EMBARASSMENT OF BLACK PEOPLE WORLDWIDE...

controlling seizures. He became the youngest chief of pediatric neurosurgery in the country at age 33. He has received more than 60 honorary doctorate degrees, dozens of national merit citations, and written over 100 neurosurgical publications. In 2008, he was bestowed the Presidential Medal of Freedom, the highest civilian award in the United States.

Someone enlighten me. How do you disregard all of your dedication, education and accomplishments to now shuck and jive for an administration and stand before an audience as a Black Man and act as if you were hypnotized by the mother in Get Out? DUDE IF YOU HAVE NOT SEEN THE MOVIE WAKE THE FUCK UP AND RUN!!!

Stop drinking the KOOL-AID!!

You, Ben Carson, can add another award to your long list of accolades. The Negro Please Award. Awarded to you for Adding To The Embarrassment of Black People Worldwide. You are in good company. Another well-known recipient is Omarosa.

You are no longer invited to any cookouts, holiday meals, spades tournaments, impromptu Soul Train Lines, any Black award shows, domino games, nothing! Your Black Card is REVOKED! PERMANENTLY!

Look! It's a Bird, It's A Plane, It's Becky To the Rescue. My Thoughts On A Day Without Women

Have you ever experienced something and it just seemed off? You couldn't quite put your finger on it but something in your gut said, "This isn't right. There is something just slightly off about this." Perhaps like when you view those Spot The Difference pictures and the pictures look so incredibly similar yet under close, eagle-eyed scrutiny you notice slight differences.

That is how I felt about the Day Without Women. I wanted to stand behind it, wanted to support it, wanted to believe that maybe this time, they got it, they understood, they learned from the Women's March. Surely Becky, UGG Boots and Pussy Cat Hats was not going to be replicated but something in my gut said this is not right.

I felt like Smokey in Friday, "You ain't never got two things that go together...cereal, no milk; Kool-Aid, no sugar; ham, no burger...damn!!" I felt like they had protests for women, yet limited, if any, marginalized women. Protests, yet no acknowledging 53% of White women voted for Trump. Protests, not acknowledging their role in the history of oppression of many women. Protests, not understanding that the very fabric of the protest highlighted privilege. A privilege to take a day off work. A privilege that many Women of Color do not possess.

Every woman does not have the privilege just to take off work. And while I know the outline allowed for this and said women on this day should wear red, I thought of women in uniforms. I thought of women that are stay at home mothers. How do they take a day off? Should they tell their children, "I am sorry, I am off today." I thought of single mothers getting up before the sun rises to head to a job that will not allow them a day to protest. I thought of many Women of Color working diligently to make ends meet all across this world.

Then I thought of women like my former teacher Ms. Brown, a Black woman, who told me my voice commanded attention even in 3rd grade. I thought of her and how her attention and nourishing of my writing and speaking, helped empower me to be who I am today. I thought of doctors, judges, bus drivers, waitresses, teachers, lawyers, professors, nurses that would be there March 8 and March 9 and March 10 and beyond because their passion and purpose are not about a National Women's Day Off. It is not about hashtags and selfies. It is about standing in the gap. It is about being a presence in a space when women need to be in those spaces. And they know standing in those spaces is an act of justice. We don't just walk off the job. We complete the job. We lay the foundation for other women to come behind us.

A Day Without Women is not symbolic of justice. It is not symbolic of equality. A Day Without Women is a day of hell. Without the backbone of this nation. A day without women is a day when the world has gone silent. And now more than ever is when we need women to shout!

Please, stop this! If you want to IMPACT this world use your power to disrupt policy that seeks to abuse the least of those. Use your privilege to stand up for someone that doesn't have the same privileges as you. Use your position to allow access for all women. Use your resources to fund a movement.

Right here in this nation reproductive rights are being taken away. Right here in this nation 10 and 11 years old girls are being trafficked. Right here in this nation Women of Color are dying from preventable diseases due to lack of health care. Right here Black women are murdered by the police and no one bats an eye. Right here they are passing laws to re-segregate schools. Right here they are passing legislation to criminalize protesting. Right here 6 Black transgender women and 1

Indigenous transgender woman have been murdered this year. Right here! Right at your very doorstep lies your protest. You don't have to look far to save the world. You don't need a spotlight to do the right thing. There are no hashtags needed when it comes to fighting for justice. As a matter of fact, we don't need you to save the world. Just save your own little corner. Start there. Forget the catchy slogans and cute knitted hats, and fancy curated posters and designer protest bumper stickers. Look around your community, your city, your state. There is where you will find a movement that needs you! Your voice! Your power! Your abilities!

Until then something will always seem off to me about these national "protests". Something will always seem "missing" like when you sit down at a meal and something just tastes off. Like it needs a little more salt. A little more "seasoning". That is how I feel about these national "protests". They need some flavor. Until then everything will continue to taste bland and leave people wanting more.

Can Black Women Live? A Black Woman's Experience Through Georgina and Rose

"I been standing with you! I been right here with you, Troy. I got a life too. I gave eighteen years of my life to stand in the same spot with you. Don't you think I ever wanted other things? Don't you think I had dreams and hopes? What about my life? What about me? Don't you think it ever crossed my mind to want to know other men? That I wanted to lay up somewhere and forget about my responsibilities? That I wanted someone to make me laugh so I could feel good? You not the only one who's got wants and needs. But I held on to you, Troy. I took all my feelings, my wants and needs, my dreams . . . and I buried them inside you. I planted a seed and watched and prayed over it. I planted myself inside you and waited to bloom. And it didn't take me no eighteen years to find out the soil was hard and rocky and it wasn't never gonna bloom. But I held on to you, Troy. I held you tighter. You was my husband. I owed you everything I had. Every part of me I could find to give you. And upstairs in that room . . . with the darkness falling in on me . . . I gave everything I had to try and erase the doubt that you wasn't the finest man in the world. And wherever you was going . . I wanted to be there with you. Cause you was my husband. Cause that's the only way I was gonna survive as your wife. You always talking about what you give . . . and what you don't have to give. But you take, too. You take . . . and don't even know nobody's giving!" Rose - Fences, August Wilson

This world takes. It robs. It covets. It specializes in thievery with no apology. No remorse. No forgiveness. No reparations. This world is like a newborn baby, mouth wide open, greedily sucking sustenance in, with no regard of what or where it pulls from. No concern for the woman. The life source. The mother. The Black woman that has suckled pain and humiliation at her breast and still managed to bring forth life.

This is the Black Woman. The Foundation of Creation. Yet often Black women are the ones overlooked. Neglected. Forced to lead a back-burner existence. So many try to understand us, attempt to tell who we are and who we should be. Black women are the most analyzed women in the world.

If it is not our hair, it is our hips. If it is not our hips, it is our lips. If it is not our lips, it is our skin. What shade is the "right" shade?

Is this shade too dark, too light? Will this shade of Black resonate with White America? Is it light enough for White America not to feel threatened? If it is not our features, it is who we date and who we won't date, who will date us.

Does our body type correlate to the stereotype? The Black woman is oversexualized. Black women aren't sexy enough. Can you see this Black woman in your bed with her shea butter and head wrap? Can Black women raise kids? Can you bring this Black woman home to your parents? Will she be acceptable? Black women are too loud. Black women always seem angry. Why do Black women have a chip on their shoulder?

It made me wonder, Can Black Women Just Live?

I never felt this more as when I watched two blockbuster movies this year, Fences and Get Out. In Get Out, I watched the maid Georgina, standing in front of the protagonist, Chris, trying and failing to hold back her tears. A Black woman wanting to speak the truth, her truth, yet finding herself stifled. Silenced in this White space. Rejecting who she was for them. Muting her voice and forcing herself to smile through her pain.

Rose, played by Oscar award winning actress, Viola Davis, delivered a powerful monologue in Fences, that summed up how it felt to be a Black woman. Many of us have been that woman. Standing there fighting with a man. Fighting for someone else's dreams. Giving your all to someone else's ambitions. One year of your life turns into multiple years gone, and you hardly know the woman that you have become morphing into someone almost unrecognizable just to please someone else.

In this world, Black women are chameleons. We hide who we are to fit in. We smile when we are crying inside. We mourn deaths of people we will never know. We stand when others sit. We attempt to be all things to all people often at the detriment of ourselves. We scream for justice even when no one is listening. We are always fighting.

But there are moments, while often few and far between, that we remember who we are. That we are women. We catch a glimpse of our greatness. We fight to find those moments. Ducking and dodging in between the hurt to stand in our humanity. We dance in between the raindrops. In and out. Finding some piece of happiness. Because it is there. In that sacred place between dew, rain, and sunshine. It is there. Reminding us that we are human. Like déjà vu, we have felt it before. We have been here before. And it feels right. It feels whole. It feels like home.

And so, we dance. Dance to rhythms strummed out on the backs of ancestors. We dance to the waves of oceans that carried sinew and bones. We dance to a live a life we never knew, yet believe we can have. We laugh, loudly. We smile and embrace our sisters. We celebrate the beauty of our skin and the strength of our bodies. We embrace our features, revel in our own beauty. We rejoice in the sound of our voices, loud, strong and powerful. We find and express our joy in the high fives and head nods, over collard greens and cornbread. Who we are does not need your analysis. Our bodies do not need your scrutiny. Our living does not require your approval. We simply are and who we are can never be explained to you. Our existence does not require explanation. You will never understand why we dance, why we sing, why we laugh. You will never understand those moments of freedom. And it is not our job to explain it. To my sisters, do not allow this world to steal those moments of joy. Find those moments and embrace them. Hold them close to your heart. Allow yourself to be human. To breathe. To dance. To laugh. To love. We are Black women. Being. Living. Loving. With no permission need.

Dear Colin Kaepernick: All You Had To Do Was Play The Game, Boy.

All you had to do was throw the ball, boy. We concealed this auction block well, didn't we, boy? You didn't know you were on sale, boy? Didn't we tell you to just run, boy? Entertain us, boy. Win championships for us, boy. Stay in your place, boy. Don't you dare get these other , Black men riled up, boy. Didn't we pay you enough, boy? Why can't you just be satisfied, boy? Stand up and salute this flag, boy. Honor your allegiance to the system, boy. Didn't we give you enough money to entice you, boy? How dare you reject your master, boy. Didn't you like your name in lights, boy? Didn't we stroke your ego, boy? All you needed to do was play the game, boy. Keep dancing for us on Monday Night, boy. Make us rich, boy. We don't care if you get hurt, boy. Our job is to break bucks like you, boy. Didn't you know boys like you come a dime a dozen, boy? We can replace you with no thought, boy. Make sure our new boy is a controlled boy. Thought you knew we don't trust Negroes to be the quarterback anyways, boy. We did you a favor, boy. How dare you turn your back on us, boy. If you are kneeling, it will be before us, boy. Ain't this game your God, boy? Don't you see how everyone else bows down before us, boy? Don't you know what we do to Negroes like you, boy? Back in the day, we let Negroes like you sway from the trees, boy. Make an example outta you, so other Negroes will stay in their place, boy. Don't you smell that strange fruit in the air, boy? All you had to do was just shut up, boy. We don't have to kill you, boy. All we have to do is silence you, boy.

The NFL is comprised of 70% African American males. Black Men have the power to dismantle an industry.

There is a story I once heard, could be fact, fiction or part fact and part fiction, however the sentiment of the story is something I will never forget. One day a man was walking through the circus passing the elephants, and he wondered how such a powerful, gigantic creature could be held in place with just a rope and a stake in the ground. The elephant's freedom was just on the other side of believing that it could break the rope. When the man saw the trainer, he asked him, "Why doesn't the elephant just break the rope and leave this place of bondage and return to his home where he will find sustenance and freedom in his original habitat where he will thrive?"

The trainer smiled and said, "When the elephant is very young and small, we tie a rope to his leg, and it's enough to hold the elephant in place. No matter how the elephant might struggle, he cannot break loose. As the elephant grows older, he has been conditioned over time to believe that he cannot break the rope so, in turn, the elephant never tries to get free."

Freedom is often connected to the ability to recognize that there is no rope that can hold you. Once you decide to walk in your power and authority you can no longer be bound. Restricted freedom is still bondage and it costs. You may not pay now, but the bill always comes due and the oppressor will always want to collect payment.

One voice can be a spark. United voices can ignite a movement. One voice can bring awareness to a system. A multitude of voices can dismantle it.

My brothers in the NFL, you are no longer enslaved. You have all the power. You hold all the cards. You have the power collectively to stand for someone that knelt for our brothers and sisters that were murdered with no regard. As Assata said, "It is our duty to fight for our freedom. It is our duty to win. We must love each other and support each other. We have nothing to lose but our chains."

You have nothing to lose but your chains…

I'm Maxine Waters, B*tch! Put Some Respect On My Name!

Dear Mr. Bill O'Reilly,

Black Women ain't new to this. Black Women are true to this! The card that you just played is one that we have heard since our mothers were pressing our hair with a smoking hot comb off the stove and Blu Magic hair grease. Let's break out the confetti another White person speaking on a Black woman's hair! Ground-breaking journalism.

It seems that is all people like you do. I often wonder how some White people get things done when 75% of their day is spent on how a Black woman should wear her hair and the other 25% is asking if they can touch a Black woman's hair.

If it isn't our hair, it's our hips. If it isn't our hips, it's our lips. Black women are the most analyzed and criticized women in the world. If you can't own it, you covet it and attempt to imitate it. We cannot be duplicated. And at best, men like you, when you cannot dispute or discredit what a woman has to say, your typical mode of attack is to mention her appearance. In this case, Mr. O'Reilly mentioned Maxine Waters hair, likening it to a James Brown wig.

Congresswoman Maxine Waters and Black women everywhere are not impressed.

While as a balding White man, ~~Mr. O'Reilly~~ matter of fact, let me just call you Bill. Bill, as a balding White man you may not understand that Congresswoman Maxine Waters didn't wake up and coif her crown with you in mind. I know as a White man on a network that is equated to the Innermost Circle of Hell, you are used to the world revolving around you. It doesn't. How Congresswoman Maxine Water chooses to wear her hair is not your issue. Congresswoman Maxine Waters hair is not on your agenda. I get it. Men like you are always secretly consumed with women they cannot have. Women they must intimidate to get their way. Women they must call and have 10 Shades of Grey phone sex with because it was nowhere near 50 shades. Then men like you attempt to discredit women that accuse them of sexual harassment, and because they are so innocent, men like you pay millions of dollars to the victims of your sexual harassment that men like you claim never happened. (allegedly) But I heard the tapes. We. All. Heard. The. Tapes. Falafel ring a bell? Refresh my memory Bill on where you wanted to place that "falafel". As a matter of fact, I can refresh my own memory because the audio is on YouTube for anyone that wants to hear how Bill gets down.

If you want to make your personal issues the news we can do that all day. Or unlike you, we can stick to the issues because Congresswoman Maxine Waters hair is not on the agenda. What is on the agenda of what you support, is a failing presidency that is in a tailspin in under 100 days. An administration that operates similarly to the Sopranos.

A federal investigation. A cloak a dagger visit to the White House by Devin Nunes who is supposed to be over the Russia investigation. The firing of Sally Yates. The rise of hate crimes since Trump entered office. A bill that sells America citizens internet privacy down the river. Trying and failing to dismantle the Affordable Care Act. A president that golfs more than he governs. The list is endless of true issues that we can cover. But in typical fashion you choose a Black woman's hair.

Men like you must always try to take from women like Maxine Waters. Congresswoman Maxine Waters accomplishments are endless. One of 13 children, raised by a single mother, Congresswoman Maxine Waters diligently worked her way to Congress. She once chaired the Congressional Black Caucus and was once the ranking member of the House Financial Services Committee. She has stood in favor of reparations for Black people and spoke out against the CIA and their (alleged) complicity in the crack epidemic that ravished Black families. She is the most senior Black woman of the only 20 Black women that serve in Congress. And you, Bill want to talk about her hair. How big of you.

The next time Bill, you want to mention Congresswoman Maxine Waters put some respect on her name! She's Maxine Waters, B@tch! Now are you finished or are you done? Cause Black women around the world have been done!

Kendrick Said He Likes an A$$ with Stretch Marks, And We Are Mad?

Anyone that knows me knows that I am a champion for women's rights. I stand on the shoulders of many women throughout history that have fought and sacrificed for me to have advantages in life. I am a proud woman and a soul survivor. I am a mother of a beautiful daughter that I have taught to stand in her authority and a niece that I pray will walk in her power.

Even with all the feminist blood running through my veins, I found myself confused with the feminist backlash rapper Kendrick Lamar is facing due to his song Humble.

I listened to the song once; then I listened again. I watched the video twice and still I could not find what was causing the problem. So, I pulled up the lyrics to the song so that I could read them slowly and thoroughly, reading in between the lines and dissecting wordplay to see if something was said that would spark this outrage.

The lyrics that are causing such a firestorm are:

I'm so fuckin' sick and tired of the Photoshop
Show me somethin' natural like afro on Richard Pryor
Show me somethin' natural like ass with some stretch marks
Still will take you down right on your mama's couch in Polo socks, ayy

Kendrick is a rapper in an industry that is filled with women and the tearing down and rebuilding of women's bodies. Women in the entertainment industry have an image to uphold that has been highly influenced by what men find sexually desirable. The images that we see have trickled down from the entertainment industry and found its way onto "Main Street, USA," where the average woman is expected to look like a supermodel. The news is filled with reports of women that have sacrificed their very lives going to back alley doctors to attain an image that is portrayed in the entertainment field.

We have seen female rappers adorn butt implants and become overnight sensations. We watched an unknown woman rise to become one of the most known and wealthy celebrities in the world on the wave of a sex tape. We watched a reality TV star swing from a shower curtain and become an internet legend. We have watched pregnant movie stars fight to get back into shape just two weeks after giving birth. Everything about being a woman in the entertainment industry is focused on image. And the buck no longer stops with those in the entertainment field. With the rise of social media, it seems everyone is clawing to become an Instagram model, the next "it" girl and many times, all it requires is that you possess a look that is often only achievable through plastic surgery.

Yet, we ridicule Lil Kim for not embracing her natural beauty. We make sure to point out that Nicki's infamous derriere is not natural. We mock those with weave and tell them to embrace their natural hair. We tell men to love us for who we are and not what we look like. Love our natural hair. Love our lips. Love our skin tone. Love Black women as we are.

And then Kendrick says just that, and it is a problem? I thought about some of the songs that many women have embraced as women, primarily the entire Lemonade catalog. I thought of Formation when Beyoncé boldly declares, "I like my Negro nose with Jackson 5 nostrils." She clearly has a preference, and her preference is for her mate to not have plastic surgery but to have his naturally given, wide-set nose which is a common trait in many African Americans. We celebrated Beyoncé for embracing the fact that as a Black woman she loved her man just the way he was born. I am unsure why this is different.

We celebrate actresses telling magazines not to Photoshop their covers and we rejoice as celebrities like John Legend embraces and loves his wife, Chrissy Teigen even as she flashes her stretch marks.

We stand up for Alicia Keys when she decides to reject industry standards and forego makeup. We feel a sense of pride when Serena Williams embraces the curves and strength of her body. So, I find myself confused. Kendrick is saying that he appreciates a woman in her natural state and not that she HAS to be in her natural state but in his industry, HE is tired of seeing women that look as if they came off a Photoshopped, filtered assembly line. And not only does he appreciate her in a natural state, but he also finds her sexually attractive in her natural state. In a world that attempts many times to reject the sexual desirability of Black women and make White women the standard for anything that is sexually desirable, I enjoyed hearing this celebrated.

We are women. We are not all supermodels. We don't wake up looking perfect. Every photo we take will not be in the perfect light. Some of us live beyond the filters. We have stretch marks. We gave birth to beautiful blessings that altered our bodies in ways we never imagined. We have edges that are kinky. And for many of us you will never be able to run your fingers through our fros. Some of us don't have a six-pack and perfectly arched eyebrows. We have scars. Our breasts are not always perky. And our asses have stretch marks. And with all that we are still amazingly beautiful and sexy. If you can see me beyond what society says I should be and just love me for who I am, flaws and all, I welcome it.

As women, we have many battles to fight. Just this week, Kentucky attempted to close its only abortion clinic which would have robbed many women of their right to choose. We struggle for equality in the workplace. We fight to have the right just to be. There are many battles to fight and I pick mine wisely. Fighting a Black man that attempts in his way to celebrate Black women in their natural state is not a fight I am willing to pick. Some battles are not mine to fight.

Dear Pepsi: How in the HELL do you Plagiarize, Whitewash and Co-Opt An Entire Movement With One Commercial?

Dear Pepsi, I have one question for you. What in the hell were you thinking?!

I suppose Pepsi was attempting to speak to the current issues of protests in the nation many surrounding the death of Black men and women due to police brutality by...wait for it...getting Kendall Jenner, one of the whitest White women that is born into a world of lily white privilege to pretend as if she has had some profound revelation while she is modeling (something she does in real life). Honey, this is not art imitating life. You have no social justice struggle, and we are smart enough to know that we will never see you at a Black Lives Matter rally or any rally. Your family treats Black people like the jewelry that you wear in your fashion shows – Black people are simply an adornment to be worn for a little while until you want to discard or upgrade them.

Back to the commercial.

After this mind-blowing revelation that people are protesting real issues while Kendall is modeling- as usual, asleep at the wheel- she tosses her blond wig aside to a Black woman, and wipes her sister's ~~overly priced might as well buy Maybelline~~ lipstick off her lips and somehow magically adorns a designer jean outfit to act as a leader of a protest. The multiracial sea of humans part and allow White Savior Kendall Moses Jenner to step forth, ~~piss water~~, Pepsi in hand and graciously give this ~~diabetes inducing~~ can of soda to a police officer. This officer has so graciously decided not to mace, handcuff, billyclub or shoot Kendall Moses Jenner but instead, smiles and takes a sip of the Pepsi. Because you know when White women walk up on the police with something in their hands it is NEVER mistaken for a gun and the police never "fear for their lives".And after he swallows down the peace, love and light in a can, Blacks, Muslims, men and women, Jews and Gentiles all hold hands, sing kumbaya and cry rainbow colored tears of joy, happy that White Savior Kendall Moses Jenner has cleaned up injustice one soda at a time.

Really, Pepsi? Really? What the fuck were you thinking? I can guarantee you the person that thought of this went to the Women's March and even knitted her own pink pussy cat hat and came back to the advertising meeting and said, "Guess what, Trisha?"

"What, Becky?"

"I totally went to like a march and stuff this weekend and people were getting soooo hype protesting like women's rights and shit. I completely understand what you have been saying about Black oppression. And I need to do something."

"Really, Becky?"

"Yes. Totally down with the system and screw the man!"

"But didn't you and most White women vote for Trump?"

"Trisha, none of that matters now. Now is the time for us to do something radical. And I know just the thing. I am going to pitch this commercial idea with Kendell fucking Jenner, and she will be like that lady from The Blind Side where she is saving all the Black NFL players, not the ones that kneel during the National Anthem because that where I draw the line. She saves everyone else but him or whatever. Anyways, Kendall is gonna be like her, a strong woman but with like Pepsi and police."

"I don't think that is the best idea. That's been done before. In. Real. Life."

"Oh, who cares what you think, Trisha. It is my job to tell you how you should see your oppression in the media. They won't care if we borrow the idea. We do it all the time. Anyways, it's going to be great! Trust me; you will love it. We will even have like Black women IN the protest but not like LEADING the protest or anything because you know, loud, Black women fighting for justice don't really do much for our product. We kind of like you know, diet justice or justice light kinda like a diet Pepsi. Ha! But we will be sure to have some of them dancing in the background, and we will just let Kendall kind of like be the face of freedom."

End Scene.

There is no way any Black person on your team, if any Black people are on your team and I highly doubt it, thought that this was a good idea. How in the HELL do you PLAGIARIZE AN ENTIRE MOVEMENT? How do you co-opt struggle? How do you Pepsi manage to WHITEWASH OPPRESSION?! How much do you stand to profit off of Black pain? This is not a game to us!

You took decades of sacrifice, struggle, pain and triumph and reduced it to a White woman and soda. Really, Pepsi is that all it takes? An ice-cold Pepsi and the police won't billy club Black people upside the head? I sure wish I could go back in time and tell John Lewis and Martin Luther King Jr. when they were on the Edmund Pettus Bridge that all they had to do was hand the officers a few cold Pepsi's, and they could have avoided being assaulted. Who knew the Kendall Jenner School of Marching for Civil Rights could make fighting for justice so easy?

The picture that Pepsi tries and fails to emulate is of Ieshia Evans attending a protest in Baton Rouge after the murder of Alton Sterling, a 37-year-old man that was shot at close range in the chest for selling CDs. Let that sink in. A 37-year-old man is now dead because he was selling CD's outside of a store. And Pepsi wants to trivialize the stand that Ms. Evans and countless others took to speak to this injustice by making a commercial seeking to profit off the struggles and oppression of Black people with some cheap ass fizzy sugar water. What Pepsi doesn't tell you is while Kendall is dancing and high-fiving in the end of her commercial Ieshia Evans was arrested and spent 24 hours in jail.

If you are going to STEAL the STORY tell the WHOLE DAMN STORY! This commercial doesn't show you Alton Sterling being shot in the chest and just days later Philando Castile bleeding out on Facebook Live. Protesting isn't about glossed over, high definition, manufactured revolution. Our revolution isn't whitewashed or ran through a filter. Revolution aint always pretty. It is death and decay. Bullet wounds and blood. It is torture and tears. It is mourning men and women that you have never met, but still, they haunt you like ghosts crying out in the night for their deaths to be avenged.

This commercial doesn't show you the lifeless bodies of Sandra Bland or Mike Brown. Would Trayvon still be alive if he was buying Pepsi and not tea? Would Alton be alive if he was selling Pepsi's and not CD's? How many sodas will it take for someone like Eric Garner to be able to breathe? How many Pepsi's do I need to purchase for police not to douse innocent protestors in teargas? How many Pepsi's will it take for our marches to be as diverse as this commercial, for people to actually care that Black people are being killed daily? How many Pepsi's should I buy to feel safe in my home? How many Pepsi's do I have to buy for this world to understand our struggle? How much Pepsi must an officer drink before he decides not to shoot an innocent Black male in the back? How many Pepsi's should we give the officer who put his knee in the back of a young girl and sat down on her with his full weight. How many Pepsi's should be allotted so an officer doesn't rape Black women he swore to serve and protect? How many sodas should the officer drink that tossed a young woman across a classroom? How many Pepsi's do I need to tell the mothers and fathers of those that have buried their sons and their daughters too soon to drink so that they will feel better? Would Aiyana still be alive if she had Pepsi before going to sleep on the couch?
How many Pepsi's is it going to take to change the world?
Let me know.

Until then, this was a foolish, insensitive campaign and it is the reason why no matter what you attempt to do, you will always be 2nd in this world.

How do you expect us to trust you with a vision to change the world when you still haven't managed to knock Coke from its number one spot? You have one job Pepsi, and you can't even manage to do that. Focus on Coke and leave the revolution to us.

This Is Not YOUR Revolution,
So Please Stop Trying to Own It.

This is NOT YOUR REVOLUTION. So please stop trying to own it.

When a house is on fire, no one cares who has the water. And indeed, the house is on fire.

Nobody OWNS a revolution.

This is not MY revolution.

This is not YOUR revolution.

The very nature of a revolution means it cannot be boxed in. A revolution is defined as a sudden, radical, or complete change and change cannot be contained. A revolution will not fit neatly within your Crayola lines. A revolution is fluid. A revolution flows where it wants. A revolution will not always possess people that look like you, that think like you, that move like you, that do what you do. A revolution is promiscuous. It goes where it wants, how it wants, attaches to who it wants. A revolution fucks someone's conscience so thoroughly that when they get up, they have wrestled in the bed of injustice and now stare at humanity who looks back at them naked and unashamed, crying out for them to see the world through their eyes. Through the eyes of father burying his child in Aleppo. Through the eyes of a Black mother praying that her son returns home safely. Through the eyes of a Muslim woman that contemplates wearing her hijab. Through the eyes of a Black mother wondering if the world will ever recognize that her daughter is missing. Through the eyes of a LGBTQ person wondering if they are safe in their neighborhood. Through the eyes of a transgender woman praying to make it in this world another day. Can you see the revolution through their eyes?

A revolution will not look how you want it to look. The very nature of the word revolution means it revolves. It is circular. Ever moving, ever changing, ever evolving.

And who are we to say what the revolution looks like? Gil Scott-Heron told us, "The revolution will not be televised," but it is. Because the revolution has been "technologized". The revolution takes place on Twitter. The revolution is on SnapChat in 10-second increments. The revolution is streamed live on Facebook. Instantaneous images of atrocities for us to tweet, retweet, post, and repost. We have witnessed the revolution on Iphone's, Androids, PC's and Mac-books around the world. Beaten and dead bodies lying in streets, images burned into our psyche, which opened the world to our reality- life ain't been no crystal stair. And who are we, to mock those that give us the information? Information we would have never known unless it was shared on social media? Who are we to judge those that are doing their part the only way they know how or can do their part? Who are we to say how you must do your part when it comes to revolution? The revolution is big enough not to be homogeneous. As a matter of fact, I prefer my revolution shaken and stirred, mixed up, undefined and inclusive.

It does not matter what you do. What matters is that you DO SOMETHING! It is time out for selective vision, pretending that you cannot see the horror, injustice and suffering all around you. However, everyone is not called to be Martin Luther King Jr. Everyone is not called to be Assata Shakur. Everyone is not called to be Angela Davis. Everyone is not called to be Malcolm X. The body cannot function as a unit if every part is the hand. So, find your part in the body of justice.

My answer to those that ask me, "What can I do?" It is simple. DO YOUR PART!

If you can write a poem, write. If you sing, sing a song. If you cook, make the sandwiches and fry the fish. If you dance, dance for justice to bring awareness. If you get on social media, post information to keep the masses aware. If you draw, make the signs for a protest. If you code, design a program that will bring awareness. If you build websites, offer your skills to an up and coming organization fighting for justice. If you are good with children, babysit while parents are at a march. If you have a peaceful home, offer someone a place to come collect themselves. If you have a car, drive someone to a protest. If you have financial resources, invest them in the revolution. If you a place of position and influence, use it to speak against inequality. If you are in political office, stand up for policies that benefit the least of those. If you own a business, hire the qualified and often overlooked minority. If you stand in a pulpit, preach against injustice. If you are a journalist, write unbiased news. If you have privilege, use it for someone that doesn't. If you are breathing…do something.

I do not stand in a position to judge what you do. EVERYONE HAS A ROLE IN THE REVOLUTION. Your mission is to do SOMETHING! What isn't an option, if you desire that this world change, is to do nothing. Find what you can do and do it! The revolution is as close as your own front door. Vow to impact those around you. Vow to make a difference in YOUR corner of the world. I am not asking that you boil the ocean. I am asking that you pick up a glass of water and help put out the fires of injustice that rage all around us in this world!

The best activism is the ONE THAT YOU WILL DO! DO THAT! And be amazed how WE can change the world one act of love, compassion, and humanity at a time.

Dear (Some) White People, Please Stop Comparing Yourself & Others To Black Civil Rights Leaders

Dear (Some) White people for the love of Martin, Malcolm, Rosa, and Harriet do us a favor, and please stop comparing yourself and other people that are not Black to Black Civil Rights Leaders.

You would have to be living under a rock not to have heard the shitstorm United unleashed around the world when officers dragged Dr. David Dao off a United flight so , employees could catch a flight from Chicago to Louisville. What is about an hour flight or a 4-5 hour drive turned into a public relations and what will soon be a very expensive nightmare for United. Dr. David Dao was left a bloody mess after this encounter and United has been apologizing because they care about their passengers. To add insult to LITERAL injury, the Courier-Journal, a local paper where Dr. Dao resides, published a sensationalized piece, digging up Dr. Dao's past and essentially blaming him for getting his ass kicked. We learned about alleged pill mills, and of course, other publications tossed in gay sex to add the cherry on top of the victim blaming sundae. Because what is digging up someone's past if we don't exploit gay sex?

Many felt all of this was done to somehow make an excuse for what happened to Dr. Dao. For the first and what I pray will be the only time in my life I thought to myself, "That's that bullshit Donald Trump be talking about." We rallied around Dr. Dao as if it was the 90's and we were fighting to Free Tupac.

And then today happened...

Dr.Dao's attorney, Thomas Demetrio, said that he got an email describing Dr.Dao as the modern-day "Asian version of Rosa Parks." **Say what now?**

The modern-day who? Cause I know this man didn't say Dr. Dao was the modern-day Rosa Parks. Which Rosa? Rosa Jenkins from 34th and Crenshaw? Cause I know, he didn't mean OUR Rosa. Not Rosa Parks that became the face of the Montgomery Bus Boycott. Rosa that refused to give up her seat to a White passenger in segregated Montgomery, Alabama in 1955. Where she risked her very life to say, "Not today. Go on with all that bullshit. I ain't in the mood for all that. I done worked all day, and I'm tired."

While what happened to Dr. Dao should not have happened and was a clear abuse of power, let's not go overboard. We are rooting for you! We want to see you win! We want to see you get a fat check, retire and then ride on United in first class just to be petty. Don't let your attorney ruin the support the world has for you with his ignorance.

Dr. Dao is in no way comparable to Rosa Parks or any other civil rights leaders that sacrificed everything so that Black people today could have an ounce of freedom.

Just this week CNN political commentator Jeffrey Lord said, "Think of President Trump as the Martin Luther King of health care." On what fucking planet?

This is a man that wants to STRIP people of having a modicum of peace knowing they have health care, can afford their children's medicine and can be treated even if they have a preexisting condition. And we are supposed to hold this man up as a modern-day Martin Luther King Jr.? This man that has incited racial violence across this nation against everyone that is not White? This man that allowed Black men and women to be assaulted at his rallies? This is the man that we should consider the Martin Luther King of health care? If that's how we are making comparisons, give me a wig, rhinestone encrusted leotard and call me Beyoncé .

Just a few months ago, people wanted to compare Education Secretary, Betty Devos, to Ruby Bridges. A person hell bent on ruining the educational system compared to a little girl fighting her way through the educational system because she was Black. There is no comparison.

On behalf of former and current Black activists, please stop comparing people that are not Black to Black Civil Rights Leaders. I know, you don't see color, but it cheapens the accomplishments that Black Civil Rights leaders have made in this world. Black people have sacrificed and have died to have basic, CIVIL rights. To this day, we are still fighting. To this day, there is no collective outrage when a Black person is shot down in the street. There is no collective outrage when a Black person is assaulted by the police.

Just days after the collective outrage that occurred with Dr. Dao, Demetrius Bryan Hollins, a Black man, had his head stomped into the ground even as he was on the ground, handcuffed and subdued by an officer and the world at large remained silent. There was no outrage for him. No one compared him to Civil Rights Leaders that were assaulted and arrested. To this world, he is just a Black man being put in his place and "we shouldn't rush to judgment" or "he should have just complied."

If you are outraged at Dr. Dao's treatment but not outraged at a Black man having his head stomped into the ground by an officer, look in the mirror. If you are going to compare anything, compare the reaction of the nation concerning both incidents and then maybe you will understand why we continue to fight. And why we will not let you co-opt the sacrifices of our leaders.

Dear America, Why Do You Keep Researching Issues Black People Have Already TOLD You Were True?

A recent article published by the Washington Post declared, "Racism motivated Trump voters more than authoritarianism." Another article published by The Nation reported, "Fear of Diversity Made People More Likely to Vote Trump."

And in other GROUND-BREAKING news, water is wet, fire is hot, ice is cold, the sun rises in the East and sets in the West, dogs bark, cats meow, roses are red, and violets are blue… Sigghhhhh Really?

How many more studies does America need? Tell me the correct number of studies that will make America believe what Black people are saying is true?

You are researching. We are living this nightmare. You are researching. We are fighting to survive. You are researching? We can see that White heroin addiction is being treated differently and more compassionately than the Black crack epidemic. You are researching. And our communities are still suffering from redlining. You are researching. And we know that Black and Brown men and women are incarcerated quicker and longer than White people. You are researching. And we know our children are suspended from school more than White children. You are doing surveys. We are mourning the loss of Trayvon, Eric, Ayiana, Sandra and many other people of color. You are crunching numbers. While. We. Are. Dying.

Were the racial slurs, not enough evidence?

Was the KKK supporting this President, not enough evidence?

Were the physical assaults on Black and Brown people, not enough evidence?

Was the defacing of mosques, not enough evidence?

Was the vandalism of Jewish headstones, not enough evidence?

Was the hijab being ripped from a Muslim woman's head, not enough evidence?

Were the screams of, "Go back to your country", not enough evidence?

Was the murder of innocent people due to hate, not enough evidence?

What more evidence will it take? How much blood needs to run in the streets to validate your research? As you may know, many of my people complete your surveys in blood and tears.

We have been shouting this truth, and this nation has turned a deaf ear and blind eye to our screams. This nation pretends it doesn't hear the innocent blood shouting just beneath the soil. The cries of injustice are what haunts you at night. When our ancestors scream, now we all scream. You should have listened.

You have only quantified and validated mathematically and scientifically, what Black people already knew to be true. What we have attempted to tell you was always true. And we know it, because we live it, live and in color every single day.

However, now that you have scientifically proven what we have been TRYING to tell you since Trump first started to run for President, now what? Now that you have this concrete data of what we have already known, now what? Now that you understand the campaign slogan, "Make America Great Again," was just a cry to Make America Racist and White Again, now what? Now that you know that race was indeed a factor in electing a man without an ounce of political savvy into the highest office in the land, now what? Now that you might have a modicum of understanding of why we are protesting, now what? Now that you know that people will sacrifice even their own benefits to have a man in the Oval Office that supports their racist agenda, now what? Now that you know what Black people have been saying since our ancestors first arrived in this nation, now what?

What will you do with this "newfound" knowledge?

You don't get off the hook because you published a study. Thank you for now admitting what we have already known. But you see, here there is no cookies and milk being served for acknowledging a longstanding and well-known truth. What we are serving up is a cold dish of crow and reality. Because knowing comes with responsibility which is why many people would rather remain in the dark, cloaked in the illusion that we are a post-racial nation that sings kumbaya, eats Ballpark hotdogs, all while sipping a Kendall Jenner ice cold Pepsi.

Knowing means working to change a system. Knowing means, you can no longer pretend. Knowing means, you have a responsibility to advocate for transformation. Knowing means, you must support policies that benefit People of Color. Knowing means, you must acknowledge injustice.

My momma used to say when you know better; you do better. So now that you know, according to how YOU needed to know, what will you do, to "do better?" Don't worry. I'll wait.

But let's be real. You didn't need a study to know what is going on all around you. You never needed a study. All you had to do was open your eyes.

Stop Stealing From Black Artists-Creative Place Taking and Black Art

It is ironic that I write this blog on the evening that HBO is debuting the made for television movie about Henrietta Lacks, an African-American woman who, while being treated for cervical cancer, had her cells stolen to create the HeLa cell lines. While most cells eventually stop reproducing, Henrietta's cells were what the medical field called an, "immortalized cell line", in which her cells would reproduce indefinitely. Henrietta Lacks cells have been used in the research for cancer, AIDS, gene mapping, instrumental in the polio vaccination and to this day her cells are used in almost every molecular –biology lab. Henrietta Lacks cells have generated billions of dollars, yet the descendants of Henrietta Lacks have not fared as well financially. As is often the case when people steal from others.

Sadly, this is nothing new, since the beginning of time people have made a fortune stealing from minorities. Land, people, resources, music, ideas, culture, art, food, style…the list is practically endless.

Such is the case with the article by Dismas Sanfiorenzo that came out in OkayPlayer featuring a Chicago "artist" and "urban planner" that completed a "large mural of Michelle Obama that is located a few blocks from the former First Lady's childhood home." The mural is of Michelle Obama in green and gold royal African attire. A photo that I recall seeing floating around Facebook, so I surprised when reading the article that this "artist" was representing the work as if it was something that he conceptualized, when in fact, the artist is actually a talented young, Ethiopian female artist named Gelila Lila Mesfin who can be found on Instagram.

The "artist" that took Mesfin's work stated in the dnainfo article, by Andrea V. Watson and Tanveer Ali, "I wanted to present her [Michelle Obama] as what I think she is, so she's clothed as an Egyptian queen. I thought that was appropriate." Really? You were sitting at home and thought, "I want to depict Michelle Obama as an Egyptian queen?" Really? Something in me finds that very hard to believe.

What I see is someone that saw an opportunity to steal a young Black woman's work and profit from it never believing that anyone would notice.

But we did.

We noticed because we recognized the picture and we recognized it because a Black woman that many of us admire was depicted as an African Queen. Images that we do not often see so the picture resonated with us, connected with us especially in a world where Black women are rarely if ever, presented as royalty.

The "artist" goes on to say in a statement on his GoFund Me page, "Our nonprofit urban planning projects often include paintings inspired by "found" images. We were blown away by a wonderful image we stumbled on and only found out after the fact who the source of the inspiration was. We in no way meant to impinge on anyone's creativity." After the fact? In this day and age of technology, you found out after the fact who the artist was? Okay, wait. Let's play Law and Order detectives for a minute. I thought the "artist" said he wanted to present Michelle Obama as an Egyptian queen as if it was his idea? Now the statement is, "It was inspired by a found image." A found image. Kind of how Christopher Columbus found America.

But wait the statements get better. In another statement the "artist" goes on to say, "We recognized the importance and power of this piece to Chicago youth, particularly at this time in history." Really? So, to inspire Chicago youth and what I can easily assume will be African American youth, this "artist" inspires them by stealing the artwork of a Black artist. How does that work? What message does that send to Chicago youth? Steal, and you will get ahead? If you cannot create something on your own just take it from a Black person? It is okay to lie to a community about conceptualizing a mural, because who is really going to notice this artwork from a Black artist that is not well known in the art world?

This is a huge problem I see when artists enter spaces and want to do creative placemaking. Newsflash: It is not creative placemaking when you steal another artist's work. Just because you steal artwork and give it a "hip" and "trendy" name does not make it creative placemaking. It is creative placetaking, plagiarism, and thievery.

What this so-called "urban planner" doesn't understand is he didn't just steal artwork from Gelila. In my opinion, he didn't care about taking the image because he has no connection to the image. He doesn't understand what it feels like as a Black woman to see a Black First Lady. How many Black women stood a little bit taller during Michelle Obama's eight years of service because in the history of the White House no one had ever held that position that looked like us.

How we admired her because she didn't lie and steal to get to the top but worked diligently to graduate from Princeton and Harvard. He doesn't understand the power we felt as Black women when we watched Michelle Obama navigate the Oval Office with dignity and class even in the face of being ridiculed. He doesn't understand how we felt her silent pain as she was called ugly and a monkey because of her features. So, he doesn't understand that seeing Michelle Obama in traditional royal African attire connected her and us to a history that has been STOLEN through slavery or maybe I should call it creative placemaking.

He never had to understand those things so for him it was okay to just steal the image. He probably never understood how Black women have had to fight for everything and his "creative placemaking" stole art from a young Black artist that is working to make a name for herself. Black women have always been on the auction block. Our stories, our bodies, our art, even our very cells are stolen with no regard, no thought, no concern. You didn't just steal from Gelila. You stole from every Black woman in this world that is attempting to simply be great any way we know how. There is no justification for what you did. You are in a long line of men and women that have profited off the backs of those that just wanted to be! That's all we ever wanted. To use our skills, talents, and gifts to simply be great! And for people like you, that is just too much. For people like you, it didn't matter that you stole someone's piece of sunshine. It never mattered in your "creative placemaking." Because it was never about the power of the image it was about you and how you could profit off the back of someone else.

I Do Not Weep For Melania. I Understand Melania.

It was a love story that rivaled the best of Hollywood movies. Young up and coming African American Columbia graduate, president of the Harvard Law Review and community organizer meets Princeton and Harvard graduate lawyer from the Southside of Chicago, and they fall in love. Barack & Michelle Obama go on to rewrite history becoming the first African American President and First Lady of the United States of America. We smiled when Barack serenaded his wife, did a historical fist bump with her that was felt around the world and showed a genuine, authentic love and appreciation for the woman he was destined to be with. The Obama's relationship photos were tagged with hashtags like "#goals."

During his final address to the nation when Obama said Michelle's full government name - Michelle LaVaughn Robinson Obama-as Black women we all melted. We knew what that meant.
That was almost equivalent to Beyoncé 's and Jay-Z's Drunk In Love song:
"We woke up in the kitchen saying
How the hell did this shit happen?", oh baby
Drunk in love, we be all night
Last thing I remember is our
Beautiful bodies grinding off in that club
Drunk in love
We be all night, love love
We be all night, love love"

We knew it was gonna be on and poppin' at the White House and we loved that. We related to that. We wanted that. It was incredible to see pure, unadulterated Black love on display, live and in color for the world to see. That this man loved his wife, the mother of his two beautiful children and was as physically attracted to her that day as the first day that he met her.

The Obama's spoiled us with their love which is why seeing the stark contrast of the Trump's marriage is a shock to many people. We caught a glimpse of the Trump's marriage during the inauguration when Trump and Melania exited the car. Trump did not open the door for Melania; he didn't lovingly hold her hand as they walked together up the stairs to greet the Obama's. Memes were made across the world depicting what was in the Tiffany box that Melania gave to Michelle Obama-many saying a simple note crying for help was in the box. More images consumed social media of Melania looking solemn, stoic and at times sad . The images of Trump exiting Air Force One show a man that feels he is the center of the universe, reveling in his power and she is just a bit part in his production.

From the moment Trump decided to run, I felt this was not something that Melania signed up for, never wanted and could do without. Video of her awkwardly reading to sick children surfaced online. I cringed as I watched the video. English not being her first language, it was not her accent that shocked me as that was to be expected. It was that she seemed not to understand how reading a book to kids worked. This was clearly not the role that she had signed up for. In her mind, perhaps they had a deal and casting a woman that has been fairly absent from the spotlight, into the global spotlight was not a part of the arrangement.

Some people have started #FreeMelania threads, but I do not weep for Melania. As a woman, I understand Melania. Many of us at times have been Melania. I have been Melania. Perhaps we have never known that degree of wealth, but in our own way, many of us have all been Melania. We may not have dined in five-star restaurants, stayed in the finest hotels or flown on private jets, but we have been Melania. We have been a woman that has settled for a man. Settled because we didn't think we had any options. Settled because he seemed like the best option. Settled because we needed to get away from a home that was not ideal. Settled because someone could pay the bills and provide for us when we needed it. Settled because as women, many of us don't chase love, we chase security. Settled because we have always been raised with this clock ticking in the back of our minds. A clock with hands that beat steady to remind us that our beauty will one day fade. That our breasts will not be as perky at 45 versus 25. That our bodies will change. That on the heels of our beauty is another woman that is faster, stronger, prettier, better that your mate will find desirable. So, we clutch on to what we have, hold it tightly as if we are fighting against the currents of life that threaten to wash us away.

And we smile when we want to cry. We laugh to hide the pain. We speak when all we want to do is be silent. We are silent when we long to shout. We sit pretty and poised. Not one hair out of place because we must project and protect the illusion. We become mechanical in our movements, our actions, our love. We do what is required to sustain the myth. We fuck men we do not want to fuck. We leave pieces of who we are on satin sheets, our voices hidden in empty moans. We fold inside of ourselves. Create bends and creases in our souls. We make excuses. We find reasons to forgive and pray that we can forget. We hide the woman we long to be for the woman that we must be in order to survive. We cover the puppet strings in fancy clothes and red bottoms hoping that no one will see them.

I have been Melania. I have done all those things, not to that degree of wealth but in my own way, I placed who I was aside to gain a life that was substantially different than the life I knew. Until one day I realized my value, my worth and no amount of money could buy that. I was no longer for sale to the highest bidder. My life was my choice. Who I fucked would be my choice. Who I built a home with was my choice. Who I had children with would be my choice. And it would no longer be a choice built on the foundation of settling. I deserved more. I deserved to be loved, truly loved. I learned that material things come with a price that I was no longer willing to pay. I had paid that debt with my body, my heart, my soul for too long. Shiny trinkets no longer impressed me. It took years to find me. To value me. To love me enough to walk away from it all with the clothes on my back, daughter in tow and know that somehow, I had the strength to make it.

Once you realize your value, you will no longer settle. Once you recognize that everything you desire to be is held within you, you will no longer settle. Life is far too short. Do not chase what can be temporary, blaze your own trail to forever. Your happiness is just on the other side of realizing that you hold all the cards, all the power, all the ability to build the best life you desire on this earth. Should any tears will be shed, it will be tears for women that do not yet know their worth and I pray that one day they realize just how exceptionally amazing they truly are as they step into their freedom.

Dear "Woke" Black People: It Is Possible for Black People To Do Two Things At Once

Dear "Woke" Black People,

It is inevitable when a current event issue comes across my social media feed or a "fun" internet challenge, there will be several "woke" members of the Black community that will let us know that we are not allowed to think about anything but one issue. And how dare we become distracted doing a mannequin challenge, singing about "beans, greens, potatoes, tomatoes", laughing as James Wright eats a Patti Pie or get "caught up" in companies misrepresenting or ill representing African Americans.

While I know this may be difficult for some in the "woke" community to understand, it is possible for Black people to do two sometimes even three things at once. It is also possible for Black people to be concerned about two, three and sometimes even four issues all at the same time. I know. It is shocking and groundbreaking.

The following is just a short list of several things that I am able to do simultaneously:

- Walk and chew gum
- Drive and sing Lemonade songs and do all the moves to Formation flawlessly
- Like my baby heir with baby hair and Afros and like my negro's nose with Jackson Five nostrils
- Listen to Biggie and Tupac
- Whistle and juggle
- Cook and watch YouTube videos
- Love children and still be pro-choice
- Walk and think
- Fight for liberation and enjoy Real Housewives of Atlanta
- Twerk on a video and still not want to sleep with you
- Go to college and raise a child
- Be bougie and ghetto
- Hold United accountable for abusing customers and care about affordable healthcare
- Be Solange on the red carpet and Solange in the elevator
- Be Black and fight for LGBTQ rights
- Wear a miniskirt and still not be asking to be raped

- Speak with eloquence and string cuss words together like a melodic soliloquy
- Care about world issues and still watch the New Edition Movie
- Care about police brutality and homicides in my neighborhood
- Have a perm, weave or braids and still believe Black women should be allowed to wear their hair any way they want
- Fight for liberation and take time to be concerned about my personal well-being
- Be pro-Black and have White friends
- Care about Shea Moisture leaving behind their base customers and justice for Black people
- Reject Pepsi co-opting the Black struggle and protest against injustice
- Resist 45 and watch Love and Hip Hop Atlanta

- Be petty and throw shade
- Bring home the bacon and fry it up in a pan

The list is practically endless of what many people that fight for liberation and I can do at the same time. Please do not paint us into a box of what the fight for justice must look like and what we must be concerned about. I never did well coloring in lines. When you make those comments, you reduce us to a people that do not possess the ability and aptitude to use our God given mental prowess and common sense. Black people have some of the most brilliant minds in the world. We have invented things that have changed the course of the modern-day existence for all people. From the stoplight and peanut butter to super-soaker water guns and blood transfusions, Black people are capable of using our mental mechanisms magnificently to transform the world. And we can do it all while walking and chewing gum.

Beyoncé , Serena and Black Women Around the World Don't Owe You Shit

This week on the anniversary of Lemonade, Beyoncé announced her new initiative the Formation Scholars designed to (as stated on Beyoncé .com), "encourage and support young women who are unafraid to think outside the box and are bold, creative, conscious and confident. Four scholarships will be awarded, one per college, to female incoming, current or graduate students pursuing studies in creative arts, music, literature or African-American studies. The schools selected for participation are Berklee College of Music, Howard University, Parsons School of Design and Spelman College."   As most of the world celebrated Beyoncé taking up this initiative, The New York Times journalist Vanessa Friedman decided not to focus on Beyoncé trying to advance educational attainment for young women but instead chose to focus on Beyoncé 's pregnancy.

Yet again Black women are blessed with another White woman speaking about a Black woman's body. OH GOODY!!! THANK YOU!!!

You know every day that I wake up, I am just dying for White women to write articles about my hair, body, lips or hips. The list is endless of the analysis of Black women and our appearance. I don't know how I would get through my life unless a White woman told me what I should think about myself.

I wondered if Friedman wanted to speak about Black women and pregnancy why not use such a high-profile pregnancy and her platform to draw attention to the health inequities many expecting Mothers of Color face? Draw attention to how poverty, lack of employment and education can impact the health of a newborn. Highlight the fact that a growing body of evidence points to racial discrimination as to the reason so many Black babies are dying. Write about the fact that the infant mortality rate is 2.4 times higher among Black infants than White infants. Use the popularity of Beyoncé to highlight something that can actually impact the readers. But of course, that is asking for too much. Why would she want to write about any of that when she can tell us that Beyoncé is setting the bar too high because she dances to Formation while pregnant?

In the article, Friedman states that Beyoncé has set the bar "uncomfortably" high not just for pregnant women in the public eye but pregnant women in general. Set the bar too high? Too high for who? You? Beyoncé is living her life. She is pregnant. Not dying. I love how Beyoncé is criticized in the article for doing her job yet, Friedman celebrates Amal Clooney, who is also pregnant with twins, as someone who, "has effectively gone about her business, appearing last month in the United Nations to talk about the female victims of the Islamic State." So how do you criticize Beyoncé who is effectively doing her job but celebrate Amal for doing her job? Should Beyoncé apologize because her job entails singing in sold out stadiums? Beyoncé is an entertainer. Her job is to entertain. She didn't sign up to entertain White women in a way that would make them feel less intimidated by her. Same with Serena Williams. One of the greatest tennis players this world has ever known and once again Friedman feels it is her business to say how Serena should celebrate her pregnancy stating, "here's hoping she does so in a humanizing style." What it really sounds like she is saying is, "I cannot believe these Black women are achieving such a level of greatness in their lives and doing it while pregnant. Who do they think they are?"

Listen, Beyoncé, Serena and Black women around the world do not owe you shit. Black women have worked in your fields, your homes, your kitchens, for nothing. Black women didn't have the time to celebrate their pregnancies because their bellies were swollen with a child due to rape by your husbands. Black women didn't have time to enjoy their pregnancies because they knew they would be birthing them into a life of hell on your plantations. And when Black women did have babies they couldn't worry about nursing their own babies because they had to play wet nurse to yours. As a Black woman, trust me when I say, we have paid our dues. We are no longer indentured servants to your feelings of inadequacy. Did Beyoncé set the bar high? You're damn right she did! Did Serena set the bar high when she won the Australian Open while pregnant? You're damn right she did! Does every Black woman that aspires to greatness set the bar high? You're damn right we do.

Our ancestors didn't just give birth; our ancestors birthed A NATION!

We were raised knowing to get half as much as anything that someone like Friedman has we would have to work twice as hard. You have no understanding of what it means and how much work it takes to be great and Black in this world.

We will never lower the bar to fit your standards. I suggest you no longer write anything that discusses Black women and our bodies unless it is done in a way to bring awareness to the systems that are designed to continue breeding the injustice that this nation continues to deny that benefit women like you. Until you do that I suggest buying a pair of sunglasses, so you do not get blinded by our shine!

Don't Just Get Yo Money Barack, Make it Rain On 'Em!

Oh, joy. Another day and another White columnist telling Black people about themselves. First it was Beyoncé and how she has set the bar too high for pregnant women and now it is how much money should be "enough" for Black people. Beyoncé can't even enjoy her pregnancy, and now Barack Obama can't even enjoy his money. Thank you, Ruth Marcus for your article, "Is $60 Million Really Not Enough For The Obamas?" In honor of Marcus's column, I feel it is my duty to send her and other journalists that have a problem with Obama's finances a nice letter.

Dear (Some) White People,

Please know that when you judge President Barack Obama for how much money he is receiving for giving speeches, this is how you sound: *"Obama sure is acting like an uppity Negro. We gotta put this Negro back in his place. Who does this Negro think he is? We let that Negro become the President and now he wants to get grand. Walking around demanding money for his time and services. How dare this Negro demand the money that he is worth? We should go back to the days when we didn't have to pay Negros anything. Who authorized this Negro to make the system work for him? Negro went to some Ivy League school probably because of "affirmative action". Now, this Negro wants to get paid for giving speeches. You know it wasn't too long ago we didn't even let them read. Back in the day, we used to have Negros like Barack working for us. I sure do wish we could go back to the days when America was I mean, no, I really mean racist. I would put Barack back in a field and let's see how his big fancy words work then. Negro probably thinks he's too good for the field. Make him a house Negro. Let him shuck and jive for us. Use his big words to entertain us. Let him keep our records for us. The only time a Negro should be making money is when he is making it for us."*

Marcus states in her article, "I don't begrudge the Obamas their reported $60-million-plus joint book deal, of which their publisher has said a "significant portion" will be donated to charity. That should leave plenty for the Obamas to live as luxuriously as they could want."

Who are you to judge how much Barack Obama makes for giving speeches? Who are you to determine what amount of money is enough for The Obamas and the legacy they want to leave in this world? Who are you to monitor the type of lifestyle the Obamas should live?

When White people gained their wealth from slavery, no one said a word. When the blood money from slavery is still circulating and has built entire industries, no one cares. When entire industries are established to showcase plantation homes in the South, it's fine. When White people leave generational wealth to their children, often gained off the backs of those they enslaved, no one complains, they make reality shows highlighting southern charm. When White people gained wealth by stealing land, it was all good.

When White people acquired wealth by redlining communities only to go back into those communities and make money, tearing down projects and rebuilding homes, it's fine. When White people do land grabs in low-income communities and gentrify the neighborhood, no one says anything. When White people make billions of dollars with subprime loans, this nation is silent. When White people bring down the financial industry only to get bailed out, it's called, good business. When you vote a White man into the highest office in the land that is a billionaire, and he refuses to show his tax returns, the nation keeps right on going and in fact attempts to justify him NOT showing his tax returns. When former Presidents set up foundations, for the most part, the nation says nothing. When Ivy League institutions are given astronomical endowments by White people, it is fine. When White CEO's are paid enormous bonuses, even when a company is failing, it is fine. When FOX News pays 25 million dollars to a man accused of sexual harassment, the nation as a whole doesn't bat an eye.

Now all of a sudden, it is a problem. Now all of a sudden, "you don't begrudge the Obama's for their 60 million dollar book deal." Oh really? Thank you so much, Ruth for not begrudging the Obama's for getting paid 60 million dollars. I am sure the Obama's are sleeping a little better tonight knowing that you are okay with their book deal.

While you may not believe your stance has anything to do with race, I beg to differ. Trust me, it is 100% about race. Because you are covering an issue about a Black man, who is no longer in office. Should the Obama's contact you first before they decide to order a pizza to make sure that lines up with how you feel they should handle their income? Should the Obamas contact you first to make sure the lifestyle they are leading is in accordance with what you believe is enough for them?

Are you asking George Bush about his money? Are you asking him how much money he and his family makes? Have you asked them about their family wealth and Prescott Bush? How was that wealth obtained?

Better yet, here is an option, why don't you focus your energy on asking Donald Trump about his money? Did he acquire every dollar ethically? How do you feel about the reported millions of dollars it costs to cover Trump golfing in Mar-a-Lago practically every weekend? I know, you can't begrudge a President for wanting to golf every weekend at a place of business that he owns so essentially his business is making money every time he decides to go golfing, right? No problem with that, huh?

What about Eric Trump taking a trip to Uruguay to look over the family's business interests which cost almost $100,000? The list is endless of where your attention could be focused if it was truly about politicians and money. If you want to speak about holding Barack Obama to a standard, what standard are you holding any of them to? It seems the "standard" only applies when we are discussing Barack Obama. As a matter of fact, I am curious, who sets the standard? You? Why do White people get the option to set the standard?

Now ya'll want to start asking about money? Now ya'll care? Now every dime any former President makes must fall under scrutiny? Now we must hold former presidents to a standard? What changed? Why now is this standard being set by White America? In a nation that prides itself on making money by any means necessary, what is different this time? The only reason why it is an issue is because Barack Obama is Black. Give me a break. Get yo money Barack and don't only get it, make it rain on these people!

His Name Was Jordan Edwards. A 15-year-old Boy. Murdered By The Police.

I scrolled through my Twitter feed and I saw the headline 15-year-old killed by police. I paused as I felt the lump grow in my throat as I wrestled with my emotions. 15. The number echoed in brain like I was screaming it in a valley. Screaming and no one could hear me. I didn't want to click the link. My finger hovered over the link as I tried to will myself not to click it. Not to read it. But I knew I had to. I needed to. I could not let his death go as a blip on my social media feed. I had to know the details. Had to absorb this truth that a 15-year-old boy was now dead. I clicked the link and read through the details. Very few were given at that time but as the hours went by more details surfaced. The police officer lied. His name not yet released because in this world we do not protect the innocent. We protect the murderer. The body cam footage did not show a car being used as a weapon. His brothers and friends saw smoke coming from the head of Jordan Edwards, who was murdered by a police officer with a rifle at 15 years old. Smoke coming from his head. The image of his smiling face now tainted with this ugly truth.

I didn't read the comments. I knew the inevitable cries of "He should have complied," "What was he doing at the party?" or "Why was he just existing?" would be there. I couldn't handle that. Not this time. It was all so routine. The shooting. The lies. The press conference with the obligatory, "Don't rush to judgment" pleas. The outrage. The hashtag. The R.I.P. shirts. The media attempting to vilify Jordan. Searching for any social media pictures that coincide with their way of making Black people animalistic and criminalistic. What evidence would they attempt to dig up that Jordan was a "thug worthy of being murdered at 15"? Then it comes out that he had "good grades" as if those that do not deserve their fate in America. That they deserve their lot in life to be the usual suspect murdered with no regard.

I do not know if I have it in me to go through this again. In this fight we bury sons, daughters, mothers, fathers, sisters and brothers we have never known. We mourn men and women we have never known. We shed tears for boys and girls we have never known. We place their pictures on t-shirts, hoodies and prom dresses vowing to remember. We chant their last words like prayers that keep falling on deaf ears. We wait for justice that never comes. We bury a little bit of ourselves each time a headline comes across our phones, TVs or computers. Pieces of my heart are buried in Florida, New York, Louisiana, California, Texas. Sprinkled across this country like a blood offering for peace that we never find.

His name was Jordan Edwards. A 15-year-old boy. Murdered by the police. He died from a gunshot wound to his head. Jordan Edwards

died as smoke came from his head. And the world as we know it keeps right on turning.

Been There, Done That: How To Spot & Deal With A Phaedra In Your Life

If you happened to feel the earth shake last night at 8:03 p.m., that was thud of the collective mouths of every Real Housewives of Atlanta fan dropping wide open as we finally learned that housewives' attorney and recent divorcee, Phaedra Parks, was the low-down, doesn't know how many months pregnant she is, lying, conniving, manipulator that started the rumor about Kandi Burruss. A rumor that Kandi and her husband Todd wanted to drug fellow housewife star Porsha and take her to their sex dungeon. The lie was already ludicrous enough as most fans know, Kandi is very open about her sexual escapades and does not indulge in drugs or alcohol. What Phaedra essentially accused Kandi of was attempting to ply a young woman with drugs and take advantage of her sexually or in a shorter word- rape. It was a shocking and potentially career damaging accusation that extended beyond reality TV and manifested in the "real world" with Kandi being forced to defend her character on social media as fans called her #BillCosby.

I sat watching Kandi fighting tears on the couch, and I could immediately relate to what she was feeling. I, too, have had a Phaedra in my life. A person that attempted with all her might to ruin my character, with lies that not only could impact my career but lies so unbelievably outrageous could impact my life. When you have worked hard to maintain your character, it is heartbreaking to watch someone you once considered a best friend and confidant do everything in their power to ruin who you are.

If you have made it through your life without a Phaedra, you are truly blessed. If you are like me and have had a Phaedra in your life or are currently dealing with a Phaedra, I pray this blog helps you.

What Is A Phaedra?
A Phaedra is someone that:
- Smiles in your face and talks behind your back
- Pretends that they are happy for your accomplishments when really, they are loathing that you got something that they didn't
- Makes you feel as if you can be open and honest with them when in reality they are taking notes in order to be calculating at a future point
- Secretly wishes that they had your life i.e. career, mate, house, money, etc.
- Colludes with your enemies to cause you harm
- Keeps a straight face will lying to your face
- Feels they are more deserving of your blessings
- Loves you while they consider you beneath them or equal to them and hates you when you are surpassing them
- Attempts to set you up for failure

- Serves you shade and attempts to laugh it off as a "joke"
- Will not do the work or be as dedicated as you but feel they should have what you have worked hard to gain
- Is very helpful and giving at the beginning of the friendship in an attempt to have things to "throw in your face" later or tell others how much they have done for you in order to make them appear innocent
- Works to get those that love and care about you to think negatively about you
- Calls you to only talk about their problems and overlooks your concerns
- Covets your gift and talents
- Secretly rejoices if anything negative happens in your life
- Wants you to remain the same and not attempt to better your life
- Gossips relentlessly and seems to know everyone's business
- Will attempt to get ahead of you by any means necessary even if it means lying or trying to damage your character

Having a Phaedra in your life can catch you off guard because typically a Phaedra is someone that you consider a best friend. A Phaedra is someone that you trust, that you share your innermost secrets with, that you would willing give the shirt off your back and if you have a dollar, without question they have fifty cents. A Phaedra is someone that you think would never do you any harm, so you have no reason to suspect them of any ill doing. You gloss over backhanded compliments, the fact that when they call they only seem to talk about themselves, that you are always there for them much more than they are there for you.

How To Spot A Phaedra

Pray - If you want to know something ask God, the Universe, the Ancestors, a Higher Power and it will be revealed to you. However, be prepared for what is shown to you.

Do Not Ignore Your Gut Feeling - When I was dealing with a Phaedra in my life, there was something in my gut that kept telling me something was off with this person but because this was my "best friend" I was second guessing what my gut instincts were telling me and making excuses for her behavior. I actually felt guilty for feeling suspect about her because of course there was no way she would ever do me any harm. In fact, my gut feeling turned out to be correct.

Pay Attention To The Signs (There are no coincidences in life) - Before I found out anything about my Phaedra, one Friday, I found out my daughter was dating the nephew of one of the church members that I like quite a bit. I thought, how neat. I will have to tell her that my daughter is dating her nephew. Well lo and behold she JUST SO HAPPENED to sit next to me in church.

As we were leaving, she said, "I have something to tell you. I don't want to sound spooky, but God wants me to tell you there is someone around you, that is very close to you that means you harm." For days, I thought about this and milled it over and thought surely no one close to me wants to harm me, at least no one in my circle. Little did I know, my Phaedra had been plotting, scheming and manipulating to harm me and this was God's way of warning me, but once again, I assumed there was no way that could happen.

Pay Attention To Who Is In Your Circle - Always take the time to re-evaluate your circle. As you grow in your gifts and talents, not everyone will truly celebrate you. People pretend well, and people will pretend as if they are happy for you when in reality they are upset that you are rising and they are remaining the same. Take note of your circle and do not be afraid to readjust as needed.

Listen To Those Around You That Have Your Best Interest At Heart - There are people in this world that truly love you and want the best for you. Often, they are on the periphery watching you excel and cheering you on. Because they are not intricately involved in the friendship, they can see things from the outside that you may not be able to see on the inside. Everyone is not hating on your friendship some people can see and are warning you so that you avoid a world of trouble.

How To Deal With A Phaedra

Never Wound A Snake, Kill It - This is a quote by Harriet Tubman that sums up the way that I feel about Phaedras. Do not entertain a Phaedra. Do not believe a second chance will make it better. Do not believe if you do anything differently Phaedra will behave differently. A Phaedra is a Phaedra. You do not entertain snakes. You do not give a snake a second chance to bite you. If you are lucky, you survived the first bite. The second bite could be deadly. Completely cease the "friendship". It is over.

When Someone Shows You Who They Are, Believe Them The First Time - Maya Angelou was correct with this statement. People can only pretend for so long. Eventually, who they really are will always show. Because you are connected to a Phaedra you believe what they have shown you, they will never do to you, but someone's character is their character. If they gossip about others, they will gossip about you. If they lie on others, they will lie on you. Never think that you are exempt from the true character of a Phaedra.

Recognize That Some Friendships Are For A Season - Everyone that joins you on the journey will not complete the journey with you. Some friendships are for a lifetime and others are just for a period of time. Know that seasonal friendships are okay. Take what you learn from the friendships that are seasonal and continue on your journey. It is always okay to bid Phaedra goodbye.

Maintain Your Integrity - Do you have tea you could spill about your Phaedra? Of course, you do! Do you hold secrets that you swore you would take to your grave? Sure you do! Would it be easy to retaliate and start serving up a piping hot mug of Earl Grey? Sure it would! Would that benefit you in the long run? No, it will not. While it would be easy to start running your Phaedra down, you place yourself on a level with Phaedra, and you want to maintain your character and integrity. While it may kill you not to seek revenge, please know life is truly cyclical and what goes around does come around. Don't get yourself dirty rumbling in the mud with a Phaedra. Trust that karma is indeed real.

Dealing with a Phaedra was one of the most trying time in my life. Someone who I considered a sister turned out to truly be one of my worst enemies. However, one thing I was determined to do and one thing I encourage you to do if you have a Phaedra in your life, is to be wise about new friendships BUT understand that everyone is not a Phaedra. There are people that will be placed in your life that love you, support you, care for you, rejoice when you succeed and truly want the best for you. Do not allow a Phaedra to alter your view on friendships. There are amazing people in the world that will hold you up and support you. That will keep your secrets as close as their next breath. That will be the hype man while you dance into your destiny. That will watch your back like a solider. Cherish those friendships but always be aware that snakes slither to and fro always waiting to strike.

Dear White People, Sex, Intimacy and Black Love

After many disgruntled tweets, Facebook posts and tears from those that just could not understand why Netflix would be debuting a series based on the acclaimed movie, entitled Dear White People, the original series was finally released this month. I immediately knew that this was a series that I would binge watch. I watched each episode back to back only taking a few moments in between for snacks and bathroom breaks. Dear White People is a clever, comedic commentary that opens a dialogue across sectors and one that I hope brings awareness to many issues that Black people experience that many White people claim they are oblivious to. The series follows a group of young African American students at the predominantly White Ivy League college, Winchester University. Many of the issues Dear White People addresses, I could immediately relate to, primarily being in college and trying to discover who you are amidst being in White spaces trying not to get swept away in the raging current of racism and micro-aggressions. Overall I was very pleased with the series and look forward to the next season however, there was one issue that I did have with Dear White People...

Where is the Black Love, Sex and Intimacy?

Yes, we saw Troy- the All-American, I-am-the-next-Obama-in-the-making -have sex with Colandrea aka Coco but their sex was more of the animalistic sex that is often stereotyped between Black men and women. Don't get me wrong, there is always a time and a place for some body rockin', headboard bangin', I bet the neighbors know my name, whose is it sex but I wondered why couldn't we see sex displayed between a Black man and woman that was intimate, erotic and sensual? Even when we did see Troy and Colandrea have foreplay and he was performing cunnilingus (which he seemed to love because not only did he perform it on her but also Nia Long's character that he was cheating with) her mind seemed a million miles away, instead of enjoying every single tongue grazing, body shaking, legs quivering moment.

In contrast, one of the first love scenes we see in the series is of Sam, the African American female lead, and Gabe, her secret White male lover, engaged in a passionate display of love making of course all shown to us in slow motion with perfect lighting. The scene is set flanked by the Autobiography of Malcolm X on the bedside table, violin music and Sam moaning passionately as she rides herself and her lover to a breathtaking orgasm. Gabe politely asks, "Did you, uh?" And Sam replies, "Uh huh, twice," as she giggles and wraps herself up in his sheets. She proceeds to pick up her cell phone afterwards and plays Candy Crush as she is wrapped in Gabe's arms and they playfully give each other love bites. The scene continues as they kiss and Sam giggles before being summoned via text to come attend the Black

Student Caucus. The scene was romantic, passionate and shows a couple that was not just having sex but that have an intimate connection.

I kept watching, hoping that with the progressiveness of Dear White People, I would have a chance to see a scene between two Black people that was just as passionate and erotic as Sam and Gabe. I thought that moment would come when Sam slips into Reggie's dorm room. Unfortunately, we do not get to see them have sex. We get a glimpse through the mind of Gabe of what their sexual encounter looked like with strawberries, ramen noodles and ice. Why couldn't we actually see the encounter? As a viewer, and a Black woman, I would have loved to see what a sexual encounter between Sam and Reggie looked like. I would have loved to see a Black man and woman, making love on my TV screen. Not animalistic, YouPorn sex. But sex that is erotic and sensual. Sex where there is deep kissing, licking on the soft part of her neck, whispering sweet nothings in her ear, telling him how much you want him, him entering her slowing, absorbing the way that she feels, both of them moaning softly than louder, him on top of her and her on top of him and him back on top of her as he moves in and out slowly than faster than slowly again until he takes her to the edge of ecstasy pushing inside of her deeper until they both release and lay tangled in sheets covered in a mist of light sweat, shining with the contentment and afterglow of love making.

However, that did not happen.

Before Sam entered Reggie's dorm room they have a conversation about him passing off the duties to lead the Black students on to her. Reggie says that he was not trying to pass the duties on to Sam but he always saw her as a leader to which Sam asks, "Don't you think there is a woman under here?" And as they say good night, Reggie enters his dorm but leaves the door open, silently inviting Sam in. And she enters. As a viewer, we know they are going to have sex but as a viewer their sex was shrouded by too many questions. Is this guilt sex? Obligation sex? A way to assuage her guilt for sleeping with a White man? A way to soothe Reggie's manhood after he has an encounter with the police? Does she feel they should really be together? Does fighting against the machine bring them together? There are too many questions that surround their encounter to make it comfortable or romantic for the viewer.

Can Black men and women ever make love without revolution between them? Is it possible for Black men and women to make love and not be overwhelmed with injustice? Can Black men and women truly be intimate if the woman feels as if she is bearing the weight of the world on her shoulders? Can Black men see Black women as sexual creatures? Can a Black man see a Black woman as a woman that just needs to be woman? Can Black men and women take off their armor and be vulnerable, naked, exposed and that is okay? Can Black men and women be passionate without thoughts of oppression? Is there ever a time to just be a woman and a man? Is there ever a time not be the face or voice of a movement and for a moment just be a man and a woman that wants to make love? Because sometimes making love has nothing to do with revolution but everything to do with desire, need and longing.

And perhaps that is why Sam found herself in the arms of Gabe. With Gabe, Sam is able to find refuge because he allows her to just be Sam the woman and not Sam the activist. Gabe brings her ice cream, supports her going to rallies, acknowledges their relationship on social media, listens to old school music with her, supports her radio show, checks his privilege at the door and invites her to dinner with his friends where she can discuss her love for old movies over cheap wine. As Sam's friend Joelle said to Gabe, "She smiles with you. Not a self-satisfied smile but with you it's a whole body thing, Head to toe. With you she smiles from her socks." With Gabe, Sam is allowed to just be Sam. She can just be who she is without the clouds of oppression, police brutality and racism engulfing her.

Perhaps that is what Black men and women need and as an activist what I need to see. I need to know that a show as forward thinking as Dear White People does not succumb to the myth that Black men and women are incompatible, argumentative and destructive. I need to know that this is not just another show that highlights Black men and women in dysfunctional relationships. I need to know that Black women can rest in the arms of Black men and feel safe. I need to know that not every Black man is cheating and looking for the next best thing. I need this world to know before there was ever 50 Shades of Grey there were 100 Shades of Black. I need to see that Black men and women can be passionate and erotic. I need to know that Black men still look at Black women like Barack looks at Michelle. I need to see that because I am that. I am woman that loves, love and that loves intimacy and passion and all things kinky and erotic and discreet. And sometimes we need a break from the machine. A moment to pause, to exhale, to breathe deeply. To connect and moan and tingle in the arms of a lover. A time to just pause and to truly make love with no thoughts of revolution between us.

White Women Are Always Allowed To Be The Victim

As the not guilty verdict hit social media feeds around the world, it left many Black people just nodding their heads, as Officer Betty Shelby was able to exit an Oklahoma courtroom a free woman. Officer Shelby would not be held accountable for fatally wounding African American motorist Terence Crutcher. Justice once again found a way to laugh in the face of African Americans. If Lady Justice is blind, she sure has 20/20 vision when it comes to allowing White officers to walk free after they murder Black civilians. While I would like to say that I am shocked and stunned by the verdict, I am not. Betty Shelby joins a long a line of White women in America who are afforded the permission to be the victim especially when it comes to encounters with African American men.

When Shelby broke her silence about the fatal encounter with Crutcher, she made sure to note that he was "about 6 feet tall and 240 pounds." While Shelby contends that Crutcher's race and body size did not influence her decision to murder him in the middle of the street, it echoes an officer's comments made from the helicopter that was recording the encounter, that Crutcher looks like a "bad dude." I am curious, if Crutcher had no weapons and admittedly Shelby said that Crutcher was not acting aggressively, what would make a man all the way in a helicopter ascertain that Crutcher looked like a "bad dude"?

It is always funny to me how when a Black man is involved in a situation with the police their height, and weight always becomes a determining factor when deciding if they should live or die. We saw this countless times over when Mike Brown was made to appear as the Incredible Hulk and Tamir Rice, a 12-year-old boy who was shot and killed by an officer on a playground in less than 2 minutes. The news media focused on the height, and weight of Tamir instead of an emphasis on the fact that this was a 12-year-old child was murdered by the police.

This is often how the media generates the story when it comes to race relations. Black men are always painted as large, dark, menacing, evil and overpowering figures. And White women are painted as the innocent, demure, vulnerable victims that need to be coddled and protected especially from Black men that seek to harm them usually in a sexually violent manner. This is a narrative that has been generated since slavery. However, we know that indeed it was White slaveowners and their wives that abused, humiliated, whipped, raped and murdered Black men and women.

White America has created, perpetuated and sold this myth to the world that it is not them that have committed some of the most if not THE most heinous crimes against humanity, but it is Black people, especially Black men that seek to harm White women.

The media continues to bolster this narrative with the damsel in distress theme. It is always a White woman that must be rescued from impending harm. From books to movies to fairytales White women are always portrayed as the innocent, demure, feminine and sexual being that must be rescued from the stereotype of the wild, savage and brutal Black man. Little girls are born and raised with images of Disney Princesses like Snow White and Cinderella, that must be rescued by their knight in shining armor. Black women are never portrayed in a way that would allow them humanity and vulnerability. Even when Disney did finally make a movie, The Princess, and the Frog, with a Black female lead character, it was not the prince that saved Tiana; it was Tiana that saved the prince. Black women are never allowed to be seen as vulnerable and in need of being rescued. Black women are never allowed to be the victim.

Similar to the narrative White America has sold about the savage and brute Black men, White America has developed and perpetuated the narrative that Black women are always the strong, wide-hipped, asexual, sassy, loud talking, side kick that is always there to provide a shoulder to cry on for White women with a finger snap, neck roll and an ounce of humor. This myth is bolstered in Hollywood with the mammy character in Gone With the Wind, Hattie McDaniel, the Black assistant coming to save the day played by Jennifer Hudson in Sex And The City, and Regina Long's character in Miss Congeniality. Black women are never portrayed as needing compassion and understanding.

This manifest beyond the big screen to real life when White women are often glorified and made into heroes for committing violent acts. Instead of portraying White women as violent murderers the media will often portray them as meek, innocent and as a woman that was pushed beyond her control. Even when White women commit some of the most heinous crimes, they are portrayed as the victim, and we are not called to vilify them but to understand them and sympathize with them. From murderers Jodi Arias, Laurie Bambenek, and Betty Broderick to child molesters, Mary Kay Letourneau, Deborah LaVave and Pamela Rogers Turner, the world attempts to make White women that commit crimes heroes and their actions excusable and acceptable. Betty Shelby stands in line with a list of White women that have circumvented justice.

White America continues to perpetuate the strong Black women myth because it absolves them of any guilt for how they treat Black women. Indeed, Black women are strong because we have always had to be strong. Society never gave us the luxury of breaking down. Society never gave us the luxury of taking a day off. Society never gave us the luxury to mourn. Society never gave us the luxury to be vulnerable. And because it never did, it does not have to see us that way, and that is why we can be abused, overlooked, overworked, raped, and beaten, and we are just supposed to be able to take it with a sister girl smile and a high five.

I understand that Black women make this look easy but we are not leprechauns or your magical Negro. Despite us declaring that Black women possess Black Girl Magic, there is nothing magical about this. What you don't acknowledge is Black mothers burying their sons and daughters, Black women putting up with sexual harassment at work because they have to put food on the table, Black women that are raped by an officer and too afraid to speak out because who would believe them anyway? What you don't see is a Black girl with an officer's knee in her back coming from a day at the swimming pool, or a Black girl thrown across a classroom like a ragdoll by a White officer because she is not moving as quickly as he would like. What you don't recognize is that Black women hurt and bruise and bleed. There is nothing race specific about pain and hurt and depression. There is nothing race specific about vulnerability. There nothing race specific about being the victim. For centuries Black women have had to go to rest in a bed of despair, crying tears into our pillows of heartache and no one ever stops to recognize that we hurt too. Sometimes we need to be rescued. There are days that we need to be seen as meek and soft and gentle and kind because that is who we are. Being a Black woman does not absolve us from heartache and pain and it certainly never seems to absolve us from the long arm of the law.

Am I surprised Betty Shelby walked out of a courthouse free to go home to her family while Terence Crutcher's family visits him at a graveyard? Not in the least bit. Betty always had two things working in her favor. She is an officer, and she is a White woman. America believes that officers are always innocent and White women are always the victim. Betty was never going to be convicted because she had everything working in her favor. It's the American Way.

Dear (Some) White People: Why Is Black People's Hair Always on Your Agenda?

In yet another episode of White People Being Too Damn Concerned About Black People's Hair, seventeen-year-old Jenesis Johnson, a student at North Florida Christian in Tallahassee, Florida was reprimanded for wearing an afro. Jenesis's teacher asked her, "How long are you rocking that hairstyle?" Okay, let me start there. Rocking that hairstyle? You mean the hair that grows out of her scalp? After this question, two days later Jenesis was called to the office and told by the assistant principal that her hair was, "extreme and faddish and out of control. It's all over the place." She was also told that her hair violates the school hair policy because you know, White people love to make policies about Black people's hair. The policy states, "No faddish or extreme hairstyles, and hair should be neat and clean at all times. The administration will make the decision on any questionable styles."

Faddish? Extreme? Questionable? Explain to me how the hair that grows OUT OF YOUR HEAD is faddish? What type of fad causes your natural hair to grow? It is not a fad to reject White societal norms and embrace your natural hair. It is not extreme to dismiss what White America says is beautiful and embrace your God-given beauty. A fad is Miley Cyrus deciding she is going back to country music now that she has pimped and profited from Black culture.

A fad is Khloe Kardashian rocking Bantu knots and acting like she invented them. A fad is Kim Kardashian rocking cornrows and trying to the pass them off as "boxer braids." Wearing the hair that naturally comes from your head is not a fad. It is not extreme, and it is certainly not questionable. This hair policing extends beyond Black women with college graduate, basketball star and NBA prospect Nigel Hayes.

Hayes received a letter from Jenny Madden, a client of the White People Being Too Damn Concerned About Black People's Hair Club telling him that in order to get into the NBA he needs to let go of his "bizarre hair-do".She encouraged Hayes to, "get all cleaned up with a nice haircut and side-bur(n) trim and professional appearance." Jenny believes if Nigel does that he will, "for sure get picked up by a pro basketball team looking better and more classy for their team and community." Clearly, Jenny of Sun Prairie is not only a client of the White People Being Too Damn Concerned About Black People's Hair Club, but she's the club's president. Trust me, Jenny, Nigel is going to be just fine, locs and all.

While White America is frightened by Black students rejecting what they say is "neat" and "acceptable" hair in the classroom, White males like Dylan Klebold and Eric Harris (two students that executed one of the worst mass shootings in America at Columbine High School) with "nice" haircuts are shooting up your schools. Perhaps White America needs to stop worrying about Black people's hair because clearly there are some more pressing issues that should be on your agenda and believe me Black hair is not one of them.

What is it with White America and this incessant need to police Black people's hair? I do not understand why Black people's hair is ALWAYS on some White people's agenda. It is as if some White people wake up every morning wondering how they can focus on a Black person's hair. What is it about Black hair that intimidates you? What is it about Black hair that scares you? What is it about Black hair that makes you covet our hairstyles and attempt to pass them off as your own? What is it about Black hair that sends a vibe through your hand that you must reach out and touch it? Why does White America get to set the standard on what is acceptable for Black hair?

I believe what bothers White America about Black hair is that they cannot control it, and they cannot contain it. They do not like to see Black people in their natural state. They get nervous when Black people start embracing who they are. They are worried when Black people start rejecting White norms. They are intimidated to see a Black woman standing in all her natural glory. They are fearful to see a Black man with his natural hair being great. Because they don't know what is coming next. They are frightened by Black people embracing their hair and who they are because they want Black people to stay in their place, conform, go along to get along, stay in the box of oppression that they have built for Black people. They are aware that once Black people begin to realize who they are they will no longer be content being confined, regulated and oppressed. And that is what it is really about. It was never about the hair. It is always about Black Liberation.

Dear Newsweek - Yes, Black Women Do Like Men Outside of Their Race

While it may not have been evident to some in America, for many Black people we understood for Rachel Lindsay to be the new star of season 13 of The Bachelorette, she would have to be damn near perfect without a blemish in sight in order to stand on that platform. In the history of the show which has been on the air for 14 years, there has never been a Black Bachelorette. (Nor has there ever been a Black Bachelor.) I was not surprised to find out that Rachel was a lawyer at a prestigious law firm in Dallas, Texas. At 31 years old, Rachael has been described as career driven and passionate. She is an attractive Black woman that appears to be confident in who she is and that understands that the world is watching her.

Indeed, for many Black people to be accepted into any position that America sees as a typical "White" space, Black people must be flawless. Look at President Barack Obama and his exceptional credentials. Barack Obama went to Columbia, worked as a community organizer, attended and graduated from Harvard where he was the first Black president of the Harvard Law Review. He was a civil right attorney and a professor that taught Constitutional Law. He was a United States Senator. On top of that, he has never been caught in any marital scandal, meeting, falling in love with and marrying, successful attorney, Michelle Obama. They have two beautiful daughters that have managed under the scrutiny of being a child in the First Family, to maintain who they are and be intelligent, well-rounded young women. Everything about Barack Obama had to be perfect, and finally, America felt in the history of the United States Government that it was time to allow a Black man to sit in the Oval Office.

Similarly, The Bachelorette decided it was finally time for a Black woman to hand out the roses to would be suitors. While the perspective husbands-to-be varied in race, and it was the first time I saw so many Black males on the show, research has shown that 59% of the Black contestants on the Bachelor exit in the first two weeks.

Ultimately, who Rachel decides to be with will be her choice. Black or White. That is the thing about love and relationships. The heart wants what the heart wants, and while I am a fan and champion of Black Love, I am also a fan of love and how love looks, no one knows. Love is promiscuous, it goes where it wants, how it wants and does what it wants with whoever it wants. Which brings me to the point of this blog. Newsweek decided it would be a good idea to write an article that leads with this headline on Twitter:

New "Bachelorette" Rachel Lindsay is Proving Black Women Actually Do Like Men Outside Their Race. What? Really? I had to read it again to make sure it was not 1917. (I would link to the article, but apparently, someone at Newsweek woke up and realized the dragging they were getting was too much and removed the article. But screenshots are forever, and something told me they would delete the tweet, so I took a screenshot of it. My petty is strong.)

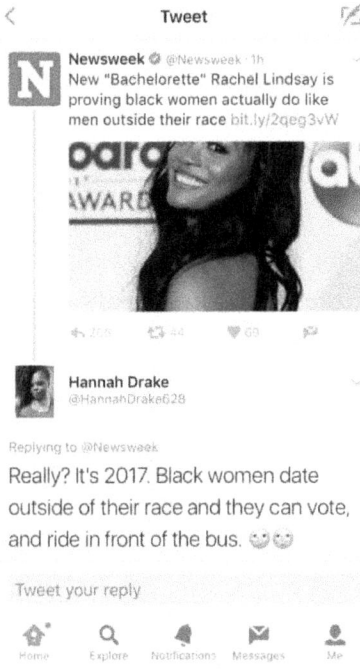

Photo 9 Courtesy of Hannah Drake/Twitter

Yes, Newsweek Black women actually do like men outside of their race. I am going to go a step further and tell you;Black women even love men AND women outside of their race. And sometimes, and I know this may be hard for you to comprehend, Black women even marry men and women outside of their race. And sometimes, wait for it...Black women have babies with men outside of their race. I know! Crazy, huh?

While I know you may not believe it, Black women actually have rights to do things now. Here are just a few things in the list of endless things that Black women can now do:

- Vote
- Ride in front of the bus
- Own homes
- Go to school
- Eat anywhere they want in a restaurant
- Swim in pools with White people
- Not put up with your stupid shit
- Star in movies and not only be cast as the maid
- Be the CEO's of companies
- Start their own business
- Excel in politics
- Nurse their own kids
- Love whoever the fuck they want

While it may have taken The Bachelorette 14 years to have a Black woman on the show, Newsweek, you lose for setting us back years with your Twitter headline. Black women can do all things and we will not allow the world to place yet another box around who we are "permitted" to love. We didn't work this hard, looking this damn good not to love whoever we want to love! Simply get in line behind The Bachelorette, Newsweek if you are just now waking up to the realization that Black women indeed are amazing!

Dear White People, No You Cannot Use the N-Word

In today's episode of, "Why Can't I Say The N- Word?", meet Valerie Smith who is running for the Village Board in Southampton, Long Island who feels it is okay that she used the N-word in describing a group of African-American men that were allegedly standing in front of her house drinking Hennessy. (Because of course if you are Black and having a drink, it is required that it must be Henny. They were also crip walking and pouring out a lil liquor for their dead homies. Okay I added that part.) Smith feels it is acceptable for her to use the N-Word because she grew up hearing it, comedians have used it, and it should be her right to use the N-word. In addition, because she is White and has chosen to graciously live in a Black neighborhood, she should be given an I-Can-Use-The-N-Word-Neighborhood-Association-Pass.

Valerie falls in line with many White people that have attempted to find ANY reason under the Sun of the Motherland to use the N-word.

But Jay-Z said it
But Kanye said it
But my Black friend says it
But Eddie Murphy said it
But Dave Chappelle said it
But ya'll say it all the time
But it sounds so cool
But it gives me street cred
But I don't see color
But I am down with Black people
But I didn't say it was an "er" I said it was an "a"
But I went to an HBCU
But it's just a word
But I donate to the NAACP
But I Milly Rock on any block…Can I finally use the N-word? The answer is NO. The answer will always be NO. At no time on this planet or any other planet in the universe will it ever be acceptable for White people to use the N-word. We don't even give Eminem a pass, and he will always be invited to the cookout.

While some people, even Black people, may or may not agree with how this word has been integrated, reclaimed and repurposed, into the African-American lexicon, that is something that is left for Black people to debate.

However, there will never be a degree of Blackness that you will ever accumulate that will ever make it acceptable for you to use the N-word. Even on Bravo's reality show, Southern Charm Savannah, when Nelson said "schvartze" which is a Yiddish slur for Black people equivalent to the N-word, it will NEVER be acceptable. In any language, in any country, even in Paris, White people will never be allowed to say the N-word. So get over it!

Truthfully, I wonder why so many White people feel compelled to want to use the N-word? It is almost as if some White people cannot understand that some things just are not for them. I know when you have a history of stealing things that are not yours like ideas, culture, food, human cells, music, hairstyles, land, people it may be difficult to understand that everything is not yours. Everything is not up for the taking just because you want it. Everything is not for you because it will fit in with you appropriating all things Black.

And I know it is killing you to know why? If I were to allow a White person to say the N-word, something deep on the inside of me would rise up. I don't have time to sit around and decipher, "Did they mean this in the 'we are down' way or are they having some plantation flashback and I am gonna have to get all Amistad on them?" It is too easy for us to be cool one minute and the word n*gger fly out your mouth the next minute. I don't want to guess did I hear an "er" on that or an "a" on that? I would rather not have to decide are you cool or are you an undercover racist?

And saying the N-word is a slippery slope. Cause one minute you are wanting to say the N-word and the next minute you are saying, "I don't mean you, I mean those n*ggers. Why don't we just round up those n*ggers and keep the cool n*ggas to make up dances for us and sing us songs? You know, like how my family used to have those "house n*ggers'. Of course, I don't mean you; you are one of the good n*ggers. You are my n*gga. I mean those thug n*ggers we need to hunt like dogs. My Daddy used to say, "The only good n*gger is a dead n*gger. But of course, I don't mean you."

And inevitably just when I think we are cool, the word n*gger will slip from your mouth to describe me because I look like those n*ggers. I am Black like those n*ggers. I disagree with your public policies like those n*ggers. I despise police brutality like those n*ggers. I stand with Black Lives Matters like those n*ggers. I believe in reparations like those lazy n*ggers. And just imagine the shock and surprise you would feel when you realize there is no difference between Black female, college educated, poet and writer Hannah and those n*ggers.

We are all Black and "those n*ggas" are my family, my friends and me. My n*ggas.

Tiger Woods, What Is You Doing?

Tiger, Tiger, Tiger...

All I can do is shake my head like one of the old church mothers on the front pew. Child, what is you out here doing?

You think you can get away with drunk driving? You are no longer America's golden boy. Your "I Can Be Out Here Acting A Fool and Get Away With It" card has been revoked. You no longer have a pass to just be doing some stupid shit. Tyler Perry, he might be able to get away with doing some stupid shit. Oprah might be able to get away with doing some stupid shit. Hell, Drake might even be able to get away with doing some stupid shit. You? No. Not today. Not tomorrow. Not even next year.

The minute the curtain was ripped and revealed that you were a serial cheater and cheated on the blondest of blond woman, your card was revoked.

Don't you get it? They let you in and you messed up by cheating. They just needed one thing to make you the villian. They let you on a GOLF COURSE! They don't care that George Franklin Grant invented the golf tee. In a world where Clifford Roberts, golf administrator and co-founder of the Augusta National Golf Club, said, "As long as I am alive, golfers will be White, and caddies will be Black", you were never expected to be allowed to play. In a game where Lee Elder, the first Black man to play in the Masters had to rent not one but two homes so he could move in between them to avoid racist attacks, you were never expected to win. Haven't you watched Bagger Vance? Your job was never to be golfer in their eyes. You were supposed to be the mystical Negro that carried the bag.

What you don't realize, Tiger is that you had the audacity to be great at their sport! You weren't just great you dominated their sport. You didn't just dominate their sport; you became rich playing their sport. You didn't just play golf; you were the face of golf! You weren't just the face of golf, but you opened the door for Black boys and girls to know if Tiger can do it, I can do it! Not only that, you had the nerve to win the Masters. The first and only Black man to put on the green jacket. You beat them at THEIR GAME!

And now they say you out here drunk driving?! Nope. Not today. Come on now! You have to be strategic in life the same way you were on that golf course. You must now learn to navigate this world. Trust me, if they cannot do it, they will always give you enough rope to hang yourself. The same way you aced golf, you must ace your new normal - that you are a Black man in this world and there is no margin of error for slip ups.

"Thank Ya, Guvanah Bevins. We's Just Gonna March & Shutup Just Like We's Marchin' 'Round Jericho"

"Why, it's mighty fine of you Guvanah Bevins to come down here to this here colored part of the city. Where did my manners go? Let me remove my cap. Like I's was sayin'. We's so glad you came down to our neck of the woods and you even got people to bring those fancy cameras. Guess we's gonna be on the news! Look momma I'm on TV.

We's just so thankful that you and your friends came down here and don't mind us, we's good colored folks. We's just gonna sit right in the back while you and ya friends sit up front. Anyways, Guvanah, we's so thankful you are here! Lord knows we's aint seent ya in these here parts in a mighty long time. Must be real busy up there in that there Frankfort. Where ya'll makin' all da laws to get us here colored folk right.

I see you brought your gal with you. Always nice to see one of us with the Guvanah. We sho do appreciat' ya comin' up with this here plan to get us colored folks togetha. Why I don't know why us silly old country, backwoods preachers neva thought about askin' these colored folks to pray. That's what da Good Book says. And dats what we's gonna do. Guvanah, we's gonna march around this here community like it's Jericho! You hear me?! I said we's gonna march around this here community like it's Jericho! And you's right, Guvanah. We's ain't gonna sing no songs. Lawd no! We's ain't gonna shout. Lawd no! We sho ain't gonna wear no shirts with no slogans. We ain't gonna carry no signs. And I done told that boy to put up his bullhorn. Oh no, Guvanah! Won't be no bullhorns. We's just gonna come outside, when ya'll tell us we can come outside, and we's gonna march and just pray in silence. Gonna zip our big lips and get to walkin'. Might walk so much we end up North!

We's so happy you came up with this here plan to stop these Negros from pulling out they pistols on one another. I done tried to tell these Negros a million times but dey just hard headed Guvanah. Dey hard headed. Head as hard as des broken sidewalks ya'll aint fixed. We's just so thankful Guvanah, that you thought of us in that big, old fancy house we's been seeing on da news. And here you are in da flesh! Praise Gawd! Our Savior done arrived!"

Perhaps that is how Governor Bevin thought the conversation would go when G, he decided to hold a "conversation" in Louisville, Kentucky with local Senior Pastors and/or a church representative to address the ongoing violence in Louisville. (Let me preface this blog by saying, I resigned from a church where I worked for 16 years, so I understand church, church politics and politics that intermingle with the church like the back of my hand. I have been saved since I was 12 years old and I believe in the power of prayer and the power of God.) Having said that, as soon as I heard his call out for Senior Pastors the first thing I thought was, "What a complete and utter waste of time." If Bevin really wanted to have a true conversation about the violence that is rocking the city of Louisville, I wondered why he would not start with people that are actually in the trenches, doing the work? While that may include Senior Pastors, it is certainly not exclusive to Senior Pastors. That would be mistake number two.

Mistake number one was foolishly presuming that HE, D, Bevin, had a plan that was going to "fix" the Black community. As if the Black people in Louisville flashed a light in the sky and asked for Bevin to come to our rescue. Bevin in his naivety believed he could mount up his white horse and gallop down Broadway, West of 9th Street, with a plan that would fix the ills of the West End and primarily fix the ills of the Black community. Bevin's actions are typical of having a White Savior Complex Mentality. We never asked for a White Savior. We never needed a White Savior and we certainly never needed Bevin to come into the West End with his ill-conceived, moronic and condescending plan to get the Negros in line.

Mistake number 3 was going online with the announcement of a "plan" without saying what the plan entailed. Did Bevin discuss this "plan" with anyone in the Black community? If this "plan" was so marvelous and would reduce homicides in Louisville, why keep the "plan" a secret? Why not fully announce the "plan"? Over the course of the last few months we have been subjected to a "leader" that always has a "huge plan that is going to be great", yet we never see the plan. Why didn't Bevin discuss the "plan" with community activists, business owners and residents? It appeared as if Bevin had a great plan to reduce violence that he was holding on to until his schedule was clear enough and the holiday weekend bourbons were consumed to announce this great "plan". Meanwhile, Black people in Louisville were still dying.

Mistake number 4 is treating Black people in Louisville like we are the problem. While redlining and city planning may have divided up the city like momma's sweet potato pie, what happens in the West End affects everyone in the city of Louisville and beyond. We are inescapably intertwined. Let's not pretend as if White people are not dying from heroin and pain killer overdoses every day in Louisville along with a multitude of other 'we-can-conceal-them-because-we-are-White' problems.

While Bevin may believe he must get us Negros in line, he fails to recognize the undercurrent of racism that is prevalent in Kentucky. Not just Louisville. But Kentucky. He needs to acknowledge that paddle boats ain't the only thing that flowed down the Ohio River. Kentucky has a history of slavery that it wants to hide with horses, bluegrass, and bourbon but the stench of your sin still lingers. We have not forgotten. We will never forget. And if you want to deal with violence in Kentucky truly, I suggest you, GUVANAH BEVINS, take a long, hard look in the mirror. This is what you inherited when you decided you wanted to be GUVANAH of Kentucky. I suggest you look at your friends that you golf, sip mint juleps and hobnob with. I advise you to ask them about the 9th Street divide. Ask them what would we find if we shake their family trees? Ask Meade County, where a Confederate statue was relocated, about a slave named Lucy, that was hung for killing her White slave master and rapist. Go to Lexington the capital of the Kentucky Slave Trade, where thousands of children were separated from their parents. Men and women that were sold and shipped "down the river".

You want to understand being Black in Kentucky? Start there and work your way through Kentucky history and then come back and humble yourself before you stand before us in your suit and tie and kumbayah entertainment. Start talking about a plan to fix wrongs that your people committed and NEVER righted. Start talking about funding and policy changes to make right the wrong your people committed against Black humanity. The seeds were planted in Kentucky years ago, and it is all entangled in the roots of the bluegrass.

We will no longer be hidden. And oh no, GUVANAH BEVINS, we will no longer remain silent. The revolution will not be met in shadows and whispers. In the spirit of our ancestors, we come with songs and shouting! Since you want to cherry pick scripture, let me pick some out for you today. We will not be silenced. We are called to fight for liberation like Esther because perhaps we are here for such a time as this! And we will not stop, we will not be moved. We stand like Amos, shouting for freedom, until justice rolls on like a river and righteousness like a mighty stream!

"The Talk"...Driving While Black

Recently, Blavity published an article titled, One Maryland Doctor Wrote The Prescription For Surviving Police Encounters. Really? Immediately, I was intrigued. A doctor with a prescription for police brutality. With the onslaught of Black people being murdered by the police, I was very interested in the article and what Dr. Geoffrey Mount Varner had to say. In the article, Dr. Varner states, "that his book isn't intended to be a cure-all or policy prescription to reduce the number of people killed at the hands of police each year. Rather he calls it a way to bridge the gap." His tips are common sense tips that most Black people have had drilled into them since they were born- be humble, don't make any sudden moves, ask permission before reaching for anything, etc.

It is not lost on me that the responsibility for an African- American driver not to be killed by the police falls not on the officer but the Black person operating the vehicle. A Black person driving is at the whim of the officer that initiates the traffic stop, never knowing if the officer is racially biased, is having a bad day or just doesn't give a damn about Black life.

Understand that many Black people never grew up with the myth of Officer Friendly. In my family, no one ever told me to distrust the police. Truthfully, it was something I inherently knew. I grew up seeing enough that I could understand that the police were not on my side to serve and protect my family and me. My first encounter with the police was them storming in my house when I was just 11 years old, eyes trained on my father as my mother ran by me as I was sitting on the stairs and up to her room to get her things. She was leaving my dad. Leaving like a thief in the night, only coming back to get her clothes but leave her children. All while the police watched daring my father to make a move. I do not remember if my mother ever said goodbye as she left the house but I do remember the police officers leaving with her. It was at that point I resolved never to call the police for any issue in my life and thankfully in 40 years, I have never called or asked the police to assist me with one thing, and I pray I never have to. I have even told my daughter if, by chance, something happens to me and I appear as if I am losing my mind, do not call the police to assist you in dealing with me. Call your aunt, call your uncle, call on Jesus but do not call the police.

It is not because I believe that all police are inherently evil, racist and corrupt. I believe the system they work in is evil, racist and corrupt. While many people mocked Colin Kaepernick when he posted a meme comparing the current police system to slave patrols, indeed, Colin was correct. As stated in   Wikipedia,   "slave patrols called patrollers, patterrollers, pattyrollers or paddy   rollers   by   the slaves, were organized groups of white men who monitored and enforced discipline upon black slaves in the antebellum U.S. southern states. The slave patrols' function was to police slaves, especially runaways and defiant slaves. They also formed river patrols to prevent escape by boat. Slave patrols were first established in South Carolina in 1704, and the idea spread throughout the colonies." In over 300 years, the system has not changed. So, the current system is fruit from a poisonous tree that was rooted in slavery.

Knowing this, many Black parents understand that for their child to survive an encounter with the police, it is imperative that they have "the talk" with their children. I wrote a poem about "the talk" titled 10 & 2. While many White parents look at their child earning a driver's license as a rite of passage and something that will make their lives easier, the minute that small piece of laminated paper is placed in our child's hands, we understand that our lives have not gotten any easier, but have gotten a million times harder. We understand that there will be many sleepless nights as our kids make a trip to a party or the mall. We understand waiting to hear the phone ring so they can tell us they made it to their destination safely. We understand that we will not truly sleep until our child is back underneath our roof. We understand that every time they drive, they are taking a gamble with life and death.

While most parents can celebrate their child receiving their driver's license, we remind our children that a trip to the store for Skittles and tea could be their death sentence, that playing their music too loudly could lead to us picking out caskets, that driving while Black could be criminalistic, that walking will Black could be deadly, that breathing while Black some have found to be lethal, that running while Black can be costly, that wearing a hoodie could have life or death consequences, that being Black in this world meant staying on guard...being smart. Driving is not merely driving for Black people. Driving is an art of survival, navigating the streets, highways, and byways so that they do not become the next hashtag.

There is no room for error. Have your license. Your registration. Your insurance card. Wear your seatbelt at all times. Don't play your music too loudly. Make sure your brake lights are working. Always signal. Make a full stop at all stop signs. Don't race through yellow lights. Do… not…make… any… mistakes. While these are normal things that most good drivers should do, we understand that failing to do any of these things may not result in a minor ticket but can lead to their death.

And when, not if, but when the police pull our children over, we have given them tips to survive the encounter because we want to believe that maybe, just maybe, if we have told our children what to do we will not be getting a phone call that our child has been murdered. We want to believe that if our child is respectful enough, calm enough, kind enough, dressed well enough, complies, has all their paperwork in order, no lights out on their car, that they will not be the next trending name on Twitter. We want to believe that maybe, just maybe, our child will be cut a break and not vilified and criminalized because they are Black. So, we have "the talk," trying to ignore the shouts in the back of our minds that nothing we say will ever matter.

We remember Jordan Davis, just 17, killed for playing his music too loudly. We remember Philando Castile, 32, killed while saying, "I wasn't reaching for it." We watched in horror as he bled out on Facebook Live in front of his girlfriend and daughter. We remember Sandra Bland, 28, who died on a jailhouse floor, after a traffic stop for failing to signal. We remember Samuel DuBose, 43, murdered during a traffic stop for a missing front license plate. We remember Sean Bell, 23, shot at 50 times in his car. We remember Jordan Edwards, 15, murdered by the police as he left a party in a car and his brothers said they could see smoke coming from his head.

We remember all their names, and we know that "the talk" really doesn't matter. We know that every time our child places the key into the ignition, they are playing Russian roulette. We know that no matter how many "talks" we have with our children, that there is no guarantee that our children will make it home safely. No matter how many talks we have we are at the whim of those that can say, "He was reaching for something." "I felt threatened." "I pulled him over because he 'fit the description.'" "I thought his wallet was a gun." "She seemed aggressive." "I didn't like her attitude." Any excuse seems to work when it comes to the police murdering Black people that are driving while Black.

My question is if we are doing our part of having "the talk" with our children, who is having "the talk" with the police? Who informs the police that Black people behind the wheel of a car, do not need to be feared? That Black people driving, want to get to their destination just like anyone else. That slave days are over, and Black people have the right to traverse across the country freely and should do so without fear of death. Who sits the police down to have "the talk" with them letting them know that driving while Black is not a crime?

Is There Room In The Movement For Mistakes?

Recently we have been inundated with celebrities that have made what many consider colossal mistakes in the public eye. From Kathy Griffin, Bill Mahr, Kylie Kardashian (well damn, really all the Kardashians), Elizabeth Banks, and even Cardi B, celebrities have been caught in a web of racial, gender and political missteps.

In a 24 hour and truthfully, a 24-second news cycle, you can be on top of the world one minute and dragged within an inch of your life the next minute, all for saying or doing one wrong thing. (Before I go any further, this blog is not about people that are clear cut racists, homophobes, Islamaphobes, etc. This is not a blog about excusing continuous bad behavior or blatant disrespect. This is a blog about everyday people that have made some unfortunate faux pas and now find themselves on the wrong side of the movement. Usually, the mistake is one that is online, screenshotted and shared across the world before the offender can even wake up and grab a hot, steamy cup of Folgers.)

We have seen this with celebrities and even locally in my hometown, Louisville, Kentucky, two institutions came under fire for artwork that was racist and anti-Semitic. Beyond institutions, I have even seen this play out with local activists and well-meaning White allies that are doing their best to "check their privilege", use the correct acronyms, go to the right meetings, make the best protest signs and do what they can do to stand up for racial justice, only to find themselves vilified and called racist because they have said something incorrectly. And often it is something they do not even understand is wrong.

I remember a few months ago I was asked to speak at a Black Trans Lives Matter event, honoring and bringing awareness to the many trans women that have been murdered in 2017. When I was asked, I immediately said yes. I write and speak for the liberation of all Black people. However, after I said yes, I felt this immediate swarm of anxiousness that I would use the wrong pronoun to describe someone, that I would use a word that was antiquated, that I would say, "girlllll" in my 'hey sister girl vernacular' and it is taken as me misgendering someone. As I prepared my speech I felt with every click on the computer keys, I was navigating a landmine. Thankfully the speech was well received, and I lived another day not to be dragged online.

However, in my anxiousness I wondered, is there room in the movement for mistakes? Do we allow people the space to make mistakes, to learn and grow? Or are we quick to jump on the 'let's drag them' bandwagon?

I will be the first to admit that I have participated in the 'let's drag the unaware offender' bandwagon. But over time I got to thinking, is this behavior productive to the movement? Recently, I have made a conscious decision to not jump on every bandwagon but to think about a few things in my process. I believe the following steps can allow room for mistakes and continued growth.

1. Do I know this person? Before you jump on the bandwagon to drag someone within an inch of their life, ask yourself, "Is the person that made the comment someone that I know? Do I know their character? Is this someone that would say or do something to hurt people or have they made a misstep?" One online or even real life mistake does not mean throwing out the baby with the   bathwater.

2. Am I getting caught up in the online drama? Who doesn't love some good online drama? It is interesting and often adds enjoyment to a typically dull evening spent scrolling through Facebook. But before you chime in and give your two cents, ask yourself, "Am I getting caught up in drama that is not productive to the movement?" "Will this matter tomorrow?" "Am I allowing someone to take me out of my character?" "Am I adding anything that will be productive to this conversation?" Every post does not need your comment. If you are not adding something that is productive perhaps it would better not to say anything.

3. Does this person really mean any ill intent with their comment? Many times, people say or do something that they have no idea is offensive. Before you "read" someone, have you considered that they just may not know that what they have said or done is problematic? Gay, homosexual, trans, transgender, LGBT, LGBTQ, LGBTQIA+, POC, WOC, Black, African-American, Latino, Latinx. Native American. Indigenous People. Don't label me. Do label me. Don't use pronouns. Do use pronouns. Don't call me Black. I'm not a color. CIS. Non-binary CIS. In an attempt to include everyone, the list of labels and acronyms are endless and not everyone knows what the new acronym of the month is and which one is acceptable. Even when you ask around just to be safe, the answers vary. Language is fluid and ever changing. What was acceptable to say 10 years ago is no longer acceptable now. Because things are ever-changing, allow room for people to learn and grow. Try to assume good intentions with someone that is seeking to learn and contribute to the movement and may have inappropriately said the wrong word.

4. Can this incident be used as a teachable moment? While it is not the job of the oppressed to teach the oppressor, some moments are teachable moments and you usually can spot someone that truly has a desire to learn. Remember someone took the time to teach you. But be aware, no one is open to learning if you are cussing and name calling. It is always acceptable to state your opinion, thoughts and beliefs directly and forwardly without cussing someone out. Also remember a moment of going off can lead to a lifetime of trouble. The same way their words are cemented forever on the world-wide web, so

are yours. Trust me there have been a million times I wanted to serve someone the same evil, racist drama they were serving me but it doesn't benefit me to come out of my character. When I my poem Formation went viral, people went back YEARS to read and comment on things I had posted. It was an eye-opening moment for me. Part of me felt like they were really attempting to verify that I was the person I was representing online. People are watching you, reading you and often taking their cues from you on how to treat problematic situations in the movement. Your words can be the deciding factor in someone taking the plunge into social justice. Are your words motivating people to join the movement, leave the movement or stay away from the movement? While you may not have signed up to be a leader sometimes the very nature of your lifestyle causes people to look up to you. 5. Is it necessary for me to drag this person online? While I know dragging someone gets a lot of likes and comments, is it necessary? While it may not get you the attention and retweets you desire, it is okay and oftentimes more productive to have a conversation offline. There is something magically organic when people can just talk without the eyes of social media watching. To be honest, most people chiming in are not commenting to diffuse but only escalate a situation that is often fueled by lack of knowledge and not ill intent. Also, be leery of someone that always feels the need to point out the mistakes of others. Some people enjoy seeing the movement in a state of confusion. Before you write the next New Jim Crow response, pause, and ask yourself, "Why am I responding to this and will what I say benefit the readers and advance the movement?"

6. Have I gathered all the information? Sally said that Sue said that Jerome said that Curtis said that Bobby said something racist yesterday. And then all hell breaks loose. Because we take the word of those that we labor with as truthful, we often never question their statements made online. However, I am finding that some people feed off drama and their lives are not complete unless the movement is in disarray. They will yell fire in a crowded room and sit back eating popcorn while watching everyone scramble. While it is great to trust the statements of those made online, it is wise to go to the source and ask them directly before you assume ill intent. Many things can be avoided by simply having a direct conversation and deciding for yourself how to proceed.

7. Give people space to make mistakes. No one came into this world knowing anything. Everything we know is because we were taught and/or learned from the knowledge that others have placed into the world. It is not our job to point fingers because someone is genuinely not aware of something. If someone makes a mistake give them a moment to correct it, to sincerely ask questions about their behavior and learn from it so they do not make the mistake again.

Do not shame others for making mistakes. Remember it is them today but could very easily be you tomorrow.

8. Allow people the space to discover and fight for justice the way they choose. Who made you the judge of determining what fighting for liberation should look like? Many problems arise because someone has appointed themselves the Grand Master of Social Justice and feel Sally should be doing what they determine instead of doing what Sally is doing. Relax. No one is the President of Liberation. Their way might not be your way but people are attempting to do something and that is what matters. Allow people space to find their fit and do not drag them because they are fighting for liberation differently than you.

9. Remember we are all in this together. A house divided against itself cannot stand. If we are fighting for liberation, it is imperative that we are not fighting one another. Will we have challenges and disagreements? Of course, we will. We are all human. Instead of stoking the flames of drama, have you considered speaking directly to the person that you are having a disagreement with? If you have done that and you still have not found common ground it is okay to separate. Not everyone in the movement will be best friends, but it is possible to have a mutual respect for the work that everyone is doing. Try not to speak ill of them on or off line. When asked about them encourage people to speak to them on their own so they can determine if they want to be involved with them.

Remember, we all will make errors, but I believe there is room in the movement for mistakes. Liberation work should be a safe space where we allow people to learn and to grow. No one is perfect, and mistakes will happen. Let's not be so focused on the "dragging" that we forget we are laborers together and what is most important is healing and rebounding from a mistake so that we all stand tall to fight another day. As George Bernard Shaw said, "A life spent making mistakes is not only more honorable, but more useful than a life spent doing nothing."

When It Comes To Men Like R. Kelly, Parents Must Stop Giving Them Prey

This article is not another write up about R. Kelly and if you should or should not support him. We know who R. Kelly is and what he has done (allegedly) and I am not going to debate that case again. However, let me be the first to say, I do not excuse any of R. Kelly's behavior. I was a huge R. Kelly fan and listened to 12-Play at least a million times. R. Kelly was the introduction to everything musically erotic with a unique mixture of R & B, hip hop, and sex appeal. His talent for songwriting and performing is immeasurable. There was nothing that R. Kelly touched that was not pure genius. Then the "secret" marriage to Aaliyah. Then the allegations came. Then the infamous video tape and enough was finally enough. The writing was on the wall. As much as I didn't want it to be true, there was no denying the many accusations made against R. Kelly. There would be no more Bump N Grind, no more rocking to Ignition and no more believing that I could touch the sky while listening to I Believe I Can Fly. It was over.

R. Kelly was what his accusers alleged R. Kelly was. A man that used his fame and fortune to prey on young women. Inherently we knew the truth; it was just that we didn't want to believe. We didn't want to believe that R. Kelly could do such a horrible thing because he doesn't fit the description of how we think a pedophile should look. R. Kelly is talented, wealthy, and assumingly could date any adult woman he desired. What we failed to understand is that money doesn't make you a different person, money just brings out more of who you truly are. And who R. Kelly is, has been shown to us over and over again. Indeed where there is smoke, typically there is a fire. And this one has grown into an inferno.

R. Kelly has his issues, and they run deep. However, my focus in this blog will not be on R. Kelly, but the parents mentioned in the Buzzfeed article that allege R. Kelly is holding their daughter in a cult like environment. In summary, the parents KNEW the allegations brought against R. Kelly. They KNEW the things whispered about R. Kelly in quiet conversations. They KNEW about the trial. And STILL, they sent their daughter to be with him all under the belief that their daughter would advance her singing career. As stated in the article the mother says "In the back of our minds, we were thinking [my daughter] could be around him if I was with her. It didn't really hit home. Even with the Aaliyah situation, now that I think about it, 'Age Ain't Nothing But a Number' ... but you don't think about that. You grew up with the song, and you like the song."

That is the problem- "You don't think about that." While R. Kelly has a wealth of alleged sins and guilt that he must contend with, the parents, in this case, are equally as complicit. They led their daughter like a lamb to the slaughter. There is blood on everyone's hands. And that is my problem.

Parents we MUST stop selling our children to the highest and most convenient bidder. While they were chasing fame and fortune, they offered their child to an accused predator. However, it is not just them; many parents will offer their children to the highest bidder because the predator pays the rent, they buy you nice things, they keep the lights on, they pay for your car. And in exchange for cheap tokens, you turn your head. You pretend you don't see. You tell your daughter to be nice to "Uncle" John when he comes over. You sexualize your daughter so that "Uncle" John will be pleased when he comes to visit. You pretend as if you do not see the way he looks at your daughter. And when your son or daughter comes to you and tells you that "Uncle" John or "Pastor" Johnson touched them inappropriately, you tell them to shut up, to hush that noise, not to say anything because you will lose your tokens. You sell your children to those that prey on them in increments. Every time you turn your head, every time you make your child sit on "Uncle" John's lap or give "Uncle" John a kiss, even when they say they do not want to, you are selling your child in small increments.

What is the going price for your child's innocence? How many tokens must he buy you for you to remain silent? How many hits of dope does it take to bribe you not to say anything? How many handbags and red bottoms must he buy you for you not to contact the authorities? How much does someone have to pay for you to look the other way and pimp your son or daughter? How long will you continue to pretend as if you don't know what your mate is doing to your child? What is the going price for a grown man to share your bed AND your daughter's bed? How many pieces of silver does it take for you to pretend that nothing is going on?

As parents, we are called to be the first line of defense for our children. It is our job to protect our children at all costs. We cannot be blindsided with shiny trinkets. Our children are not be pimped and prostituted for monetary gain or fame. Our children are not to be served up on an auction block for men or women that will give you your next hit or pay your rent. You are supposed to protect your child from threats not hand them over to the threat. We must do better in our families and our communities. We must work harder to protect our children. Children are not a commodity to be sold to the highest bidder while we look in the other direction and pretend that we do not see that for 30 pieces of silver we have sold our child's soul to a predator.

Issa & Lawrence- We All Need Spontaneous Couch Sex At Least Once!

Yesssssssssssss! Sometimes that is just how you need to get it done! And Lawrence and Issa got it done! That was one of the sexiest, spontaneous moments I have witnessed on TV lately. It was guttural and primal and erotic and everything that made me wonder, "Where have I went wrong in my life that I am not having hot, spontaneous couch sex?" I have only had that type of chemistry with one person then I remembered in a moment of mental clarity I deleted his number from my phone. After Lawrence and Issa's get down, I was trying to remember those digits, but God and my wise ancestors blocked it. Sighhhhhhh...

Anyway, the long and short of the story is that Issa has cheated on her longtime boyfriend Lawrence and they are in that awkward stage of a breakup where you might get back together, you might date other people but it's nothing serious because you are not quite sure what the next steps will be in the relationship. Is it really over or will you be getting back together? Issa hopes that they will get back together, so she calls Lawrence to come to their apartment and pick up his mail. Because you know that is what we do when we really want to see someone after we broke up. We call them and tell them to come pick up their belt, a half a box of cornflakes and three paper towels. Anything will do as long as we can see them again and maybe rekindle that spark.

After a few delays, Lawrence stops by the apartment to pick up his mail, and at this point, Issa has just given up on his stopping by and is emotionally depleted after a failed party and a job assignment that is not going well. She is not dressed up when Lawrence unexpectedly comes to the door; just in some boy shorts, a t-shirt and her natural hair pulled back. But don't get it twisted, Issa lounging around the house and most people lounging around the house are two different things. When I lounge around the house, I might have a stain on my shirt and half my braids taken out. (Maybe that is why I am not having spontaneous couch sex. I need to get my life together.) Issa looks remarkable even though she is feeling defeated. Her legs are toned and go on for days, booty popping, cocoa skin flawless and her natural hair is glistening with jojoba and coconut oil.

Lawrence walks in and gets the mail and says he also left some stuff in the bathroom. When he comes out, he makes small talk and then heads for the door and babbbbbyyyyyyyyy in one quick move, slams the door, drops his bag, said fuck that mail and he was ready to fuck Issa. Right there on the couch! And it was one of the best sex scenes I have seen on TV in a while! It wasn't neatly choreographed; there were no candles, Lutha (not Luther) Vandross was not playing in the background. It was just two people that still had amazing chemistry and sexual energy that could not keep their hands off each other.

It reminded me of Biggie Smalls song, Fuck You Tonight

"So no, caviar, Shark-Bar, uh-huh

Strictly sex that's sweaty and leftover spaghetti

I know you used to slow CD's and Dom P's

But tonight, it's eight tracks and six-packs while I hit that!"

And Lawrence hit that! And honey I was like REWINDDDD! Let me see that shit again!

And sometimes that is just how it is. I don't want to hear long conversations about what went wrong, and where we are going from here and what should we call this thing and are we in a relationship or not? Sometimes it is just about that moment, and we will figure the rest out the next day. Or we won't. And sometimes that is okay. Everything is not going to fit neatly into some box or can be labeled. Sometimes shit really is complicated. Sometimes relationships can't be defined, and sometimes you just need to have hot, spontaneous couch sex on top of a 'Miley, What's Good' pillow because you can, and you want to, and you're a grown ass woman.

Confederate: How Long Do White People Want to Profit From Black Pain?

I should have known when the creators and showrunners of the hit TV series Game of Thrones, David Benioff, and Dan Weiss, had "Daenerys Stormborn of the House Targaryen, First of Her Name, the Unburnt, Queen of the Andals and the First Men, Khaleesi of the Great Grass Sea, Breaker of Chains, and Mother of Dragons", being lifted into the air by a swarm of Black people, shit was gonna go left real quick with David and Dan.

Before I start this blog, in full transparency, you must know that I love Game of Thrones. I have watched Game of Thrones since the dire-wolves still had milk on their fur, since Cersei had long hair, and her brother, lover and father of her children, Jamie Lannister, had both hands. I have watched Game of Thrones since Arya was play fighting with "Needle" before she became a skilled assassin and a girl with no name. I am so emotionally invested in Game of Thrones, when Khal Drogo called Khaleesi his, "Moon of My Life," I imagined that he was speaking to me. When Khal Drogo died, I thought, "What is the point of going on with this show?" But I was invested in the fan outcome of finally seeing the long-held theory manifest that Daenerys and Jon Snow are brother and sister meant to rule the kingdoms.

I watch Game of Thrones faithfully, pulling in friends and family to join me each Sunday as we hum along to the opening tune. I waited with bated breath just to hear Arya say, "Winter Came for House Frey," one of the greatest lines in TV history. And then, the next day came, David Benioff and Dan Weiss announced that they were greenlighted to create a show called Confederate, that will explore an alternate timeline where the Confederate States of America won the Civil War, and take place in a world where slavery is a "modern institution."

SAY WHAT NOW?

I should have known. Y'all have put me through the beheading of Ned Stark, the abhorrent evil of Joffrey, the sadistic actions of Ramsay Bolton, the emotional turmoil of the Red Wedding and now to top off this emotional ride; you now want me to follow you to another show about slavery never ending?

Have you lost your damn mind?

I have several issues with this new show Confederate:

1. Why do White people always find a way to profit off Black pain and suffering? For White people to always use the "Get over it that was so long ago excuse," when it comes to slavery, it seems this excuse flies out the window when it is time to make a profit. White Hollywood (which does include television) always loves to relive slavery. It is like telling the story of slavery is a guaranteed Oscar/Emmy win or nomination. Haven't White people taken enough from Black people? Why do White people feel compelled to continue to profit from our suffering? Were Black people picking cotton in the fields, not enough? How much more money do you want, David and Dan, from slavery?

2. Why do White people always want to hijack Black stories and history? Our history is not YOUR story. Our history is not for YOUR profit. If the story of Black history is to be told, it must be told by Black people. We do not need White people to whitewash OUR history. White people have done that enough. White people CONTINUE to benefit from slavery by telling OUR stories and STEALING our art and creativity. Black people are gifted and equipped to tell THEIR OWN STORIES! Someone posted that David and Dan are Jewish. Hmmm... Why not write a story about what if the Holocaust never ended? Why not tell YOUR story if you want to fantasize about history? You don't want to pimp your history, but you are fine pimping ours.

3. If White People are so obsessed with Black History, why don't they portray the truth and just speak on their collusion in the slave trade, Jim Crow, and Civil Rights? If you are going to tell the TRUE story of slavery, Jim Crow, the struggle for Civil Rights, why not tell the REAL story? Why not tell the story from the White perspective? How did White people act during slavery? How did White people act during Jim Crow? What is the TRUE story of White history regarding slavery? What did your father, mother, grandfather, grandmother, great grandfather and great grandmother do during slavery? How many slaves did your family own? How long has the plantation home been in your family? How much money still benefits your family due to slavery? Which side was your family on, friend? Tell that story. I would be curious to see that movie. The REAL TRUTH! Stop telling the story of slavery without mentioning YOUR PART. Show us YOUR PART.

4. Why do White people love to fantasize about what the world would look like if slavery never ended? As a Black woman, I fantasize too. I fantasize about what Africa would be like if White people had left Black people alone. I fantasize about what Africa would be like if White people did not rape it for its resources. I fantasize about what it would be like to know my heritage, to speak my language, to eat food native to me. I fantasize about the advancements Black people could have made without White people stealing our ideas and creativity. I fantasize daily about what this nation would be like, if Black people were never brought to this land. Make that TV show. How would America look if Black people were NEVER brought here? Would White people have picked their own cotton? How would White people do without peanut butter, the fold out bed, potato chips, riding on a train, shoes, the light bulb, blood transfusions, receiving mail, the telephone, pacemakers, video games, cataract removal, any movie with 3-D special effects, super-soaker water guns, the refrigerator, birth control, the elevator, the computer, the microphone, the traffic signal, sugar, the cell phone, scooping ice cream, the dustpan, the squeeze mop, the clothes dryer, the ironing board, diamonds, paper, home security systems…The list of our contributions is endless. What would White people do without Black people? Tell THAT story.

What David and Dan fail to realize is that they do not have to write and produce a show based on the theory of what if slavery didn't exist. Michelle Alexander already wrote the script with the New Jim Crow, and Ava DuVernay already made the movie with the documentary 13th.

David and Dan do not need to fantasize about what slavery would look like in modern times. It is taking place all around you but when you are White sometimes you cannot see that. Take a step from behind the camera lens and look at the world. Black people live this reality every day. What White America has done is simply fool the world by changing the name slavery to mass incarceration. To be Black in America is to live under a state of slavery. To drive and wonder if you will make it to your destination alive, is slavery. To have your head cut off in Jackson, Mississippi like Jeremy Jerome Jackson, is slavery. To be lynched by dragging from the back of a truck, like James Byrd Jr. in Jasper, Texas, is slavery. To be choked and murdered on a New York street, like Eric Garner, is slavery. To be imprisoned for three years without a trial, like Kalief Browder, is slavery. To die on a jailhouse floor, like Sandra Bland, is slavery. To have corporations financially benefit from the incarceration of Black men, is slavery. To create policies to secure inmates to produce products for corporations, is slavery. To still be fighting for basic civil rights, is slavery!

YOU, DAVID AND DAN, see a profit! Because Black trauma has always been made to tap dance for your pleasure! Black pain has always added coins to your coffers. BLACK PAIN, LIFE, SUFFERING, HEARTACHE IS NOT AN HBO, MADE FOR TV SERIES! This is the REALITY OF THE WORLD THAT WE ARE LIVING IN!

If you want to tell A STORY, do not point the cameras at us. Point the cameras at men and women that look like you. Tell that STORY!Until you do that, I borrow a phrase from your hit TV show, Game of Thrones; YOU KNOW NOTHING! AND YOU WILL NEVER KNOW NOTHING ABOUT OUR STORY!

Dear White People: This Is Why I Will Never "Get Over" Slavery

I have seen the beginning, standing in the Door of No Return at Goree Island in Dakar, Senegal. I was almost afraid to walk through the entrance of what many call a slave castle. There was nothing majestic or regal about the building. Had history not recorded the reason the building stood, many would walk by it and think nothing of the structure, never knowing the horror that took place beyond the entrance. Still, I knew the ground that we stood on was sacred.

Photo 10 Goree Island

I walked into the small, dark stone rooms with just a sliver of space for a window, running my hands along the walls. Rooms separated for men, women, girls, and infants. I tried to imagine what it would have felt like being captured, confused, not knowing what was happening. Being separated from my daughter, who according to the museum curator, would have been raped and/or sold to White slave traders. I imagined the screaming, the cries, the moans, the suffering, the stench of urine and feces all intertwined with agony.

I listened to my daughter as she sat in the room for young girls, and it was the first time as a mother that I heard my daughter's soul scream. Her cries were piercing, echoing throughout the castle as she crouched on the floor and wailed for her ancestors absorbing the pain that we imagined took place in the room.

I stood at the room located underneath the stairs, a room for those that dared to resist. It is a room similar to a crawlspace, and the museum curator said they are unsure how many people could fit in that space, the only goal was to close the door. I imagined the broken bones of Black bodies being shoved into the space, legs entangled in arms, feet atop of heads, bodies broken and bruised merely for resisting.

Just above the holding cells was the space for the slave traders. Just. Above. Right on top of the horror was the space where the slave traders dwelled. I wonder what type of monsters could reside in a space just above unspeakable pain, terror, and suffering? Upstairs was pristine with artifacts of the slave trade. One thing that always remained with me the museum curator shared with us is that five cowrie shells were equal to the price of one Black man. Five. Cowrie. Shells. I could not wrap my mind around something I wear as jewelry was the going price for a slave. I made a mental note to always respect this shell when I wore it from now on. It was sacred. This shell cost a Black person their humanity.

Then it was time. I had to go to the door. I walked down the dark hallway slowly, staring into a sea of nothing. Water going on for miles looking as if you would drop off the edge of the earth if you went too far. I stood in The Door of Return and looked out at the Atlantic Ocean, tears streaming down my face wondering what my ancestors must have been thinking. "Where am I going?" "Will I see my family again?" "Will I be allowed to come home?" "What have I done to deserve this?" This was truly the door of no return as many would never return to their home. While it may sound foolish to the reader I must say as I stared at the ocean, I reminded myself this was before the age of Facebook, Twitter, and Instagram. This was before the age of the common knowledge that on the other side of this vast ocean is more land. My ancestors were entering the space of the unknown not knowing the horror that awaited them on slave ships and in America...

Photo 11 Brianna Wright standing in The Door of No Return,
Goree Island

Dear White America: At Least Acknowledge Your Hypocrisy and Bullshit

By now I am sure you have heard of the domestic terrorist event, fueled by racism, which has taken place in Charlottesville, Virginia. What the media has chosen to call the "alt-right") instead of what they are-the Ku Klux Klan, Neo-Nazis, bigots, racists, took a trip to Home Depot and bought hundreds of tiki torches and attempted to intimidate a group of "counter-protestors" at Emancipation Park. It is being reported that this event was organized to Unite The Right (whatever the fuck that means) against the removal of a statue of the man that lost the South in the Civil War, Robert E. Lee.

Watching this riot unfold on Twitter, I was overwhelmed with the response from White America. White men walking down the streets of a town in America shouting, Heil Trump, with torches, helmets, sticks, some decked out in camouflage and guns, and somehow, this was okay. What was strangely missing from many of the pictures were police in riot gear, people being tear gas, rubber bullets, and tanks.

It used to be against the law for Black people to gather in groups of 2 or more. And even now when Black people come together to protest injustice, the police come out in full military style regalia ready to tear gas anyone on the spot. Had this been a Muslim person that drove into a group of individuals, Trump would have spent every second of the day tweeting about it. It would have immediately been called an act of terrorism. We would have heard a million talking points about immigration. If Black people had gathered with tiki torches and guns, White America would have been in an uproar. The police would have tear gassed, billy clubbed and arrested many people.

Yet somehow when it is White people involved in acts of terrorism fueled by race, White America has amnesia. Almost worse than the white sheets and hoods, White America pulls on the cloak of hypocrisy.

I could deal with White America if it were consistent with its bullshit and fuckery. But it is the blatant hypocrisy that White America displays that makes me livid. I would do better if White people just said, "Yeah, we are cool with this because they are White and not Black." JUST ADMIT IT! It is the BLATANT HYPOCRISY like we are not seeing what we are seeing. You are not going to gaslight your way through racism!

You have Tamir Rice, a 12-year-old boy killed in less than two minutes for having a toy gun on a playground but White people can march down the street with AK's, and the police don't bat an eye.

You have Sandra Bland dead on a jailhouse floor, jailed for failing to signal but the police take Dylan Roof hours after murdering 9 Black men and women in a South Carolina church, for a burger and fries.

You have people protesting the murder of Mike Brown in Ferguson met with rubber bullets and tear gas, but the police look the other way in Charlottesville.

You have Indigenous People fighting for their land and the right to have clean water met with water hoses and vicious dogs, but the police do nothing in the wake of impending violence in Charlottesville.

You have Colin Kaepernick that silently protested by taking a knee during the National Anthem, vilified by White America, but White America is fine with White men walking down the street screaming, "Heil Trump!"

You have Trump that wants to get into a pissing contest with North Korea yet doesn't have the courage to stand up against the KKK and racists right here in America. (Trump is a joke to the world.)

You have Trump that can dip his nose in and offer his useless comments on other countries fighting terrorism, but doesn't have the courage to say an act of domestic terrorism has taken place on American soil if it is committed by White people.

You have Black people that desire intervention by way of policy, legislation, and funding to combat violence and when the Governor of Kentucky says, "Just pray about it," we were supposed to be okay. But when he told White people to paint rocks to combat opioid addiction, NOW White America is enraged at his fake drug addiction policy.

This White America is you. Take a long hard look at your hypocrisy.

You are the SAME White people that want to tell me, "Why do you say, Black Lives Matter. You should say All Lives Matter."

You are the same White people that want to say my blog is race baiting and send me hate mail. You are the same White people that believe if you don't talk about race it will just go away. You are the same White people that don't want to own any responsibility or understand a sound argument but are so quick to say, "Not All White People." You are the same White people that believe just "being kind," as Lady Gaga said, will fix racism. You are the same White people that believe because Barack Obama was the President racism is over. You are the same White people that call Black Lives Matter protesters thugs, yet Richard Spencer is declared as dapper and fashionable. You are the same White people that want to know all the Black slang, dances and hairstyles but don't care anything about our suffering. You are the same White people that want Black people to jump on your causes but never stand up for ours. You are the same White people that tweet and post pictures of cats and dogs but won't take the time to post anything about Black issues. You are the same White people that want to find soft terms to label racists in the media and call a riot a skirmish as the You are the same White people that say give Trump a chance when he cannot even condemn hate groups. (BECAUSE HE IS IN COLLUSION WITH THEM!!!) You are the same White people that dare to tell me, "We should just wait and see how the Confederate show turns out."

This is what "waiting to see" gets you.

A woman is dead. Dozens are injured, some with life threatening injuries and White America has the nerve to stand around looking shell-shocked like, "What happened?"

What happened is you didn't listen. What happened is you chose racism over common sense and the good of humanity. What happened is you didn't care. What happened is you didn't give a damn because it wasn't affecting you! What happened is our word wasn't enough. What happened is that you were asleep at the wheel! What happened is you are fighting for a show like Confederate to be on HBO all while disregarding the racism going on around you live and in color every day! What happened is you have raised sons and daughters to be in that "alt-right" crowd because you never took a stand in your home as a parent to teach your children about righteousness and the reality of racism.

White America this one is on you. The blood was shed in the streets of Charlotteville is on you. You have been a passive and active participant in the hatred that continues to fuel this nation. If you want to start healing, mending and fixing this divide in America, the first step is shedding your cloak of hypocrisy and owning your part. Only then will this nation begin to heal.

Newsflash Lady Gaga, THIS IS YOU!

In the wake of the racist violence that took place in Charlottesville, Virginia, Lady Gaga took it upon herself to start a hashtag #BeKind, and another soon popped up on Twitter, #ThisIsNotUS.

Really? This is not us? Be Kind?

Newsflash, being kind is not a solution to systemic racism. Kind people were sold into slavery. Kind people were lynched. Kind people are serving life sentences in prison for trumped up charges. Kind people are murdered because they were transgender. Kind people are vilified because of their sexuality. Kind people are murdered in the streets by the police. Kind people were run over in Charlottesville, Virginia. Kind people have been murdered fighting against injustice. A kind woman, Heather Heyer, sacrificed her life for justice.

Lady Gaga and others that jumped on the #BeKind trend do a disservice to those that have sacrificed their very lives to fight for justice. Being unkind is not what caused these issues. And simply being kind to people that seek to destroy you, is not going to fix them. Being kind is not a solution to racism and hatred. Confronting racism will not always be roses, daffodils, fluffy clouds and sunshine.

For the people sharing the, This Is Not Us hashtag, if it is not you, then who is it? THIS IS YOU! This is America. This has been America since its inception. Making up a hashtag so that you can sleep better at night will not erase racism. Trying to exclude yourself from White people that commit heinous acts will not make racism go away. This is You. All of it.

This is the system that you benefit from. While your hand may not be on the murder weapon every time you do not stand up against injustice, you are a part of the problem. If you are fighting to have the show Confederate on HBO, you are a part of the problem. If you voted for a man because you chose racism over humanity, you are a part of the problem. If you allow your friends and family to make racist jokes and you remain silent, you are a part of the problem. If you see injustice happening and refuse to speak up, you are a part of the problem. If you are raising children with racist beliefs and don't want to "get in their business," you are part of the problem. If you are not using your privilege and influence to benefit those that are marginalized, you are a part of the problem. Every time you create a hashtag to absolve yourself from guilt, you are a part of the problem.

The reason this nation along with the world remains broken and cannot heal is because White people have taken on a "This is Not Us" attitude. White people have difficulty admitting THIS IS US. Nothing will ever change until you accept responsibility for what your race has collectively done to innocent people around the world. It is time for you to look in the mirror and take a good hard look at what you have done.

You enslaved innocent Black men, women, and children. You murdered innocent Black people. You raped a nation of its resources for your profit. You lynched Black people and took pictures smiling as their bodies hung from trees. You raped Black women while your wives pretended not to see. You bought and sold Black people for your financial gain. You continue to profit off the backs of Black people. You continue to profit financially from slavery. You stole land from Indigenous People. You relocated Indigenous Tribes leaving them to suffer from disease, exposure, and starvation. You sent innocent people to gas chambers. You made lampshades out of the skin of innocent Jewish people. You profited from the murder of innocent Jewish people and still reap the benefits of that blood money today. You performed medical research on Black people without their consent and withheld treatment. You sterilized Indigenous and Black women without their knowledge. You stole human cells from a Black woman and used them to advance medicine and your profits all without her consent. You turned your back on America and bombed American citizens. You walked into schools and slaughtered innocent children. You sent tainted blood to foreign countries for profit. You drove a car into innocent people, injuring many and killing one. You have committed some of the most heinous, egregious crimes against humanity and that is who you are.

And I know it ain't pretty. But sometimes the truth doesn't come decked out in lipstick, eyelashes, and stilettos. This is who you are.

All of this happened, and this is just the tip of the iceberg. This is not a figment of our imagination. White people did this. And for there to be any progression part of that is owning your responsibility. And before you give me the, "I wasn't involved in that" line, if you are White, you have benefitted from everything that I have listed. Making a cute hashtag, will not absolve you of the guilt you do not want to face.

What would have been a better hashtag is to say THIS IS US and what can we do to correct the mistakes that we have made? That is how you start to make a difference. You don't make a difference by sticking your head in the sand and pretending you are not a part of the problem.

When will White people collectively step up to the plate and own responsibility for their crimes against humanity? When will White people finally say," THIS IS US"? When will White people admit their complicity in systemic racism?

Only then can this nation and the world begin to heal. Some of the very steps to healing is admitting there is a problem and admitting your role in the problem. Until that happens, Lady Gaga, your hashtag does nothing to move America towards healing.

When Black People Go Rouge Quiz

Recently, it seems every media outlet is attempting to find any Black person other than the Embarrassment to Black People Trifecta, Ben Carson, Omarosa and Sheriff Clarke to speak up for Donald Trump in the wake of him cozying up to Neo-Nazis, the KKK, and White Supremacists. It almost seems unreal considering everything Trump has stood for that anyone that is Black could actually continue to support him. They act as if they have been doused in magical Negro racist repellent shea butter oil sheen and the hate and vitriol that is spewed from lips of White supremacists will somehow ricochet off their melanin, and they will not be affected. Indeed, we know that this is wrong.

What is striking to me is just like I cannot tell the difference between tiki torch yielding racists and Donald Trump due to their "we-hate-Blacks-Jews-Muslims-small dogs-and babies"-, polo shirt and khaki pants uniforms, it's hard for me to tell the difference between Black people against Trump and Black people for Trump.(On a side note I wonder when the Tiki Torch Posse went to buy their Abercrombie & Fitch uniforms what did they say, "I will take the polo shirt in a shade of White is superior in my delusional mind and a pair of khakis in a shade of I hate anyone that is this shade of tan and beyond?")

You can never be too safe in this charged climate so from this point on ANY Black person that wants to friend me online must FIRST take and PASS the following test. I have included Black Crib Notes to assist you.

WHEN BLACK PEOPLE GO ROGUE QUIZ

1. What's that number one _____ sign?!
Black Crib Note: Phrase made popular by Luke that women love to hear on their birthdays. A phrase that can get women in their 40's to start twerking, reliving college parties, egged on by a hype woman sipping Crown Royal and Coke.
2. I got _____ on it!
Black Crib Note: A monetary amount that you are willing to donate to the group to smoke marijuana.
3. "What ya'll going?" "We got board." "We going 10 on 'em!" "Run a Boston!" "Quit talking across the board!" What game is being played when you hear these phrases? _____
Black Crib Note: A game played at many Black family reunions that causes many fist fights and your cousin cussing under his breath at your grandma for reneging.

4. Finish this statement. I got _____, _____, potatoes, tomatoes! YOU NAME IT!

Black Crib Note: Phrase from Shirley Caesar hit gospel song, Hold My Mule, remixed by Suede the Remix God that made Black people laugh thinking about good old fashion homecooked food at Big Mama's.

5. God is good, all the time and all the time, _____ _____ _____.

Black Crib Note: Standard Black Baptist Phrase that must be said EVEN when you are going through hell and just drove your car to church on E.

6. Black folks who make a habit out of sinning all year long only come to church on C.M.E. What does C. M. E. stand for? _____, _____ and _____

Black Crib Note: Standard holidays Black church folks that hide their sins well mention to look down on those that come to church infrequently.

7. In the summertime Black children are given 2 rules: "Close the door! You are letting all the _____ _____ out!" and "Stop Running _____ and _____!"

Black Crib Note: Two phrases that every Black child hates to hear and cusses their parents out in their head every summer when they hear it.

8. I brought you in this _____ and I will take you _____.

Black Crib Note: Phrase that all Black parents say knowing good and well they ain't gonna murder anyone.

9. When you were a child and asked your mom for McDonald's, her response would be, "You got McDonald's _____?

Black Crib Note: A phrase every Black mother has said knowing good and well you did not have a job because you were only 7.

10. Finish this statement from Black parents: Stop crying before I _____ _____ _____ _____.

Black Crib Note: A phrase that every Black child hated to hear. We were already crying. Why do we need something else?

11. See I'm not your little _____.

Black Crib Note: A phrase your mom usually says right after she has said, ya'll are besties. You wonder if she is lying.

12. I got _____ problems but a _____ ain't one.

Black Crib Note: Popular song by Jay Z before he married Beyoncé and attempted to act right. We now know the lie detector has determined that was lie. Jay Z had many problems. Thank God for 4:44 and growth.

13. Okay Ladies, now let's get in _____.

Black Crib Note: Beyoncé 's hit song that made many White people very upset because it rallied Black people to get informed, get aligned, be prepared.

14. Trump was elected into office by 53% of _____ women.
Black Crib Note: A statistic you can post on any social media forum and piss off anyone named Becky.

15. You need to call _____
Black Crib Note: Phrase made popular by Erykah Badu and often used when a woman is done dealing with you and your bullshit and wants you to leave her house.

16. I got broads in _____.
Black Crib Notes: No one knows what the hell Desiigner is saying, but you MUST know that line.

17. When Rose takes you to meet her White parents for the weekend, you GET _____!!
Black Crib Notes: Blockbuster movie that used horror and White liberalism to highlight racism.

18. You better call _____ with the good _____.
Black Crib Notes: Phrase used on the hit album by Beyoncé , Lemonade that made us all try to figure out who Jay Z had cheated with and gave us a clear understanding of why Solange served him a two piece and a biscuit with butter and grape jelly in that elevator.

19. Cash Money Records taking over for the _____ and the _____.
Black Crib Notes: Song that will get any Black woman up and twerking on the dance floor, Ciroc in hand!

20. Reclaiming my _____.
Black Crib Note phrase made popular by Maxine Waters that reminded those that didn't know, she is boss, and all Black people can step up and do this as an act of self-care.

BONUS QUESTION: Put some _____ on my name!

SCORE RESULTS

20 and Bonus Question Perfect Score. You are certified, Black! You have made the ancestors proud! You get the big piece of chicken at the next cook out!

15-19 - You are doing great but need to step your game up, or we will revoke your Black card.

10-14 - You are suspect. Black people around the world are watching you closely with a STRONG side eye.

0-9 -REALLY? You have infiltrated the system. All the ancestors are looking down at you in shame. You have reached threat level Kanye! Black card REVOKED!!

ANSWERS

1. Zodiac
2. Five
3. Spades
4. Greens, Beans
5. God is good!
6. Christmas, Mother's Day and Easter
7. Cold air, in and out
8. World, Out
9. Money
10. Give You Something To Cry About
11. Friend
12. 99 B*tch
13. Formation
14. White
15. Tyrone
16. Atlanta
17. Out!
18. Becky, Hair
19. 99, 2000
20. Time
21. Bonus Question: Respeck

The Problem Is Not The KKK; It is Well-Meaning White People

In the Letter from Birmingham Jail, Martin Luther King Jr. wrote, "First, I must confess that over the past few years I have been gravely disappointed with the white moderate. I have almost reached the regrettable conclusion that the Negro's great stumbling block in his stride toward freedom is not the White Citizen's Counciler or the Ku Klux Klanner, but the white moderate, who is more devoted to "order" than to justice; who prefers a negative peace which is the absence of tension to a positive peace which is the presence of justice; who constantly says: "I agree with you in the goal you seek, but I cannot agree with your methods of direct action"; who paternalistically believes he can set the timetable for another man's freedom; who lives by a mythical concept of time and who constantly advises the Negro to wait for a "more convenient season." Shallow understanding from people of good will is more frustrating than absolute misunderstanding from people of ill will. Lukewarm acceptance is much more bewildering than outright rejection."

Similarly, to Dr. King's thinking, while the KKK and other racist groups exist, I am not overly concerned with the Richard Spencer's of the world. In fact, if I may be honest, on some level I can respect Richard Spencer for saying exactly who he is and exactly what he stands for. There is no in between or gray areas with Spencer. He wears his beliefs about race on his sleeve. Please do not misunderstand, I do not agree with any of the racist rhetoric that spills from his mouth, and I certainly do not condone any of his tactics or the tactics of others that seek to harm and disenfranchise people due to their race. However, when it comes to racism, I like racists to be the same way I like my Kentucky bourbon, straight with no chaser.

It is not the Richard Spencer's of the world that are causing me any problems. It is well-meaning White people that believe they could never be racist, that think because they are married to a Black man or woman or have Black friends they are not like "them." It was well-meaning White people that owned slaves. It was well-meaning White people that remained silent as Black people were lynched. It is well-meaning White people that read my blog and send me messages that say, "I should speak about love and not hate." It is the well-meaning White people that say, "I understand slavery but y'all should get over it." It is the well-meaning White people that believe they are not racist because they do community work in Black neighborhoods, donate to the NAACP and know all the dance moves to Single Ladies. It is well-meaning White people that believe there is nothing wrong with Confederate statues, trying to convince Black people that this issue of removing them is truly about history. It is well-meaning White people that will cheer for their NFL team powered by Black men but refuse to understand why Colin Kaepernick is kneeling. It is well-meaning White people that chose race over humanity when they voted Donald Trump into the highest office in the land. It is well-meaning White people that refuse to believe the statistics about the election results because they are too embarrassed to look in the mirror. It is well-meaning White people that can look at a video of a Georgia police officer, Lt. Greg Abbott saying, "We only kill Black people," and try to convince Black people that have suffered under the weight of police brutality that he was "only making a joke." For the mere fact, well-meaning White people are trying to convince Black people that this officer was making a joke, means they never understood our fight against police brutality. If so, they would understand that there is no humor when it comes to the death of Black men and women at the hands of the police.

When it comes to racism, well-meaning White people are a part of the problem.

While I applaud well-meaning White people for marching, tweeting, sharing an article, attending anti-racism meetings, if we are going to combat racism, it must be a little bit more personal to you. There is no benefit of continuing to preach to the choir. The choir is not your audience or your amen corner. It is time for you to decide which side you are on, friend. And should you choose the side of righteousness, compassion, liberation, and humanity, it will mean having some uncomfortable conversations, some that must start at your dining room table. There are conversations well-meaning White people need to have with their husbands, wives, children, girlfriends or boyfriends. There are neighbors that you will need to address. There are jokes that cannot be tolerated in the coffee break room. There are words you cannot tolerate in your presence or out of your presence. There is Facebook friends and family that you need to educate about racism. There are policies that you must speak out against. There are sacrifices you will have to make for the good of the many. There are Black people fighting that you must stand with on the front lines. Liberation will not be won in the shadows. Liberation demands the spotlight. It is time out for hidden allies. If you stand with us, stand with us in word and deed.

Well-meaning White people have stood by long enough. Well-meaning White people have remained silent long enough. Well-meaning White people have wavered in the winds of justice long enough. In the words of Florence Reece, "Which side are you on, friend?" The line has been drawn in the sand.

And for those well-meaning evangelicals that believe they are doing their Christian duty, like Paula White, let me quote Revelation, "I know your deeds, that you are neither cold nor hot. I wish you were either one or the other! So, because you are lukewarm—neither hot nor cold—I am about to spit you out of my mouth."

Make a choice. And if not, at the very least, stop pretending.

To The "Not All" Posse, PLEASE, STFU!

Typically, as a writer, I take time to work through my thoughts, research statistics, develop a compelling opening and storyline and know that I am working towards a conclusion that will challenge the reader and invoke dialogue across sectors to move a conversation that is generally centered around race relations.

However, this time, I have done none of that. This time this blog will be short and sweet. Quite possibly the shortest blog I have ever written.

Perhaps I am tired. Perhaps I am pissed off. Perhaps I just don't give a damn anymore.

This is something that has bothered me every time I go online and read intriguing, thought provoking commentary that challenges the reader to think outside the box, revisit long held beliefs, and perhaps redirect the way they see the world.

If you address an argument about race relations, police brutality, feminism, etc. with the words, "NOT ALL," PLEASE, SHUT…THE FUCK…UP!

You are contributing NOTHING to the progress of these issues by saying, "not all." In fact, the people that read your "not all" statements have wasted their time, effort and energy to educate themselves about topics that are impacting society.

If you believe a writer TRULY means EVERY SINGLE WHITE PERSON IN THE WORLD when they say, "Dear White People," you have a problem. Instead of looking at the totality of a system, you want to make yourself FEEL better by saying, "not all." Because of course that, "not all" statement includes you. For instance, when I point out the fact that 53% of White women voted for Donald Trump to be President, without fail, a White woman feels compelled to tell me that SHE did not vote for Trump. As if her saying that means we are going to get together and sip hot chocolate and braid each other's hair. It still DOES NOT NEGATE THE FACT that White women helped put Trump into office. Instead of facing that fact, they would rather try to water down facts with the "not all" clause.

Similarly, when an issue about police brutality comes up without fail someone will say, "Not All police are bad." Really? Thank you, Sherlock, for adding that worthless piece of information to the conversation. Most people know ALL police are not bad. Some police ACTUALLY signed up to do the job because they care about humanity, safety, their community and making the world a better place. However, that DOES NOT NEGATE THE FACT that there is a system at play when it comes to policing Black people and Black communities.

The same goes for the "All Lives Matter" posse. Saying Black Lives Matter DOESN'T TAKE ANYTHING AWAY FROM ALL LIVES HAVING VALUE! Do you REALLY think by saying, Black Lives Matter, we mean NO other lives matter? Think for a moment. Of COURSE, all lives matter. However, it seems that the value of Black Lives means nothing when it comes to policing and policies. In October when breast cancer is highlighted I have heard NO ONE say, "But colon cancer matters too!" Cancer affects EVERYONE and if it hasn't impacted your life in some way, just keep on living. However, people took the time to HIGHLIGHT breast cancer because this cancer was disproportionately affecting women, so there was a need to place a spotlight on it for awareness, policy changes, resources, treatment, etc. Does that mean the world doesn't think ALL cancer is serious and important? OF COURSE NOT! When we say Black Lives Matter, we are bringing awareness to the fact that Black Life is often seen as expendable. Jumping on a Facebook thread to interject, "All Lives Matter," does NOTHING to advance the conversation on race relations.

And while I'm at it, let me address misspellings. This is a tactic often used by the "Not All Posse." Look, more than likely when it comes to social media people are typing on their phones. We ALL know predictive text will have you saying something you NEVER meant to say. More than likely someone knows the difference between there and their or your and you're. Mistakes happen. I probably have a million of them in this blog. Such is life. STOP DERAILING THE TOTALITY OF WHAT SOMEONE IS SAYING BECAUSE OF A SPELLING MISTAKE!! Instead of trying to seem superior due to spelling and take away from the argument that is calling you to look at yourself in the mirror, pause and ask yourself, "Am I mentioning spelling because it is central to this commentary? Outside of minor spelling mistakes that can probably be explained and edited easily, have I absorbed ANYTHING that is written about this topic?" If you answer is no, STFU ABOUT SPELLING!!

If your ONLY argument to race relations is NOT ALL, save us all the time of reading your comments. If your ONLY argument to police brutality is, "NOT ALL police," don't waste our time. If your only response to well thought out commentary is, "You misspelled a word," don't bother. The NOT ALL argument contributes NOTHING to the advancement of humanity. In actuality, it is simply a way for you to feel better about yourself rather than admit the truth of the argument.

And while I understand admitting the truth is difficult, rather than say, "NOT ALL," I would rather you scroll on by and just SHUT... THE FUCK... UP!

Nice Girls Say No

Recently, I found myself at an event that I did not want to attend. I attempted to be cordial at the event, but in the middle of the event, I thought, "Hannah, why are you here? Why are you doing this to yourself?" And for the first time in my life, I answered the questions honestly. I was not there because I had to be or someone needed me to be. I was there because of what people would think about me. And immediately I thought, "Why do I care?" If I were to leave the event at that moment, the world would not stop spinning, the sun would not stop rising in the East and setting in the West, and for the most part, life would go on just fine. With that realization, I immediately jumped in my car, turned the key to my ignition and headed home. I realized I was needlessly torturing myself over an event I should have and could have easily said no to.

As I drove home, I instantly felt a sigh of relief. I was now free to spend my weekend how I wanted to. Admittedly, spending my weekend how I wanted amounted to nothing more than wine, comfortable clothes and Netflix but still, I was in control of my time. I was in control of me. And for a woman that is attempting to establish herself in the world, the first thing I knew was I must take ownership of was me.

I remember calling my friend before the event lamenting (which is just a fancy writer word for whining) about attending, and he asked me, "Why didn't you just say no?" Just say no? Was he crazy?! What would they think? What would they say? How would they judge me on social media? I offered a million excuses, and his only response was, "All you had to say was no." Was it really that easy? As I punched the gas pedal on my car and cruised down the highway feeling like Thelma and Louise, I realized, yes it was just that easy! Instead of saying yes, I could have easily just said no.

But I am a nice girl, aren't I? I was raised to be a nice girl. A nice girl that is seen and not heard. That sits pretty and poised. And nice girls don't say no. Nice girls work later than their male counterparts for less pay. Nice girls let people steal their ideas and don't say anything about getting credit. Nice girls babysit your kids when they are tired. Nice girls attend all your events even when they would rather be home reading a book. Nice girls support your causes even when you don't support theirs. Nice girls aren't defiant. Nice girls don't reject unwanted advances. Nice girls take your phone calls even when they don't feel like talking. Nice girls tolerate your dick pics. Nice girls go along to get along. Nice girls don't buck the system. Nice girls don't say no.

But fuck all that. I AM a nice girl. And nice girls DO SAY NO!

On that drive home, I realized that nice girls could and should say no because saying no is an act of self-preservation. I started going through a mental list in my mind of all the times I didn't say no and how different my life would have been if I was not so consumed with being the nice girl, the nice employee, the nice friend in the group, the nice girlfriend. Saying no was not a curse, in fact, it was a blessing.

I realized that:

• No is a complete sentence.
• No does not require any further explanation.
• No does not need to offer an excuse.
• No does not mean you aren't a team player.
• No does not mean you are not supportive.
• No does not mean feeling guilty.
• No does not require you to make up a white lie.
• No does not mean you do not like or love someone.
• No is not beholden to anyone.
• No does not mean everyone will understand.
• No allows you the space to say yes to what you really want to do.
• No does not require that you have extravagant plans.
• No is enough.

It is with these realizations that I am making a conscious decision to pause before I say yes. I am taking the time to ask myself, "Is this adding or subtracting from what you would like to do with your life?" "Are you saying yes out of guilt or obligation or is this something you really want to do?" "Are you only saying yes because of what people will think about you?" "Does saying yes to this mean this is a good use of your time?"

I am finally stepping into my own awareness. My own authority. My own purpose. It has taken me decades to get to this point in my life. I have said yes to so many things that I wish I had said no to. I have remained silent while people stole my ideas because I was a nice girl. I have worked hard building the dreams of others while putting mine on the back burner because I was a nice girl. I accepted payment for work that was lower than what I should have been paid because I was a nice girl. I slept with men that I did not want to sleep with, because I was a nice girl. I stayed in relationships I should have walked away from, because I was a nice girl. I chatted with people online that I didn't want to speak with, because I was a nice girl. I attended events where I was miserable, because I was a nice girl. I devalued my time, because I was a nice girl. I had no one to blame but myself.

So finally, I realized, enough is enough. My no is enough and saying no allows me the freedom to say yes to things that I really want to do. It allows me to spend my time the way that I want to spend my time. Saying no gives me the time to accomplish my goals. And even if that means by saying no, I will be spending time in my king size bed, eating something deliciously decadent while watching The Office on Netflix, that is okay. My no is my power. I am taking a page out of the Book of Beyoncé , "I'm grown woman! I can do whatever I want!" And what I want is to say no. And nice girls can always say no.

Fuck Going High

I love, First Lady Michelle Obama. God knows I do! But FUCK GOING HIGH!

I was honored to see a Black woman standing in the highest office for a woman in the land. A Black woman that was not simply riding on her husband's coattails but a Black woman that was established in her own right. Michelle LaVaughn Obama was raised on the South Side of Chicago and went on to graduate from Princeton and Harvard. Bitch what?! What? Say something?! Anything! Crickets! Silence! You know why? Because she's a bad mamma jamma! SHUT YOU MOUF!

Michelle Obama is poised and confident. Michelle Obama is Harriet, Coretta, Serena, Beyoncé, Cardi B., and every little Black girl that ever dared to dream the impossible all rolled into one! Not only is she intelligent, but her body is also relentless! Have you checked out those arms?! Michelle Obama didn't come to play wit' you hoes! She likes cornbread and collard greens! Michelle Obama can sport a crop top and high slit skirt and remind you she is probably having better sex than you can ever imagine having! Why? Because she doesn't give a fuck now! She's free to be her, thigh meat and all! Watch her stunt on em!

Have you seen Barack lately? He looks like a man this is seriously fucking the love of his life and not quiet, reserved White House fucking. Barack is getting it in. Michelle is pleased.

And I want her to be happy. If this were Coming to America, I would be one of those rose petal women tossing rose petals at her feet. I love her.

But...

When Michelle Obama said, "When they go low, we go high," I died a little bit inside. The world applauded, and the hood in me was thinking, "Nah." But I'm trying to refine my hood tendencies, so I was going to give this, "they go low we go high" tactic a chance. But these "I'm-coming-out-of-the-closet-as-racist" muthafuckas done went over the top. So, no. They go full on racist because Panera Bread ran out of the everything bagel or some shit. This "go high" tactic IS NOT WORKING!

FUCK THAT!

I am from the, "When they go low, we go even fucking lower" tribe.

I am baffled why People of Color, who have been hurt, victimized, discriminated against, vilified, marginalized, harmed even to the point of loved ones dying at the hands of White people, must always take the high road.

FUCK THE HIGH ROAD! I AM ANGRY! I am from the Cardi B school of politics, PULL UP ON ME!

Pull up on me

I heard you talkin' cray, I know you hella fake

You better pull up on me

I hope you feel the same when you see my face

You better pull up on me

Ain't no backing down, prepare to shake, you better pull up on me

Now you wanna be my friend, no you ain't safe

You better pull up homie

Recently a video surfaced online of a Sikh man being accosted by a White woman, and his response was, "We welcome you, we support you and we love you." AND I GET IT! I DO! Because in that MOMENT if he says something, he is the enemy. At that moment, the media is ready and waiting to flip the story. At that moment, if he stands up for himself against a White woman that is yelling in his face, she is now the victim. So he has to eat her bullshit!

Similarly, Black people are always expected to provide sanctuary for their oppressors. Black people are always expected to offer forgiveness to those that have harmed them. Black people are always expected to take the high road. Black people are always expected to understand their oppressors. Black people are always expected to take racist comments as a joke. Black people are always expected to take racist comments from the police as "no problem." Black people are always expected to take celebrities appropriating their culture as appreciation. Black people are always expected to just "get over" slavery. Black people are always expected to wait for the evidence, not rush to judgment. Black people are always expected to understand injustice.

Why must Black people be the race that must understand hatred? Why must we have compassion for those that seek to destroy us? Why must Black people and other People of Color be the ones that go high? No one asks the White woman going ballistic because she missed out on a cup of Starbucks and decided to go full racist, to understand Black people. No one asks White men marching through the streets with tiki torches to pause and understand how their actions can be problematic. But Black people are supposed to be immune to injustice. Black people are expected to bend over and say, "We's so sorry that our existence made White people feel threatened. Forgive us, White people, for daring to ask for justice. Who was we? What was we thinkin'? Please keep "discriminatin' against and killin' us, White folks. We's just love it, and we's offer yous our forgiveness! And we's just gonna wait for justice in the big by and by."

FUCK THAT! When they go low, I'M GOING FUCKING LOWER!

I LOVE YOU MICHELLE BUT THEY MOST KNOW, KNUCK IF YOU BUCK!

Trust Black Women: Munroe & Jemele Told No Lies

Just a few weeks ago American was rocked, once again with senseless acts of violence in Charlottesville, Virginia that lead to the murder of Heather Heyer. Heather stood up for righteousness and one of her final quotes that she shared on Facebook, "If you are not outraged, you are not paying attention," has reverberated throughout the world.

Apparently, Margana Woods, the Texas representative for Miss America, was paying attention. When she was asked about Trump's response to the Charlottesville incident during the Miss America pageant, Margana replied, "I think that the white supremacist issue, it was very obvious that it was a terrorist attack. And I think that President Donald Trump should have made a statement earlier addressing the fact, and making sure all Americans feel safe in this country. That is the number one issue right now." Hold up. Someone rewind that for me! What did she just say? Admittedly even I was stunned when she stated her response. Most people avoid having open, honest dialogue about racism in everyday spaces like their dining room table. This young woman was on national television, ready to give an answer that could decide the future of her life and without hesitation, she spoke truth to power.

While Woods did not officially win the crown, America has crowned her for standing up and speaking the truth. I applaud and appreciate White women like Heather and Margana. I stand with Alex Wubbles, the nurse that stood up to the police officer and was subsequently arrested for not allowing him to conduct an illegal search on a patient.

It is nice to see the world rally behind them, hail them as heroes and fighters for social justice. However, in just a matter of a few weeks, I have seen Black women vilified for speaking the same truth about White supremacy and standing up against injustice.

Recently, Munroe Bergdorf was fired from L'Oréal for making a statement about White supremacy after the racist violence in Charlottesville. Bergdorf stated in a Facebook post, "Honestly I don't have energy to talk about the racial violence of white people any more. Yes, ALL white people. Most of ya'll don't even realise or refuse to acknowledge that your existence, privilege, and success as a race is built on the backs, blood, and death of people of colour. Your entire existence is drenched in racism. From micro-aggressions to terrorism, you built the blueprint for this shit. Come see me when you realise racism isn't learned, it's inherited and consciously or unconsciously passed down through privilege. Once white people begin to admit their race is the most violent and oppressive force of nature on Earth … then we can talk."

The backlash for her comments was swift, and the obligatory statement from L'Oréal spoke volumes to me about their real intentions when they decided to have a "diversity campaign." "The L'Oréal Paris, True Match campaign, is a representation of these values and we are proud of the diversity of the Ambassadors who represent this campaign. We believe that the recent comments by Munroe Bergdorf are at odds with those values, and as such we have taken the decision to end the partnership with her. L'Oréal remains committed to celebrating diversity and breaking down barriers in beauty."

This is what happens when you hire a Black person to represent diversity because diversity and inclusion are trendy buzzwords. Diversity sells products. Diversity gets people to endure themselves to your brand. It is not a surprise that makeup companies are rushing to compete with Rihanna's Fenty Beauty line because she developed shades for all women of color. It is not that they truly care about women color, because they would have done it already if they were that concerned. It is that they realize they are missing out on profits by not catering to diversity. Diversity they are learning, is profitable. However, when you have someone like Bergdorf that speaks about White supremacy, that challenges how some in the world view diversity and inclusion, and your company fires her because she spoke the truth, there is a problem.

Black women are not your brand accessory. Black women are not the afterthought so you can meet some quota. Black women are not to be called on to sit, smile and remain silent about the issues that are plaguing our race just so that you can sell lipstick or shoes or a can of soda. If your company really wants to hire Black women, the best thing you can do is allow Black women to have a voice to speak truth to power and stand with them as they stand in their truth.

When ESPN commentator Jemele Hill made a post on her Twitter stating that Donald Trump is a White supremacist that surrounds himself with other White supremacists, Twitter was in an uproar. While many people did defend, Jemele, because Trump's words and actions speak for themselves, others called on ESPN to fire Jemele. Even the White House Press Secretary weighed in on the issue and said Jemele's tweet was a fireable offense. Really? In my opinion, the White House has no leg to stand on. They have cast their lot with a man that is racist, misogynistic, xenophobic, transphobic and doesn't feel ashamed in the least bit about the way he thinks or the vile and evil things that come out of his mouth. This is a man that has vilified innocent Black young men in New York, has been sued for housing discrimination, is friends with known racists, is backed by David Duke, supports policies that penalize miniorites, has racists in his administration, will not commit to signing a joint congressional resolution condemning White supremacists, blames Mexicans for everything wrong in America, fanned the flames and supported the birther movement against a Black President, said that there were good people on BOTH sides in Charlottesville when only one side was shooting guns, carrying tiki torches, screaming racist chants and drove a car into a group of innocent people injuring many and killing one. And THIS is the person you want us to believe is not racist?

Unlike L'Oréal, ESPN has chosen to stand with Jemele issuing a statement only after she "apologized." ESPN's statement says, "Jemele has a right to her personal opinions, but not to publicly share them on a platform that implies that she was in any way speaking on behalf of ESPN. She has acknowledged that her tweets crossed that line and has apologized for doing so. We accept her apology."

There is a problem when Black women are penalized and vilified for speaking the truth. There is a problem when Black women must weigh their employment against speaking up against racism. There is a problem when many in White America shudder just hearing the words White supremacy. There is a problem when many in White America are afraid when Black people call racism what it is. There is a problem when many in White America want sugar coated lies instead of the bitterness of reality. There is a problem when people can hear Black women say the VERY SAME THING as White women allies and yet only Black women are vilified. There is a problem when your organization hires Black women to be the token face of diversity and inclusion, but you expect Black women to remain silent about racism.

Black women have thoughts and opinions. And our thoughts, opinions, voices, and actions are just as valid (and even more so because we ARE BLACK WOMEN) as Heather's, Margana's and Alex's. While I certainly appreciate, White women allies that stand with us, the truth is no less the truth because it comes out of a Black woman's mouth. Sometimes it appears our truth cannot be swallowed by the masses unless it is shaken, stirred, bleached, watered down and whitewashed first. Trust what Black women are telling you. It does not need to be rearranged on the tongue and ran through the mouth of a White woman for you to understand the truth. The truth is simply the truth. And Jemele and Munroe told no lies.

We Rooting For Black People

When Issa Rae was asked at the 2017 Emmy's, who she was rooting for, Issa gave the most unapologetically Black answer I could have hoped for. "I am rooting for everybody Black. I am." Black America cheered, and White America cried. And I laughed as I watched her clip over and over again! For those who claim her statement would be racist if a White person said it, look it would be redundant for a White person to say, "I am rooting for a White person," when White people are typically always nominated in EVERY SINGLE CATEGORY. If you were to randomly pull names from a hat for someone to win an Emmy 9 times out of 10, it would be a White person.

So, stop crying, "racism." Newsflash White America, we are ALWAYS rooting for the Black people.*

I don't care what it is.

Oscars? We rooting for the Black people. I don't care if it's some obscure award and the person that won won't even get on stage, we are rooting for them.

Emmy's? We rooting for the Black people.

MTV Music Awards? We rooting for the Black people.

Grammy's? We rooting for the Black people. And while I'm at it, Adele still didn't deserve album of the year, and I will never forget! Beyoncé deserved that award for Lemonade, and you know it!

If it is Family Feud? We rooting for the Black people.

New Black film? We are rooting for Black people.

Jeopardy? We rooting for the Black person to win.

Track and Field? Not like there was really a chance anyways but just in case, we rooting for the Black people.

When you have time please watch this YouTube video of Tonya Nero. (https://www.youtube.com/watch?v=timn_B1A7jA) I have replayed this video at least a HUNDRED TIMES and laugh every single time! It is symbolic of the world. White people, teaming up EVEN WITH THEIR COMPETITOR because they are so confident they are going to win and a Black woman comes and snatches the crown. The look of surprise is beautiful because they NEVER expected a Black woman to win.

New Fenty Beauty makeup line? We rooting for Black people.

A pie baking contest? We rooting for the Black people.

A hot dog eating contest? We rooting for the Black people.

Underwater basket weaving? We rooting for the Black people.

And some of y'all have said this is racist. How many times must I go over the definition of racism? Look, I don't CARE if you think this is racist. It isn't.

For the fact that in 2017 and we can still say "the FIRST Black person to _____ (fill in the blank)" shows you WHY we ARE ROOTING FOR BLACK PEOPLE! Black people have been in America for almost 400 years, and it is still likely if you do ANYTHING, you will be the first Black person to achieve it. Not because Black people are not smart, gifted, intelligent or creative but because Black people have not been afforded the same opportunities as White people due to systemic racism.

We are rooting for Black people to stand in places our ancestors suffered and bled and died for!

We are rooting for Black people because we stand on the shoulders of so many Black people that came before us, that marched, that protested, that endured so that they could kick open the door for us!

We are rooting for Black people because White people have made billions off our ingenuity and creativity without ever allowing us to profit from our own gifts and just be great!

We are rooting for Black people because for too long our talent, wisdom, and intelligence have been overlooked!

We are rooting for Black people because White America has co-opted our culture for their gain!

We are rooting for Black people because we know if we don't stand up for our own people, no one will!

We are rooting for Black people because we know how it is to stand in a space and be the first to ever stand in that position!

We are rooting for Black people because we understand a Black person that achieves anything has had to work twice as hard to have a fraction of the opportunity given to a White person.

So yes, White America, we are rooting for Black people to dream, to persevere and to win. Every. Single. Time.

*Disclaimer: On behalf of Black America we ARE NOT rooting for Omarosa, Sheriff Clarke, Ben Carson, and Black Police Showing Out For the White Cops.

Dear Women: Please Stop Apologizing, Dumbing Yourself Down and Allowing Men To Take The Credit For Your Work

"I'm sorry to ask you this but…"

"I'm sorry for calling you but…"

"I'm sorry to say this but…"

"I might be silly but…"

"This might be stupid but…"

"I hate to ask this but…"

"I'm sorry to send this text but…"

"It was my idea but…"

"Sure, you can use my business plan…"

"Of course, I don't mind working late to build your empire…"

If you have said or wrote any of the above statements, please raise your hand!

I was the QUEEN of apologizing for my input, always making some self-deprecating statement before my "real" statement, and allowing men to take credit for my ideas without acknowledgment or payment. If not knowing who you are and your worth was an empire, then I was surely the queen on the throne. Then, in 2015, the clock was ticking towards the New Year, and I chose for the New Year that I was no longer going to apologize before I made a statement. I was no longer going to make self-deprecating comments to make myself appear as if I didn't think I was "better" than the person I was addressing and one of my biggest issues that I needed to tackle was that I was not going to allow men to take credit for my ideas.

All that may seem like lofty goals but there comes a time in your life when you realize who you are and you realize that you can, and you must stand in your power.

There comes a point in your life that you realize that you do not need to apologize before you make a statement. What are you apologizing for? For being great? For having fantastic ideas? For having a thought? For having an opinion? For going against the grain? For existing? Make a point to be conscious of the words that come out of your mouth. Own your authority. You do not need to apologize before you make a statement. You have every right to say what you feel, and that does not require an apology.

"This might be stupid but…" Why do you feel the need to call yourself or your thoughts stupid before you state them? If you are compelled to say something, it is not stupid. You are not stupid. You do not need to dumb yourself or your comments down for them to be received. You do not need to call your statement stupid so that you do not appear as if you think you are smarter than everyone in the room. Perhaps you are just that smart! There is nothing wrong with being smart! You do not need to make a negative comment about your statement to grease the pathway for a man to accept what you are going to say. Speak with your authority! Your thoughts are just as valid as anyone sitting around the boardroom table, and you do not have to coat your comments in the guise of stupidity to be heard.

Stop allowing men to STEAL YOUR IDEAS!! I have had some of the BEST IDEAS! I have had million dollar ideas. I have had ideas that have elevated people and increased their income all while my income remained the same. I chose to STOP allowing men to steal my ideas! It is easy to remain silent while men steal your ideas because women have been conditioned to be helpful, to assist, to be silent and remain pretty and poised. Women who are promoted JUST BENEATH THE CEILING don't rock the boat. But do you want to remain beneath the ceiling or break the ceiling? It is OKAY to say, "I need to be credited for that." It is okay to say, "My name is not mentioned, and that was my idea." It is okay to say, "I need to be paid for my work." And even better, it is okay to KNOW if a man can take your idea and run with it, YOU can take your OWN idea and CONQUER THE WORLD! You do NOT need permission from a man to be great! I was one of those women that watched men take my ideas and act as if they invented them and I was so frustrated! And finally, I thought to myself, "Why am I frustrated? They are only doing what I ALLOWED." I allowed men to own my GENIUS! I allowed men to STEAL my ingenuity! People will only do what you allow! If you have a great idea, OWN IT! There is nothing wrong with you owning your work and your creativity and being paid for your work and creativity!

After I spent a lifetime frustrated and having my own personal pity parties, enough was enough! I realized that I was powerful in my own right! I am a woman! And women are creative, intelligent, strong, powerful, wise and host of other things. I have agency! And I am in control of my thoughts, my ideas, and my creativity! And I will NOT apologize for being GREAT! I will not dumb my statements down so that men can feel smarter! I will not allow men to STEAL MY IDEAS when I have the power to manifest my ideas into actions!

I am a woman! And women can do ALL THINGS with no apologies needed!

Trump Doesn't Give A Shit About You; He Just Wants To Win

I love winning. Who doesn't? I grew up in an era where everyone didn't receive a participation trophy. And quite frankly, I never wanted a participation trophy. I strived to be the best at whatever I set my mind to do. I wanted to win, and I wanted my winning to have precise definitions; first, second or third.

I, like everyone, likes to win, however, there is a problem when you want to win by any means necessary. That is the problem with Donald Trump. He is obsessed with winning and with this obsession it doesn't matter who gets caught in the crossfire.

It is a dangerous thing when someone wants to win at any cost, at the expense and well-being of others.

When it came to eliminating Obamacare, it didn't matter to Donald Trump that millions of people would be left without health coverage. It didn't matter if people could not afford cancer treatments or their life-sustaining medications. The American people that got caught in Donald Trump's crosshairs of winning would just be collateral damage. Because it was never about the healthcare. Trump doesn't care about your healthcare. In truth, he doesn't care about the details of who or what Obamacare serves. What Trump cares about is beating Barack Obama. Since Barack Obama became President, Trump has had a strange obsession with Barack Obama heading the birther movement as if Barack Obama hid where he was from all his life because he knew one day he would become President. Yet Donald Trump just couldn't let it go, and many in White America did then as they are doing now, jumped on this birther movement without even taking just a moment to rationalize just how preposterous Trump's claims were.

If we are honest, Trump is jealous of Barack Obama. Barack Obama is a self-made man. Barack Obama graduated from Columbia and went on to Harvard where he was the first Black president of the Harvard Law Review. He is a civil rights attorney and professor and taught constitutional law at the University of Chicago Law School. Barack Obama was a Senator where he served for three terms before going on to secure his spot in history as the first African American President of the United States. He is a New York Times Bestseller, won The Nobel Peace Prize and is a skilled orator. To add the cherry on top he is married to Michelle Obama who is equally accomplished and is the proud father of two daughters who are well mannered and will go on to do amazing things in life. Trump believes someone like Obama should be shining his shoes, cooking in one of his hotel kitchens or being his caddie while he plays golf. Trump would like to put Obama in his place. Every time Trump sees Obama or hears his name, he is filled with jealousy to the point that he has made it the mission of his presidency, to dismantle anything that Barack Obama has done. Trump is in a dick measuring contest with Barack Obama and trust me, as a Black woman I know, you are not going to win. Not today or tomorrow.

It is a sad, pathetic state when you are in competition with someone who doesn't even know nor are they concerned that you are competing with them.

The same can be said about Trump's position on the NFL protest. Colin Kaepernick started kneeling in the NFL preseason, August 14, 2016. Trump was silent. For the most part, the world was silent. This was not an issue on the campaign trails; it was not a topic in any speech he gave because Trump already had villains his base could point to- Hillary Clinton, Mexicans, and Blacks in Chicago. This only became an issue because the man behind the curtain has been revealed. The veneer is wearing off. The shouts of Make America Great Again are falling on deaf ears. So, Trump needs a new villain, and he found it in Colin Kaepernick, who isn't even IN the NFL any longer, and made this an issue about patriotism. He knows this topic will rile up his base because hyper-patriotism has become the new racism. That is why he can call NFL players that kneel son's of bitches but doesn't have the testicular fortitude to address White supremacists that terrorize an American town.

To double down on his dog whistles, Trump gets on Twitter and tries to rile up his base about NFL players kneeling, yet it backfired because more players started to kneel. But Trump isn't going to lose. Oh no! So he essentially says, "Forget the players I will go after the organization." So he gets on Twitter and mentions the NFL's tax exemptions. Essentially telling the NFL to, "get your niggers to fall in line." Is he going to do anything about the NFL tax exemptions? Of course not because often times wealthy, White men are cut from the same cloth which is why Jerry Jones can demand that African American players that have made him rich billions of times over must listen to their master.

Trump's tactics NEVER CHANGE! It is ALL SMOKE AND MIRRORS! His tactics are so blatantly obvious that I am beginning to think most of his supporters think just like him or are too ignorant to realize that they are a pawn in his game.

Trump doesn't care about healthcare. Trump doesn't care about the NFL and Trump doesn't care about the American people. Yes, even those that voted for him, he doesn't give a shit about you. If you are White and poor and by poor I mean not in the 1%, he doesn't give a shit about you. If you lost your job mining coal in the hills of West Virginia, he doesn't give a shit about you. If your loved one was killed in a mass shooting, he doesn't give a shit about you. If you lose all your belonging in a natural disaster, he doesn't give a shit about you. If you need healthcare so that you can get cancer treatment, he doesn't give a shit about you. Trump doesn't give a shit about ANYONE but Donald Trump. And the sooner you realize that, the better off you will be.

Rose, White Feminism & Intersectionality
(Or some other buzzword that's hot this month)

Rose...Rose...Rose... Really, Rose? In your righteous fight against men that have sexually assaulted women in Hollywood, you went overboard by saying being called a woman is comparable to being called the N-word. To double down on your ignorance, instead of apologizing to every Black woman that you offended, you blame your comments on smoking weed. (Don't worry, I have screenshots below.)

And THIS is my problem with White feminism and just how self-serving it is. You see, we were rooting for you, Rose. But still, I watched your comments on Twitter and never said a word because as much as I reveled in you and other women bringing down a seemingly lifelong sexual predator, I remember that it is some of these very same White women that didn't have any problem putting a man that said, "Just grab em by the p*ssy", into the highest office in the land. It is some of these very same White women standing with you, that never say a word when a Woman of Color is a victim. I have been in this world long enough to know that in your quest to bring awareness to your issue, you would say something against Black women. And without fail, you were right on cue.

Feminism and Black women aren't that difficult to understand, but for some reason, it appears White feminists continue to make misstep after misstep when it comes to Women of Color and feminism. I am going to explain this as plainly as I can from my narrative of being a Black woman and a woman that believes in the liberation of ALL women. Of course, this list is not exhaustive but these steps should serve as a good start to combat White Feminism.

Photo 12 Courtesy of Twitter/Hannah Drake

1. My name is Hannah. Hannah is a woman AND Hannah is also Black.

2. Being a woman and being Black are <u>not</u> two separate issues for Hannah.

3. Hannah fights for justice and believes in the liberation of ALL women!

4. Not just SOME women.

5. Because Feminism does NOT just include cisgender heterosexual, able-bodied, middle and upper class White women.

6.Feminism is NOT about silencing Women of Color.

7.Feminism is NOT about ignoring issues that affect Women of Color because you think they do not directly affect you.

8. Feminism is NOT about stealing the creativity and ingenuity of Women of Color and pawning it off as your own in order to capitalize on it.

9.Feminism is NOT about equating the issues White women face with being called a n*gger or other racial slurs.

Tweet

Hannah Drake @HannahDrake6... · 21s
Replying to @rosemcgowan
The n word and the word women are not equal. And THIS is my problem with White feminism.

Photo 14 Photo 13 Courtesy of Twitter/Hannah Drake

Courtesy of Twitter/Hannah Drake

10. Feminism is NOT about making excuses when you have said or done something that is problematic or offends Women of Color.

11. Feminism is NOT about valuing the legacy of White supremacy over the interests of all women.

12. Feminism is NOT about appropriating the struggles of Women of Color or exploiting a cause that is centered around Black people to champion your cause.

13. Feminism is NOT about restricting Women of Color from the table.

14.Feminism is NOT about allowing one woman of color at the table to perpetuate the illusion of inclusion.

15. Feminism means getting your hands dirty and it will not always feel comfortable or have a cute hashtag, hat or ribbon to go along with it.

16. Feminism means looking in the mirror and having some tough conversations with yourself, then your friends and family about the privilege White women have in this world.

17. Feminism means admitting that you have not stood up for Women of Color because you didn't care or you didn't have to because you didn't see our issues as your issues and then making a conscious decision to do better.

Photo 14 Courtesy of Twitter/Hannah Drake

18. Feminism is admitting that as a White woman you have benefitted from some of the very systems that have harmed Women of Color and you remained silent. You have been complicit either as as active or silent co-conspirator in some of the very systems and policies that have harmed Women of Color.

19. Feminism means remembering it is not all about you, taking your ego out of it and refraining from calling Women of Color hostile, abrasive, disruptive or intimidating when we challenge your silo style of feminism.

20. Feminism means holding the door open, passing the mic and using your privilege to advocate on behalf of Women of Color.

21. Feminism means LISTENING to Women of Color when we speak.

22.Feminism means challenging policies that negatively impact the lives of Women of Color.

23. Feminism means inviting ALL women to the table to share their voices, influence and power and not as an afterthought.

24. Feminism means if it is an issue for Women of Color it is an issue for ALL women!

White Feminism seeks to serve itself. White Feminism on Intersectionality seeks to serve ALL women. Any questions?

Which Side Are You On, Friend?

Just when I think this administration cannot 'out racist' itself, it manages to surprise me. Only a few months ago the nation was dumbfounded when Donald Trump said there were "good people on both sides" after a terror attack fueled by racism was committed in Charlottesville, Virginia killing Heather Heyer. Doubling down on the administration's racist agenda, John Kelly, who some have said was called into the administration to bring order, spun it deeper into a web of confusion when he stood at a podium and completely lied about remarks Rep. Frederica Wilson made at the dedication of a new building in Miami, calling her, "an empty barrel." Video footage was released that disputed every word he said and proved him to be a liar and instead of apologizing, Kelly stated that he would "absolutely not" apologize and in fact stands by his lies.

That was not a surprise to me. Anyone that has chosen to serve underneath a man that is a lacking the morals of a slug probably thinks and acts just like him. While many people would like to hold Kelly to a certain standard, Kelly merely has proven who he is, and I am from the school of Maya Angelou, "When someone shows you who they are, believe them the first time." The first time was when Kelly insulted Rep. Wilson. The second time was when he came on national TV and said, "I would tell you that Robert E. Lee was an honorable man. He was a man that gave up his country to fight for his state, which 150 years ago was more important than country. It was always loyalty to state first back in those days. Now it's different today. But the lack of an ability to compromise led to the Civil War, and men and women of good faith on both sides made their stand where their conscience had them make their stand." (Some White people love to relitigate the reason for the Civil War to minimize their role in and the atrocities of slavery. The Civil War was about slavery. Period.)

To add the cherry on top of their bullshit and lies sundae they prance out the 2nd Liar in Command – Sarah I-Don't-Know-How-I-Sleep-At-Night-Or-Look-My-Children-In-Their-Eyes-When-I-Am-So-Full-Of-Shit Huckabee-Sanders to echo Kelly's comments about a compromise.

Compromise? What is the compromise when the issue is slavery? What compromise would Kelly and Sarah suggest? Enslaved men, women and children would get a few days off a week? Maybe they wouldn't have to pick cotton from sun up to sun down, and the slave owners would let them off at 4 pm? What about a lunch break? Maybe Black women could only be raped once a week instead of every day? What type of compromise do you make when it is about the freedom of Black people?

Kelly spoke his heart, and this is why I continue to say when people stand behind the Make America Great Again slogan it is indeed a call to Make America White Again. There was no time in the history of America that America was EVER great for Black people. The only time it was great for White people is when they could have their foot on a Black person's neck, rape Black people freely, have Black people picking cotton making them rich, cooking food for them and saying, "Yes, Master" all while they did it. And for many people like Kelly and Trump, those were the good old days.

Sorry, Trump, Kelly and Huckabee, those days are over! I do not care what policies they try to enact; those days are never coming back. The actions of this administration have drawn a clear line in the sand. For anyone reading this blog, please know that now is not the time waver. There comes a time in your life that you must make a decision and that time is now. There are some things that are just non-negotiable. If Trump believes there are two sides, then I am challenging you, to pick one. There comes a time when you must stand for something; when you must boldly speak truth to power. There comes a time when you must say, "Enough is enough." There comes a time when you must admit the truth."Ya been had! Ya been took! Ya been hoodwinked! Bamboozled! Led astray! Run amok!"* And you fell for it. You believed you put a man in office that had your best interest at heart. You chose racism over righteousness. You chose bigotry over your own healthcare. You chose hatred over love. And now here we are today standing in a mess of hypocrisy, treason, and lies. And you are still confused over where you stand?!

This administration has shown you everything they are. They no longer hide their true feelings. They no longer disguise their intentions, and if for one minute you believe that you will not be swept up in this horror you are fooling yourself. If you believe in a sea of tiki torch racists yelling blood and soil, build the wall and fuck niggers and jews, there are good people; you are fooling yourself. If you believe there was room to compromise when it came to the liberation of enslaved Black people, you are fooling yourself. If you support people who think a White man killing over 50 people and injuring 489 is not domestic terrorism; you are fooling yourself. If you believe players in the NFL are kneeling to protest a flag; you are fooling yourself. How long will you play the fool?

If you support an administration that seeks to divide this nation, you do not stand with me. You do not stand with the people that are fighting for justice and liberation. And I don't care how many Black friends you have, how many James Baldwin quotes you can recite or how many books and articles you read by Ta-Nehisi Coates. If you are silent during this time of blatant racism and chaos, you have made your choice. For the others that are still deciding, just take a look around you, take a look in the mirror and ask yourself, "Which side are you on?"

*Quote from Malcolm X (Film)

Author's Note To Kelly: Robert E. Lee was a traitor to the nation like the man you work for and he lost. You have completely thrown away your character to stand with a man with no integrity and that is the legacy you will leave behind. As stated in the National Review magazine one thing you for certain have in common with Robert E. Lee is that you, like him, "failed the basic test of history: leaving the world better and freer than he found it." Congratulations, you played yourself.

Even Harvey Weinstein Has Standards

"It would have been more comfortable to remain silent."

This statement was spoken 26 years ago by Anita Hill during the Supreme Court nomination of Clarence Thomas, as she testified about the sexual harassment she endured during her employment as Thomas's assistant. This quote came to my remembrance after I read Lupita Nyong'o's statement about her encounter with Harvey Weinstein. A part of her statement that resonated with me was, "I also did not know that there was a world in which anybody would care about my experience with him. I wish I had known there were ears to hear me." By the time, she made her statement public, many women had come forth, and Harvey Weinstein had already been removed from his position and had not spoken much to the public about the allegations. However, Weinstein made a point to come out of hiding and dispute Nyong'o's allegations. It was as if Weinstein wanted to make it clear that he may have raped and sexually assaulted many women in Hollywood but he wouldn't dare touch a Negro gal.

Hannah Drake
@HannahDrake628

Even at what should be the lowest point in his life, he doesn't want the world to believe that he tried to sexually assault a Black woman.
twitter.com/vulture/status…

7:19 PM - Oct 20, 2017

♡ 14.6K ⭕ 5,959 people are talking about this

Photo 15   Courtesy of Twitter/Hannah Drake

When I commented on Weinstein's statement on Twitter, someone replied to me, "Because at some point, even a sexual deviant has a standard to what he will go after."

Imagine reading that comment as a Black woman. It reminded me of slavery and how Black women were nothing more than free labor and a sexual commodity. And while White men could and did freely rape Black women it was a dirty little secret on the plantation. In fact, White men have been raping Black women for centuries with almost little to no consequences. Nearly 400 years later, this narrative has not changed. A man that has sexually assaulted women for almost four decades made it clear that he didn't try to touch that Negro gal. It seemed to him, that would be more embarrassing, humiliating and damaging than the fact that he is a known sexual predator.

For weeks, I have thought about Anita and Lupita, knowing that I wanted to write about this topic yet wrestling with my own thoughts and emotions. While outwardly, I remained silent, inwardly my feelings were in a whirlwind as I thought about my own encounters and relationships with men throughout my life. These feelings came to a head when the Louisville Metro Council voted in favor of Councilman Dan Johnson remaining in position despite sexual misconduct allegations. Dan Johnson had been accused of sexual misconduct towards Councilwoman Jessica Green in addition to an allegation of harassment by a staffer. The vote came down to 13 in favor of Johnson and 6 against Johnson remaining on the Metro Council. The Metro Council have given Johnson strict stipulations that he must adhere to and have stated several reasons for their vote.

On the surface, the reasons seem compelling and perhaps legally justifiable. I am not here to argue that as I know the opinions on this can and do vary. I am here to state two things that stood out to me. The Metro Council was advised that removing Johnson would likely result in an appeal and a lengthy trial that could cost almost $100,000 in taxpayer's money. I wonder what is the right price that would have worked for the Metro Council for Jessica Green to work in an environment where she felt safe and secure? If $100,000 was considered too much for her, what would have been a feasible amount for this Black woman to receive justice? What was Jessica Green's worth to the taxpayers of Louisville? When I hear Jessica Green say that she has been, "stripped of her humanity," I want to know, how much was her humanity worth to the Metro Council? Because when I read that it would have cost the taxpayers, what I heard is, justice for Black women has a price limit. Justice for Black women has a monetary cap on it. Justice for Black women isn't profitable to the city.

I am discouraged by the vote, but I am highly disappointed in the women that voted for a man that admits his "wrongdoings and transgressions." I do not excuse men like Weinstein or Johnson for any of their behavior, but I take an issue with women that are complicit in the sexual assault of other women. While they may not have committed the offense, they have made it that much harder for women to stand up and speak out. Shame on you! How do you come back to your neighborhood and look your constituents in the eyes and justify this? Especially if the area that you serve is predominantly an African- American community. How do you explain to Black women that this vote was one of compassion and love? How do you explain this to Black women knowing that in a preliminary study, 60% of Black women have been sexually abused before they are 18? And often by someone of the same race as them. If not in their own homes, if not in their own communities, if not at their place of employment, where can Black women find justice? This vote was a slap in the face to women all around Kentucky, and it was, particularly, a backhanded slap to Black women who have been victimized. I read accounts of Weinstein, and while I was disgusted with his behavior, I am angry with the women that led innocent women to him like a lamb to the slaughter. The vote in favor of Johnson was a reminder to Black women to shut up. Don't say anything. Be quiet. Who is gonna believe you anyway? You ain't worth the money it would cost to fight for justice. So deal with it!

That is what the vote said to me as a Black woman in Kentucky. When this issue first came out, I asked the question, "If A Black Woman Yells Rape, Does Anyone Hear It?" The answer is a resounding no. Remember, Black women, even Harvey Weinstein has standards.

How NOT To Do Feminism and Intersectionality. I Brought Receipts.

I am going to present this conversation as much as I can in its entirety, periodically drop in commentary and then follow up.

Hannah Drake
@HannahDrake628

What's over? People knew he was when they voted for him and had no problem with it. When someone shows you who they are, believe them. Remember White women voted for Trump.

4:10 PM - Nov 21, 2017

♡ 266   ♡ 70 people are talking about this

This is what I wrote in response to Amy Siskind's tweet (who I follow and love reading) about Trump supporting Roy Moore who is an "alleged", pedophile. I was not surprised by Trump's support because Trump is gonna Trump all day. However, I could not sit by and watch White women act surprised by his actions when indeed Trump has not wavered from who he really is as a person. He has shown his true colors time and time again yet for some reason people want to continue to believe that he will somehow be different. I took this time to remind Twitter, because I and many others will NEVER forget, as we are stockpiling can food and water waiting for all hell to break loose, that White women supported and voted for Trump. That one sentence opened a flood of "not all". Listen, I understand why people want to say, "not all" as if that removes them from "those" people. They feel better about themselves when they do not have to look at the totality of their race and wonder how the very people they call family, sit on the PTA with, invite into their homes for tea and cucumber sandwiches could vote for Trump. Acknowledging that fact forces them to look at themselves, to call into question their friends and family and doesn't make it easy to sleep at night. I get it. I understand fully why the "Not All" brigade comes stampeding when the fact is stated that White women voted for Trump. However, like it or not, those are simply the facts. White women voted for Donald Trump and are part of the reason that he is in office. Period.

Now here comes the conversation that I would like to highlight because it shows how NOT to do Feminism and Intersectionality if we want a shot at working together and making this world a better place.

Enter Veronica & Gina in response to my tweet. (I have removed their photos and Twitter names for this publication.)

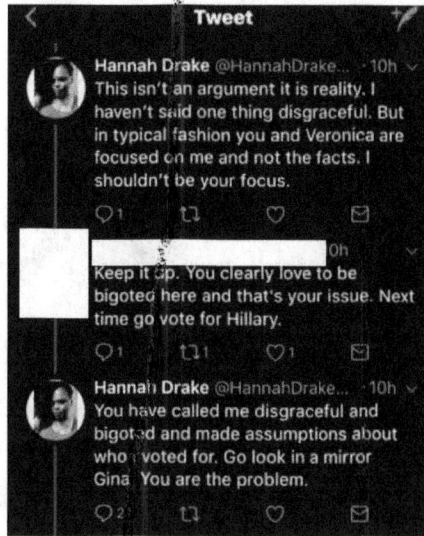

Veronica went on to agree with Gina comments and addressed me about being divisive but NEVER said one word to Gina, about calling me disgraceful and a bigot. Not ONE time did I say anything that was divisive. Facts are not divisive. They are facts. However, calling someone disgraceful, a bigot and an angry Black woman IS divisive. However, you see how Veronica NEVER once said a word about that? She doesn't perceive Gina as the problem, she perceives ME as the problem.

Gina continues...

Hannah Drake
@HannahDrake628

Replying to @HannahDrake628 @GinaMineo65
and 3 others

Stating facts isn't trashing White women. Why do facts bother you so much? It's because you don't want to face reality and THAT is why we are in the situation we are.

11/21/17, 9:08 PM

ılı View Tweet activity

Tweet

11/21/17, 9:08 PM

ılı View Tweet activity

10h
Replying to @HannahDrake628
@VeronicaSam13 and 2 others
Whatever you say. I voted for Hillary and so did every white woman I know. We're all educated. Make sure you eat lots of turkey on Thursday.

♡2   ↺1   ♡1

Hannah Drake @HannahDrake... 10h
You are the problem and I am sure when you rest at night you cannot see that. However once your emotion is out of it, go back and read how you addressed me. And check yourself. Not me.

Tweet

Hannah Drake
@HannahDrake628

Replying to @GinaMineo65 @VeronicaSam13 and 2 others

I never said you didn't however you said I didn't. As well as say I was disgraceful and bigoted as well as tell me to "keep it up" like that was some threat of some kind. Tell me Gina, who do YOU sound like?

11/21/17, 9:12 PM

View Tweet activity

(When I said "I never said you didn't", I'm responding to when she said she voted for Hillary)

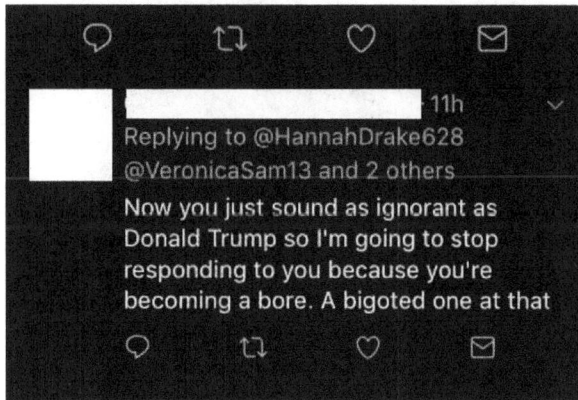

Replying to @HannahDrake628 @VeronicaSam13 and 2 others

Now you just sound as ignorant as Donald Trump so I'm going to stop responding to you because you're becoming a bore. A bigoted one at that

So, let me get this straight. I am disgraceful, a bigot, ignorant and she has made assumptions about who I voted for because I stated a fact. Okay. Let's keep going with this feminism and intersectionality. Those are the buzzwords now, right? It gets better. Keep reading. Now I was done for the night and went to bed. I said what I said and facts are facts. This morning my daughter woke up at 6 am to take our sick dog to the vet. She wanted to be there early because it gets full fast and then you have to wait for hours. Because she didn't know where she was going, I said I would drive her and while waiting I checked my Twitter. However, Gina thinks she is SO important in my life that I stayed up ALL night to talk to her because of course my world centers around her. In fact, my world was focused on my dog. (My dog got medicine and should be fine in a few days.) However, because Gina is SO important in my life and of course is one of the "good" feminist resisting, this is the comment I woke up to. (So it was not ME that was up through the night it was HER. But she cannot see that. She is blind to her own actions. You can see the time stamps. She was up over 11 hours ago responding to me. I was sleeping. Once again, blind)

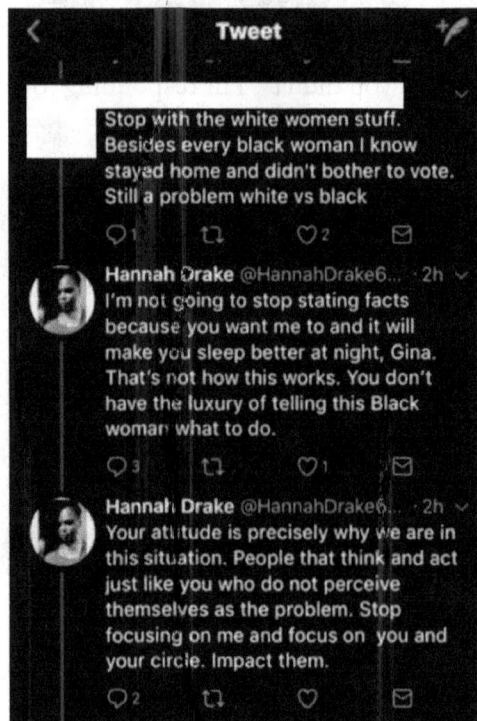

5h ⌄

Actually I have the luxury of telling this black woman anything I want. It's called Twitter. You need to get a life clearly you didn't sleep

GIF

💬 2   ↻   ♡   ✉

Hannah Drake @HannahDrake6... · 3m ⌄
Gina you are the problem. My life shouldn't be your concern. Focus on you and who you can impact. Try that.

💬 2   ↻   ♡   ✉

< Tweet ✎

1h ⌄
Replying to @HannahDrake628 and @Amy_Siskind

I voted for Hillary. While most black people stayed in bed that day because it wasn't Obama. Delusions of grandeur will get you nowhere.

💬 1   ↻   ♡   ✉

Hannah Drake @HannahDrake628 · 1h ⌄
Gina, facts are facts. The very same thing happened in Virginia and in Alabama there is actually a question if people should support a pedophile or not. I don't need to do any soul searching. I'm not your audience.

💬 2   ↻   ♡   ✉

1h ⌄
Hannah you becoming a bore now so I'm going to do the one thing I love doing. Indifference is the ultimate insult. I'll be ignoring you now.

💬 1   ↻   ♡   ✉

< Tweet ✎

Hannah Drake @HannahDrake628 · 1h ⌄
Gina I've already told you any more conversation was futile. You didn't have to start talking to me nor did you ever have to continue. Thank you for giving me work for my blog. Perhaps through you, I can show others what not to do.

💬 1   ↻   ♡   ✉

1h ⌄
You have a Blog? That's a frightening thought. I'm sure it's so full of diversity and open-mindedness. I feel sorry for you.

💬 2   ↻   ♡   ✉

Hannah Drake @HannahDrake628 · 1h ⌄
Maybe you will read it because this entire conversation is about to be on it.

💬 2   ↻   ♡   ✉

1h ⌄
Thankfully my life is so full and wonderful I don't waste time on bigoted people and their blogs. Good riddance again.

< Tweet ✎

Hannah Drake @HannahDrake6... · 5h ⌄
Gina you are the problem. My life shouldn't be your concern. Focus on you and who you can impact. Try that.

💬 2   ↻   ♡   ✉

5h ⌄
Try not being such an angry black woman and label everything as black vs white and you might have some validity to your arguments #hypocrite

💬 2   ↻   ♡   ✉

Hannah Drake @HannahDrake6... · 4h ⌄
Now I'm the angry Black woman when YOU have called me names. I've not called you a name but in typical fashion you call ME angry. Okay. Go get a mirror. This entire conversation is going to make an amazing blog to show reality. Thank you.

💬 1   ↻   ♡   ✉

Replying to @HannahDrake628 and
@Amy_Siskind

My best friend of 30 years is black.
She was the first one to comment on
you and backward thinking. Your
bigotry is showing again.

11/22/17, 7:57 AM

Hannah Drake @HannahDrake628 · 1s
Replying to @GinaMineo65 and
@Amy_Siskind
I am glad your best friend is Black.

This conversation continues and you can go to my twitter @hannahdrake628 to see the entire conversation because she continues to respond and the screenshots are endless but I believe as a reader you get the point. To top this conversation off, Gina hit me with the "I am part of the resistance Draw 4 card" the inevitable, "My Best Friend is Black" and doubled down with, "I am raising my child to be 'color-blind'".

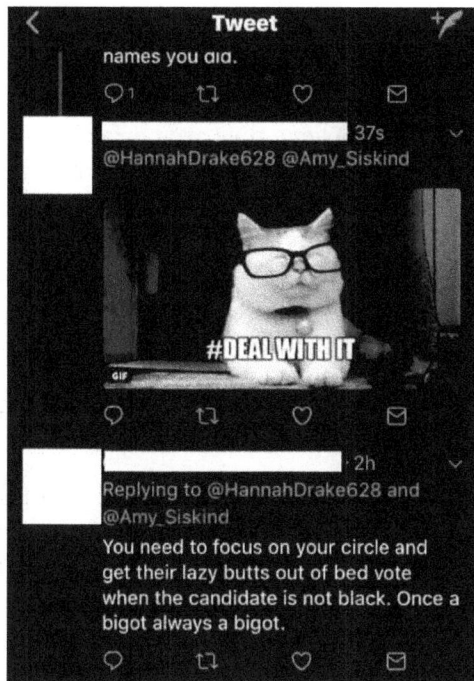

Now, I know many of you reading this will wonder, why even engage with someone like this who calls you names and talks down to you? Typically I do not. However, this time I wanted people to SEE that these are the same women that BELIEVE they have NOTHING in common with the White women that voted for Trump. These are the same women that believe they are not a part of the problem. Not ONE time did I speak to her in an angry manner yet she called me an angry Black woman, a hypocrite, a bigot, disgraceful, angry and old, ignorant, told me she had the RIGHT to tell me anything she wanted and then posted a meme that said, "Deal With It." and to top it off called Black people lazy. But THIS is a woman with her "resistance", "feminism" and "intersectionality" that I am supposed to connect with? How?

This is my PROBLEM WITH WHITE FEMINISM! It is feminism until you tell White women like Gina something they do not want to hear and cannot reconcile and then you are the "Angry Black Woman."

Until women like Gina are willing to look in a mirror, we will continue to have the same problems. Women like Gina do not see themselves as part of the problem and they do not want to do the hard work and self reflection to change. Women like Gina believe they are perfectly fine. Women like Gina believe they are the "good people". Women like Gina believe they are not like "those people". When it fact they are just two sides of the very same coin. Truthfully, I would take a White woman that tells me to my face, "I just don't like you because you are Black," rather than have a million women around me like Gina, pretending to fight for causes that affect Women of Color, any day of the week. At the very least, I can respect a racist person's honesty. I know where to put people like that. Women like Gina remain hidden in the shadows and it is those that lurk in the lukewarm shadows that are the problem.

UPDATE: Let me say, thank you to those that have read and shared this blog. I had no idea when I was posting on Twitter that this would become one of my most read blogs. I told Gina that I would post this conversation because as she was hurling racist insults at me as an "ally," I saw a teachable moment, which she could not see. For me, that is what matters. I have been called names time and time again, and for the most part, they do not bother me because I understand once people go from facts to personal they have felt attacked. Gina felt personally attacked by the facts. This is obvious when she says her and all her friends that voted for Hillary are educated. No one claimed she wasn't, so that is something internally she holding onto. And so that made it personal for her, and everything Gina ever felt about Black people came out. And I will allow her that. Her facade of resistance was lifted, and her real thoughts about Black women were exposed. However, after she was done calling me names, the fact remains that OF THE WOMEN THAT VOTED, White women voted for Donald Trump. Period.

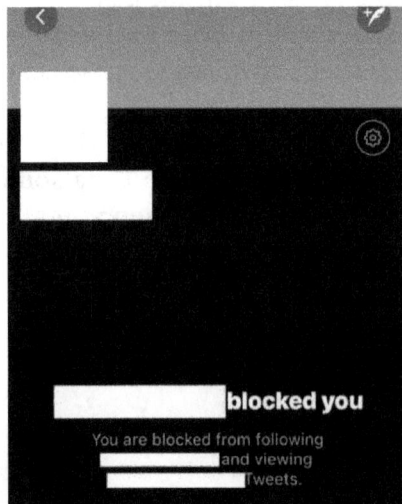

I never called Gina a name, but Gina blocked me. Blocked the truth. Because when it comes to hearing the truth about these election results and trying to progress, who needs to listen to that? However, MANY White women stepped up and called Gina out on her comments. I applaud them! And not only that, they sent me screenshots of Gina continuing the conversation with me being blocked.

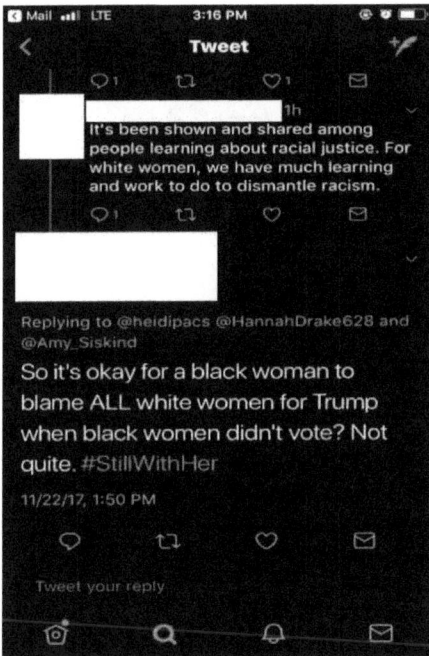

Her comments are a lie. Not one time did I say, "White women are the reason Trump won." However, White women did play an integral part in Trump winning the election. That is a fact. She goes on to call me an "Ignorant woman." (Love that intersectionality!) She also asserts that I "blame ALL White women for Trump." I never said that either. What I said, I posted on this blog, and you can follow me on Twitter to see the entire conversation. Now it may not flow because she blocked me so I do not know if you can read the totality of the conversation, but my words are there. I have no reason to lie about what I said. I do not go to bed in sheets of guilt. I feel fine. Did I love Hillary? No. She had her issues. Did I vote for Hillary? YOU DAMN RIGHT I DID! TRUMP IS TRUMP!

However, Gina and women like Gina are willing to LIE and post comments that will support their narrative. Gina and women like Gina surround themselves with people that support their LIES so they can sleep better at night. Tell me, since this is a White woman that claims she is part the resistance and on my side, how do I stand with a White woman like Gina that is willing to LIE to win an argument on Twitter?

Funny I just had an argument with a black woman on Twitter saying that white women are the reason Trump won. Ignorant woman. #stillwithher

2017-11-22, 6:16 AM

How do I stand with a woman that will block me from responding to her lies so that she can continue to tell her lies with no resistance? How do I stand with a woman like Gina that post comments on Twitter saying "this Black woman," as if that is an insult to me for being Black? How do I stand with Gina and women like Gina that claims their best female friend is Black but in the same breath says, " Every Black woman she knows stayed at home instead of voting" and tells me to get my lazy Black friends out to vote? Gina posts the hashtag #StillWithHer and never once sees me as a part of the "her." Gina and women like Gina exist in their own world of White feminism. They know all the buzzwords to say and post online but when it comes to seeing that in action, I am just one of those "lazy Black people."

It is obvious we still have a lot of work left to do. I thank the women that have stepped up and spoke out and reflected what being an ally honestly looks likes. Thank you. Gina and women like Gina, may not be able to hear me but perhaps working together, they can hear you.

Is The "Woke" Black Woman Becoming A Caricature & The New Mammy?

Caricature - car·i·ca·ture ˈkerikəCHər,ˈkerikəˌCHo͝or/ noun a picture, description, or imitation of a person or thing in which certain striking characteristics are exaggerated in order to create a comic or grotesque effect.

Several months ago, I remember I was standing at my closet looking for something to wear to a poetry event and my daughter came in my room and asked, "Why don't you just wear a poetry outfit?" I turned to her intrigued by her question and asked, "What is a poetry outfit?" She said, "You know a Black people/Black struggle related shirt, Black earrings, ripped jeans and heels."

I laughed as I scanned my mind over the latest poetry crowds and she was right. That is the "standard" look. That way of dressing is always suitable in a poetry setting. While us as poets speak of our right to be individuals and not conform, we had morphed into one another.

My daughter's assessment of the "poetry outfit" made me reflect on the poetry I heard at a recent event. Most of the poems centered around Black Lives Matter. And they do! Black lives do matter! However, I remember feeling exhausted after hearing the 10th poet, with a Def Poetry Jam cadence tell me about the hardships of being Black. I left the event early because as a Black woman going through the reality of Black pain, I couldn't bear to hear another verse about Black heartache. I recall a good friend of mine said to me once, "You write so many poems about the hardships of being Black. Do you ever celebrate what it means to be Black?"

Pause. Deep Pause.

My friend and my daughter, were right. I did not want to become a caricature of "Black angst poetry." I write on a myriad of topics and didn't want to be boxed in.

And that is what I thought as I watched, Spike Lee's, She's Gotta Have It on Netflix over the holiday weekend. Let me be clear, for the most part, I enjoyed the series and I will support the series, because I am rooting for everybody Black. However, it was difficult to watch the series and not see Issa from Insecure or Samantha from Dear White People. During the first episode, I had to continually remind myself that I was not watching Issa.

The series followed the relationship between Nola Darling and three men in her life. The original movie was released in 1986. While it does resemble the original in some ways, it has been updated for today's time. Peppered in the series are the fingerprints of "Black Twitter." Lines we have said. Lines we have typed. Lines we used as we laughed, "cut up", and formed a family in the social media world. Lines we have LIVED. She's Gotta Have It and Insecure were not just shows for us. This was the reality that we are living, breathing and often, surviving.

I wondered is this where TV is going? Is this how the stories of Black women are trending? Hollywood's Guide To A Successful Black TV Show CheckList:

- Black woman
- Black woman that is mid/late millennial age range to appeal to younger and older women
- Black woman with natural hair
- Back woman that is socially conscious
- Black woman that wears faddish, social conscious t –shirts
- Black woman that wears trendy clothes
- Black woman that lives in an apartment that we all wonder how she can afford
- Black woman that is living in a neighborhood that is being gentrified
- Black woman that is an artist or works for a non-profit
- Black woman that knows all the Twitter and Instagram hashtags
- Black woman that knows the latest songs and dances
- Black woman that dances to and loves old school music/rap
- Black woman that refuses to be labeled
- Black woman that gets her freak on
- Black woman that is unapologetically Black

Just add HBO, Netflix series and stir.

While I did watch and support She's Gotta Have It, it showed me that Issa Rae did something that has sparked an industry. She awoke an industry that for the most part overlooked the stories of Black women.

However, now the industry is paying attention. They are paying attention, not because the industry is REALLY concerned about Black women or what Black women believe and support.

I believe they desire Black women because it is profitable to curate a show around a Black woman now. Being Black and supporting Black is the "in thing." I believe the industry will become saturated with depictions of Black women speaking about albeit serious issues, however because of the saturation they will become nothing more than noise and a caricature. Just add "woke Black woman" and stir.

Is the "woke Black woman" becoming a fad? Is the "woke Black woman" now a caricature? Is the "woke Black woman" now a fixture in Hollywood like the "sassy Black bestfriend" or "Mammy"?

My issue with fads is that they fade. Here today, gone tomorrow. If enough of the "woke Black woman" character saturates our TV screens does it water down the issues we are trying to address? Will it become a fad to have the Afro-centric woman on TV that wears trendy Black slogan shirts and speaks about topics that are trending in the Black community? Will that make the message of Black women that are in the trenches and not on TV, less heard and effective?

What is the solution to this so that Hollywood does not rewind time and cast every Black woman as the "woke Black Mammy?"

ALLOW BLACK WOMEN TO TELL OUR STORIES! Every Black woman is not a millennial, wearing Black conscious T-shirts, killer shoes, working as an artist or in a non-profit, sipping cosmos. Our stories existed before time was time! Tell the Black transgender story. Tell the Black lesbian story. Tell the Black single mother story. Tell the Black enslaved woman's story. Tell the story of Black biracial women. Tell the Black divorcee story. Tell the Black Muslim story. Tell the Black asexual woman story trying to navigate in a sexual world. Tell the Black submissive story. Tell the Black Dominatrix story. Tell the Black grandmother story.

TELL OUR STORIES in ALL THEIR UGLINESS, BEAUTY, SEXINESS, DYSFUNCTION AND SPLENDOR! Black women are THREE HUNDRED AND SIXTY DEGREES OF NARRATIVE! And Black women live and write these stories EVERY SINGLE DAY! Step outside the norm and challenge your creators and writers to TRUST that WE KNOW what we want to SEE AND HEAR! BECAUSE WE LIVE IT AND WE WANT TO SEE US. ALL...OF...US!

TED Talks Broke My Heart. Mwende Katwiwa Put It Back Together Again.

In November of 2015, I decided to quit my job of 16 years as an administrative assistant. I remember as I was exiting my officer after turning in my keys and leaving a manual for the new executive assistant, I turned and looked at the office and took a picture. I wasn't sure where I would end up, but I decided that day to never remain hidden in a box again.

Photo 16 My former office

I was starting a new chapter in my life, and one of the first things I did was make a list of everything that I ever wanted for my life and as a spoken word artist. I have been performing for over two decades, and I feel that I have something that world needs to hear. One dream I had for years was to give a TED Talk. As stated on their website, TED is a nonprofit devoted to spreading ideas, usually in the form of short, powerful talks. I had listened to TED Talks over the years and was inspired, encouraged and motivated. I wanted to give those same feelings to someone else. This was my dream. So much so that I downloaded an app on my iPhone called Echo that allows you to type in your prayers and it will remind you on a day and time that you choose to pray for whatever you listed. I have Ted Talks on my prayer list for every day just before bedtime.

That is why when I saw the article "I was invited to give a TED talk — then asked to "cut Black Lives Matter" from it," by the writer, Mwende "FreeQuency" Katwiwa, I was devastated. Mwende writes, "After finishing, I went backstage only to notice the curator of the conference walk up behind me. She informed me that there had "recently been 2–3 talks on the TED platform about 'Black Lives Matter'", and suggested that I "cut the 'Black Lives Matter' portion from my talk" to make it "just be about Reproductive Justice." While in shock, Mwende states, "I spat out that I could not cut 'Black Lives Matter' from my talk, since the foundation of the talk was how the Movement for Black Lives and Reproductive Justice were inseparable for me." Mwende went on to give her poem and talk in its entirety, but still, I was heartbroken. How could an organization that I dreamed of being a part of ask a Black woman to remove Black Lives Matter from her talk? The very essence of a Black person saying Black Lives Matter means we cannot just remove it because some feel it won't play well with their audience. It would almost be as insane as asking me to remove my skin. Me being Black and saying Black Lives Matter is inescapably intertwined.

I went to bed that night and didn't pray to give a TED Talks. Maybe it was time to dream another dream. The next morning as I drove to work I couldn't shake Mwende's article. How did I reconcile my dream with the reality of what she said? But then I was reminded of my poem Spaces that was recently selected in a nationwide call for artists by the National Academy of Medicine to appear in a permanent, online art exhibition about equity, and I paused. Spaces is a poem about standing in spaces that make you uncomfortable so that one day someone else that is marginalized can stand in those same spaces. And perhaps because of what you did, they will stand in their authority knowing they have right to be in those spaces and to speak boldly in those spaces.

I thought about all the times that I stood in spaces that made me uncomfortable. Spaces where people assumed I was a server and not a speaker. Spaces where I was the only Black person in the room. Spaces where I questioned if my braids were appropriate. Spaces where I reminded myself to code switch. Spaces where people had influence and power that could affect my very livelihood if I said the "wrong" thing. Spaces where I stood afraid, voice quivering, knees knocking, but still knew that I had an obligation to stand in those spaces for two reasons. One, for every Black person that came before me that stood in spaces where they felt uncomfortable. Black women like Fannie Lou Hamer who testified at a Congressional hearing during the Civil Rights struggle.

Fannie Lou Hamer who was beaten within an inch of her life simply because she stood in spaces so that others could be liberated. Hamer once said, "I guess if I'd had any sense I'd've been a little scared, but what was the point of being scared? The only thing they could do to me was kill me, and it seemed like they'd been trying to do that a little bit at a time ever since I could remember." So, I have vowed if women like Fannie Lou Hamer can stand in spite of all the obstacles in her way then I can stand behind a microphone even when I am afraid. Two, I stand for every Black person that will come after me. So, they know they have a right to be in these spaces and to speak their authentic truth in these spaces.

We don't run. We don't change the message to make the masses comfortable. Change dwells in the realm of the uncomfortable.

It is not easy bearing the task of standing in these spaces, but when you know whose shoulders you are standing on and who is climbing up your back to stand on your shoulders, you promise yourself that you will stand in these spaces even when you are afraid and uncomfortable.

Thank you, Mwende for being a spacemaker. Mwende stood in that space to make it available for poets like me. Mwende stood in her truth and never wavered. Mwende stood in that space and spoke to truth to power.

Will I ever be invited to do a TED Talk? I don't know and even after writing this I may have ruined that opportunity if it was ever possible. Who knows? I am okay dreaming another dream. My soul can rest just fine because of women like Mwende that reminded me always to stand and speak my truth. Unapologetically.

Trump Wants to Attend the Civil Rights Museum Opening Because White.

In Peak Level Whiteness, Donald Trump is insisting on attending the opening of the Museum of Mississippi History and the Mississippi Civil Rights Museum in Jackson, Mississippi although many have called on him not to participate. U.S. Representative and Civil Rights icon, John Lewis, has said that he will not attend the opening if Trump is in attendance.

When asked about this at her ~~Weekly Lie Session~~ Press Conference, Sarah-I-Lie-For-Sport-Sanders, added insult to her own stupidity and said it was, "unfortunate that Mr. Lewis would not join the President in honoring the incredible sacrifice civil rights leaders made to right the injustices in our history." She's not too bright, is she? What Civil Rights leaders could she be referring to? Hmmmm, let me think, JOHN LEWIS! (Idiot!)

While Trump was lying about his feet hurting, men like John Lewis was fighting for CIVIL RIGHTS! Trump and his My-Daddy-Can-Buy-Me-Out-Of-The-Military "bone spurs" couldn't walk a MILE in John Lewis's shoes. John Lewis has sacrificed for this country. John Lewis has bled for this country. John Lewis was beaten so that Black people could have freedom. John Lewis was beaten on the Edmund Pettus Bridge in the same state the pedophile that Trump endorsed, Roy Moore said the last time America was great was "at the time when families were united. Even though we had slavery, they cared for one another. Our families were strong, our country had a direction." I am glad someone finally admitted what Black people have said since day one- Make America Great Again was always a slogan to make America like the antebellum South. This is the man that Trump endorses, and we are to believe that Trump cares about a Civil Rights Museum opening in Jackson, Mississippi?

The NAACP President and CEO, Derrick Jonson released a statement that said, "President Trump's statements and policies regarding the protection and enforcement of civil rights have been abysmal, and his attendance is an affront to the veterans of the civil rights movement. He has created a commission to reinforce voter suppression, refused to denounce white supremacists, and overall, has created a racially hostile climate in this nation." This is a man that spoke as if Frederick Douglass was still alive. This is a man that disrespected a Civil Rights Leader with his tweets. This is a man that insisted the First Black President of this nation wasn't born in America. This is a man that called a Black congresswoman wacky. This is a man that essentially called a grieving Black gold star widow a liar. This is a man that was sued for not renting to Black people. This is a man that said good people were on both sides when racists killed a woman in Charolettesville, Virginia. It is evident that Trump has no concern about Black people, issues that impact Black people and doesn't care about honoring history and Civil Rights leaders.

So why does Trump want to attend?

Because White.

White people are so used to defining spaces, asserting themselves in spaces and then determining who can or cannot enter those spaces that they feel like it is an affront to them if they must remove themselves from a space. Because, of course, everything revolves around THEIR level of comfortability. White people are so used to everything being centered around them that when something is clearly not about them and would, in fact, cause a damper on what should be a day of reflection and celebration, they are more concerned about themselves than others.

Trump doesn't care about the museum. Trump doesn't care about Black people. Trump is merely asserting his Whiteness in a space where he is not welcomed. But none of that matters to him. What matters to him is inserting and asserting himself and making the day about him. White comfortability is the standard in America, and that is all that matters to Trump.

I understand John Lewis's sentiments in not attending the museum opening if Trump attends. However, I am tired of Black people removing ourselves from spaces or minimizing ourselves in spaces to maintain White comfortability. How many times as a Person of Color have you shrunk yourself in a space for White people to feel comfortable? How many times have you wondered if your natural hair was appropriate in a space so that White people would feel comfortable? How many times have you switched up your vernacular in a space so that White people could feel comfortable? How many times have you wondered if you shouldn't wear your hijab in a space so that White people could feel comfortable? How many times have you avoided going to places in your own city so that White people could feel comfortable? The list could go on and on! I am tired of navigating my life in spaces so that White people can feel some sense of comfortability. What about my comfort? Do White people ever think about that or is it always secondary to their comfort?

John Lewis should not have to skip this event. John Lewis has EARNED the right to stand in this space. John Lewis deserves to be in that space, and Donald Trump should humble himself and sit this one out. The people that are honored in the museum suffered, bled, and some even died to fight against men like Donald Trump. Trump being there is a slap in the face to everyone that stood and fought for Civil Rights and that includes John Lewis.

But Trump will never see that. Because Trump is Trump and all Trump cares about is being Trump in all his peak level White glory.

Omarosa You Gonna Get This Draggin' And Rightly So

Let's get this out at this outset of this article, Omarosa, you're gonna get this draggin'. And you deserve it. However, there is an opportunity for you to redeem yourself.

You have been arrogant, rude and self-serving at best. You cared more about proximity to power than how the person that possessed that power would use it to harm People of Color like yourself. You went on national TV and tooted a horn for a man whose oppressive policies disproportionally affect the very people that look like you. You remained silent as this man sought to restrict transgender individuals from serving in the military. You didn't bat an eye when this man said, "Grab em by the pussy." You turned your head when this man stood at a podium and implied that NFL Players (mostly Black) are "sons of bitches" for protesting police brutality and injustice. You stood by as this man said, "There were good people on both sides" after Heather Heyer was murdered by a White supremacist in Charlottesville, Virginia. You said nothing when this man stood at a podium and encouraged police officers to "rough up" suspects when they place them in custody even after knowing how the murder of Freddie Gray rocked this nation. You walked into a Civil Rights Museum in Jackson, Mississippi where just this year a Black man named, Jeremy Jerome Jackson was beheaded. A town in which I was told when I was visiting Mississippi, "Do not drive through Jackson because we cannot guarantee your safety." And in 2017 my daughter and I drove into Mississippi afraid to stop to even go to the bathroom. And this is the place where you stood with a man that has no regard for the history and sacrifice of Black people during the Civil Rights Movement.

You, Omarosa, in your silence have blood on your hands.

The reward for your deafening silence was the title Director of Communications for the Office of Public Liaison of President Trump with an annual salary of approximately $180,000. You, like many people did not listen when we warned you about Trump. You walked into the Oval Office with dreams that you would be the next Olivia Pope. And even on Scandal Olivia was warned.

Apparently, you missed that episode of Scandal because, after the election that rocked Alabama and the astronomical number of Black Women that voted for Doug Jones, it was announced that you were terminated. (I understand that you say "resigned.")

Life is not without its irony. Everything always comes with a price.

My question for you today, Omarosa, was the price that you paid for standing on the wrong side of history, worth it?

The person that has the ear of the king can rule the nation. You had an opportunity as a Black woman with a strong personality and convictions to sway legislation, to stand up for others, to be a voice for those that will never have the opportunity to speak directly to the President of the United States of America. And what did you do? You flaunted your proximity to power; you took wedding photos at the White House for Twitter, you smiled smugly on Frontline and told people, "Every critic, every detractor, will have to bow down to President Trump." You forgot that meant you

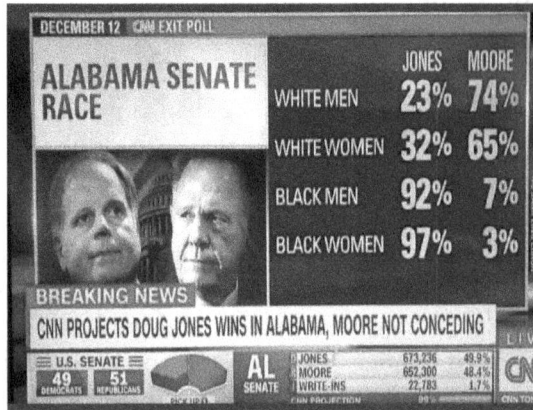

Photo 17 CNN Alabama Election Results

too. Trump didn't give a second thought about placing his foot on your back. You are the scapegoat for the loss in Alabama.

And the blowback from your choice to serve in an administration that doesn't value the fundamental aspects of humanity has been brutal. Admittedly reading some of the comments, I felt sympathy towards you. Even sharing a comment or meme, I felt a little guilty. However, for all the reasons I listed above and many more, I believe you have earned this criticism. This is a punishment that you are going to have to take. Sometimes the medicine doesn't taste good going down, but you need to swallow a heaping tablespoon of humility.

Your comments about "my community," "my people" and the obvious strain to bring forth tears as you cried about how difficult your life has been for "just trying to help" was an insult to everyone that is fighting against this administration. You turned your back on your community and your people. You turned your back on women, particularly Black women. And now, even in your termination, you are not concerned about "your community" or "your people," but your true motivation is an inevitable book deal. I am certain it will be marketed as a tell-all book since you are already branding yourself as the, "only Black person that served on the senior staff of this administration." In the age of internet fame, I understand the need for branding, however, let me be clear with you, Omarosa, in 2017 to say you are the only Black person in a position of leadership at the White House, is not a badge of honor. It is not "just words" for your rebranding ambitions. It is an embarrassment to this nation and speaks to the lack of concern about having all voices at the table to have input on the policies that will ultimately affect the lives of many People of Color.

You have stated on The View that, "You are a proud American." You cannot deny that America is weeping. If you are truly concerned about the state of this nation, you would shout everything that you know from the rooftops. Take a lesson from history as an enslaved girl stood in the dining room of Melrose Plantation in Natchez, Mississippi pulling the string of a punkah to fan the flies off her White slavemasters food. When I saw a punkah in person, my heart shattered knowing that a young Black girl was enslaved simply for White people to avoid having flies land on their food. And the Black tour guide reminded me, "Do not be dismayed. She had a job to do. While they <u>think</u> she is just there fanning flies, her ears are tuned into the frequency of freedom. And her job is to GO BACK and TELL her mother EVERYTHING she has heard. Especially if she hears the master will be leaving the plantation because it is then that they will run for freedom!"

Photo 18 Punkah- a large swinging fan moved by an enslaved child. Melrose Plantation Natchez, Mississippi/Hannah Drake

If you are genuinely about liberation then your work has just begun. Your job, Omarosa is to come back and tell everything you know, not for your monetary gain but because a nation is SHOUTING for FREEDOM!

All It Takes Is For ONE White Woman To Pass The Mic

In 1940, Hattie Mae McDaniel received an Oscar for her role as Mammy in Gone With The Wind. The Los Angeles Times praised McDaniel's work as "worthy of Academy supporting awards," and indeed McDaniel went on to win an Oscar for Best Supporting Actress.

Many people viewed this as a turning point for the Oscars. However, they fail to mention that McDaniel was not allowed to sit at the table with cast members, Vivien Leigh and Clark Gable but had to sit at a table near a far way wall because the Ambassador Hotel, where the ceremony was held, had a strict No Blacks policy. The film's director, David O. Selznick, called in a favor just to have McDaniel allowed into the building. Her final wish, to be buried in the Hollywood Cemetery was denied because "the cemetery practiced racial segregation and would not accept the remains of Black people for burial." On one hand Hollywood might appear progressive during that time in awarding McDaniel the highest award in their industry, on the other hand, her honor was still undergirded by racism. In fact, it would take over fifty years, for a Black woman, Whoopi Goldberg, to accept an award for Best Supporting Actress again.

April Reign started an #OscarsSoWhite movement in response to the lack of diversity at the Oscars, but it speaks even more to the scripts that are being greenlit in Hollywood. Women of Color cannot win awards for roles they are never allowed to have. Roles that are never written with a Women of Color in mind. Stories that are never told about Women of Color. And indeed, Women of Color have a myriad of stories. Stories that are bubbling up inside of them, waiting to be told.

However, those that control who tells the stories, share the stories that they desire. So, seeing the cover of LA Times The Envelope, doesn't shock me because White women are the default when it comes to most things in this world. White women are held up and presented as the standard. So, when the LA Times decided it was going to do a story on "A Shift In Focus: Actresses Call For A Change In The Way Stories Are Told" and placed all White women on the cover and only enlisted the voices and opinions of White women, to them this is acceptable. Because White is the standard, they cannot even see the irony of the title of the article in juxtaposition to the photo. How many People of Color are on the staff of the LA Times? How many People of Color have power and influence at the LA Times? How many People of Color, write the stories at the LA Times? How do you write a story about the hit movie Get Out that challenges people to listen to Black people more and then do a article about shifting focus that is only centered around White women?

One of the actresses, Jessica Chastain, said in the article, "I'm open with my opinions because I've only been in the industry for six years. I started pretty late — 2011 is when my first film came out. I'd already had the great

fortune of growing up out of the industry. I don't know how to not speak out."
Jessica has even posted about the "unseen women" issue on Twitter. If Jessica
was ever going to speak out about unseen and unheard women, during this
interview and cover shoot would have been a great time.

All it would take is for ONE of those women to stand up and say,
"Because we are talking about telling a new story, we should have a more
diverse selection of women to tell their story in this article." That is how you
change the world. That is how you show intersectionality not just in word but
also in deed. However, when everything around tells you that as a White
woman you are the standard, it is difficult to notice when someone isn't being
represented. It takes making a CONSCIOUS DECISION TO CARE
ENOUGH TO EVEN NOTICE AND THEN TO ACT. How could
someone like Annette Bening, a legend in Hollywood, shift the entire focus of
the article, if she stood up and said, "There are people missing from this
discussion." She has influence, USE IT. One of the BENEFITS of having
power is to USE IT for those that do not have it to impact their lives.

Representation matters. Seeing yourself reflected to you, can alter the
course of your life because you start to believe that what the world has told
you was impossible is in fact, possible. As a Women of Color, I am always
looking for someone that looks likes me in a space. For someone that I believe
will represent me and issues that impact Black women. For someone that can
tell my side of the story in a room that I may never have the power or influence
to be in. And when it is not represented it is glaringly apparent. However, it is
oblivious to people who more than likely never have to think about being "the
other." For instance, when Princess Michael of Kent wore a blackamoor
brooch to the queen's annual Christmas lunch at Buckingham Palace some
considered the brooch racist. In her apology, she said, "She has worn it before,
and it has never caused any controversy." Just to make that statement shows
how the world makes White the standard. I am going to assume in her social
circle she is around people that look and think like her so naturally, it would
not be a source of controversy. When you have always been the standard, you
see nothing wrong with wearing a brooch that many consider similar to
blackface. She never has to think about it; it is just normal to her.
When it comes to how we tell stories, I challenge White people, particularly
White women, to take themselves out of the center and then ask themselves:
1. Am I making myself the center of this story?
2. Who is telling the story?
3. Are there Women of Color that should be telling this story?
4. Who benefits from this story?
5. Whose voice isn't being heard in this story?
6. What agenda is centered in this story?
7. Who is or isn't being represented in this story?

8. Are White people the default in this story?
9. How are People of Color portrayed in this story?
10. Have I thought about "the other"?

Seeing the La Times The Envelope cover, I was reminded of Viola Davis's Oscar speech:

"Thank you to the Academy. You know, there's one place that all the people with the greatest potential are gathered. One place and that's the graveyard. People ask me all the time, what kind of stories do you want to tell, Viola? And I say, exhume those bodies. Exhume those stories. The stories of the people who dreamed big and never saw those dreams to fruition. People who fell in love and lost. I became an artist—and thank God I did—because we are the only profession that celebrates what it means to live a life."

I became a writer to tell the stories and perspectives of Black Women. I want to read about characters that look like me and speak like me, that understand my "slang" and do not chastise me for my differences. I want to read stories where I am the center, where issues that impact me are the focus. I want to see me all around me. As my friend Kiara said, "The world is so much more beautiful when you can see yourself in it." I became a writer to put those stories into the atmosphere and to use my words to challenge people to tell a new narrative. All people have a story, and they deserve the right to tell their story. Open up your eyes and be amazed at how much more rich, glorious and full this world can be if the voices of all people are heard.

Dear Black People: You Do Not Need Permission From Anyone To Dream

In The Mis-Education of the Negro, Dr. Carter G. Woodson wrote, "When you control a man's thinking you do not have to worry about his actions. You do not have to tell him not to stand here or go yonder. He will find his 'proper place' and will stay in it. You do not need to send him to the back door. He will go without being told. In fact, if there is no back door, he will cut one for his special benefit. His education makes it necessary."

Although published 84 years ago, Dr. Woodson's thesis remains true today. Woodson argued that "Blacks of his day were being culturally indoctrinated, rather than taught, in American schools. This conditioning, he claims, causes Blacks to become dependent and to seek out inferior places in the greater society of which they are a part."

Dr. Woodson's comments on controlling a man's thinking came to mind when Sean 'Diddy' Combs announced that he was interested in buying the Carolina Panthers- an NFL team that is being put up for sale after the current season, due in part to a growing investigation of sexual misconduct and racist language attributed to Carolina Panthers owner, Jerry Richardson.

Combs expressed interest via Twitter in purchasing the team.

Combs is a businessman, rapper, songwriter, actor, record producer, and entrepreneur. In 2017, he was listed in the Forbes Magazine as the highest-ranking entertainer with an estimated net worth of 820 million dollars. Other Black men such as NBA player for the Golden State Warriors, Steph Curry and blackballed NFL Player Colin Kaepernick have expressed interest in joining Combs in taking his words from a tweet to reality.

I expected many White people to tell Diddy that owning an NFL was impossible. The oppressor will always seek to keep the oppressed, oppressed. And true to form many White people did voice their opinions telling Diddy how foolish he was even to make the statement that was interested in buying the Carolina Panthers. However, many Black people decided to voice their opinions as well, with most letting Diddy know that believing that he could actually own the Carolina Panthers was a foolish dream. Henry Wofford, an African-American sports reporter, for Bay Area TV station KRON4 recently came under fire for his remarks, regarding Combs buying the team. Wofford said, "How can you take Diddy seriously? The guy looks high right there in that video. He looks like he just smoked a blunt and drank a 40." After the backlash, Wofford issued an apology.

While I would like to say that I am surprised by Wofford's comments and other Black people that think like him, I am not shocked. When you are so used to just being the player, it is difficult for your mind to conceive that you could actually own the team. When it is so ingrained in you that your success is dependent upon what a White person will allow you to have, you never seek to believe that you can have anything else outside of what they are offering you. When you are so used to allowing a White person's vision for your life to set the parameters of your dreams, it is easy to tell Combs what he cannot have. This way of thinking is nothing new. Malcolm X spoke about this way of thinking at Michigan State University over 50 years ago. Malcolm X said, "So you have two types of Negro. The old type and the new type. Most of you know the old type. When you read about him in history during slavery he was called "Uncle Tom." He was the house Negro. And during slavery you had two Negroes. You had the house Negro and the field Negro.

The house Negro usually lived close to his master. He dressed like his master. He wore his master's second-hand clothes. He ate food that his master left on the table. And he lived in his master's house–probably in the basement or the attic–but he still lived in the master's house.
So whenever that house Negro identified himself, he always identified himself in the same sense that his master identified himself. When his master said, "We have good food," the house Negro would say, "Yes, we have plenty of good food." "We" have plenty of good food. When the master said that "we have a fine home here," the house Negro said, "Yes, we have a fine home here." When the master would be sick, the house Negro identified himself so much with his master he'd say, "What's the matter boss, we sick?" His master's pain was his pain. And it hurt him more for his master to be sick than for him to be sick himself. When the house started burning down, that type of Negro would fight harder to put the master's house out than the master himself would.

But then you had another Negro out in the field. The house Negro was in the minority. The masses–the field Negroes were the masses. They were in the majority. When the master got sick, they prayed that he'd die. If his house caught on fire, they'd pray for a wind to come along and fan the breeze.

If someone came to the house Negro and said, "Let's go, let's separate," naturally that Uncle Tom would say, "Go where? What could I do without boss? Where would I live? How would I dress? Who would look out for me?" That's the house Negro. But if you went to the field Negro and said, "Let's go, let's separate," he wouldn't even ask you where or how. He'd say, "Yes, let's go." And that one ended right there.

So now you have a twentieth-century-type of house Negro. A twentieth-century Uncle Tom. He's just as much an Uncle Tom today as Uncle Tom was 100 and 200 years ago. Only he's a modern Uncle Tom. That Uncle Tom wore a handkerchief around his head. This Uncle Tom wears a top hat. He's sharp. He dresses just like you do. He speaks the same phraseology, the same language. He tries to speak it better than you do. He speaks with the same accents, same diction. And when you say, "your army," he says, "our army." He hasn't got anybody to defend him, but anytime you say "we" he says "we." "Our president," "our government," "our Senate," "our congressmen," "our this and our that." And he hasn't even got a seat in that "our" even at the end of the line. So this is the twentieth-century Negro. Whenever you say "you," the personal pronoun in the singular or in the plural, he uses it right along with you. When you say you're in trouble, he says, "Yes, we're in trouble."

But there's another kind of Black man on the scene. If you say you're in trouble, he says, "Yes, you're in trouble." He doesn't identify himself with your plight whatsoever."

It has been said that Harriet Tubman said, "I freed a thousand slaves. I could have freed a thousand more if only they knew they were slaves." While the validity of attributing this quote to Harriet Tubman has been called into question, the sentiment of the quote remains true. Some Black people will never see that they are slaves to a system. Some Black people will never believe that they can have more than what a White person chooses to give them. In a world where many Black people are content eating the crumbs that fall from the table, it is difficult to teach some Black people that they do not need to settle for crumbs but can indeed cook their own meal.

When you know nothing but oppression, it is difficult to believe that you can have freedom. But you can, and that freedom starts with the simple belief that you can have everything that you have ever desired. Black people you can dare to dream. You can dare to believe that what they say is impossible is in fact, possible. Know that when people tell you something is impossible, they are speaking out of their own fear or their desire to keep you in a specific position often for their gain. Black people, you can own and know your worth. Do not underestimate your value. White people have pimped your value for their gain for centuries. Those days are over. You do not have to settle. Black people you do not have to believe what they have told you about you. You write your own story. You are the offspring of greatness, brilliance, and excellence.

Combs dares to believe. Perhaps that is why he rose from a young Black kid from Harlem to the highest paid entertainer on the Forbes list. As Dr. Woodson wrote, "History shows that it does not matter who is in power…those who have not learned to do for themselves and have to depend solely on others never obtain any more rights or privileges in the end than they did in the beginning." Going into a New Year if I can implore Black people to do anything, I would ask for us to dream, to set a vision and then do everything within your power to act on that vision. To support other Black men and women that have a dream. Believe that we can have anything that we desire. That anything we want is possible. That we do not always have to be the players, but we can own the team. We are the masters of our destiny. We are not beholden to anyone to fulfill our destiny. Understand that we stand on the shoulders of giants. Genius is inscribed on our DNA. All we have to do is believe.

Dear Alyssa, Please Stop With Your Performative Twitter Social Justice

In January 2017, my blog begin with a critique of the Women's March, a march that was heavily and primarily attended by White women in knitted pink pussycat hats as if we had forgotten that indeed 53% of White women that voted, voted for Donald Trump. As I watched the march on TV, I struggled to figure out why it was not resonating with me. I am a woman that believes in the liberation of ALL women, but something was amiss. And then the iconic picture of Angela Peoples standing in front of 3 White women in pink pussycat hats on their cellphones and taking selfies, while she stood with a lollipop in her mouth and a sign that read, "Don't forget, White women voted for Trump,: came across my newsfeed and immediately I knew that was why I felt the way that I did.

While I support protesting, and marching I felt many of the White women during the November 2016 election were like the three White women in the background of the picture nonchalantly on their phones, taking selfies in their Ugg boots as if the proverbial plane was not on fire. However, the plane is on fire and has been on fire, but White America treated Black people, particularly Black women as if we were the stewardess giving instructions as the flight takes off for what to do if the plane goes down. We were tuned out, and our shouts ignored as White America went on about its business.

We were just those protestors fighting against racism until it was Heather Heyer. We were only those people complaining about police brutality until it was Alex Wubbels a White nurse being wrongly arrested by a Utah police. We were just overreacting when we screamed about Freddie Gray being given a "rough ride" by the police which aided in his death, and then the President of the United States encouraged police to rough up suspects. We were just those lone dissenters screaming about healthcare until you realized Trump meant your healthcare would be taken away too. We were just standing with a Black woman named Anita Hill that testified about sexual harassment against a man that went on to become a Supreme Court Justice and then it all hell broke loose in Hollywood. We told you we did not live in a post-racial America after the election of President Barack Obama and then 74% of White men and 65% of White women that voted in the Alabama Senate election, voted for a racist alleged pedophile and the world realized we were not post-racial. It seems life would be much less complicated if White America would listen to Black people, particularly Black women when we speak. And not as an afterthought but a forethought.

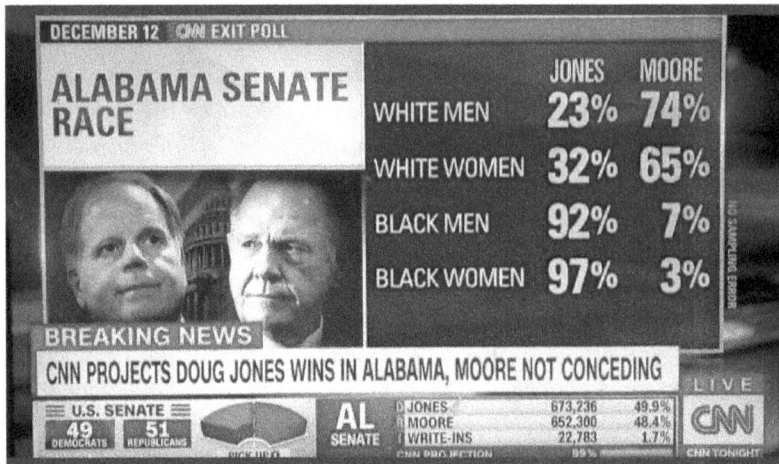

I started this year on a high note, believing that something that I wrote would shake up the world. Yet here we are just three days from a new year and actress turned activist, Alyssa Milano makes a Twitter post that revealed to me that we have a very long way to go. Alyssa was thrust into the spotlight after she tweeted a phrase "Me Too" to bring awareness to people that have been victims of sexual harassment and assault. However, the "Me Too" movement was actually started by a Black woman named, Tarana Burke over a decade ago. Alyssa later acknowledged this fact however what was done was done and many credit Alyssa with sparking a movement.

Perhaps Alyssa was feeling particularly revolutionary when she took to Twitter early in the morning to post the poem by Langston Hughes, Let America Be America Again. In her posting of the poem, she highlights a stanza by Hughes forgetting the central focus of the poem that Hughes places in parentheses, America never was America to me, almost as if he wants to draw particular attention to that part of the poem.

It is as if the ENTIRE meaning of the poem flew just north of Alyssa's head.

Alyssa's convenient performative act of justice reminds me of when White people cherry-pick quotes by Martin Luther King Jr. or Muhammad Ali that help them sleep better at night. Do not forget that while Dr. King said, "I have been to the mountaintop" he has also said, "First, I must confess that over the past few years I have been gravely disappointed with the white moderate. I have almost reached the regrettable conclusion that the Negro's great stumbling block in his stride toward freedom

is not the White Citizen's Counciler or the Ku Klux Klanner, but the white moderate, who is more devoted to "order" than to justice; who prefers a negative peace which is the absence of tension to a positive peace which is the presence of justice; who constantly says: "I agree with you in the goal you seek, but I cannot agree with your methods of direct action"; who paternalistically believes he can set the timetable for another man's freedom; who lives by a mythical concept of time and who constantly advises the Negro to wait for a "more convenient season." Shallow understanding from people of good will is more frustrating than absolute misunderstanding from people of ill will. Lukewarm acceptance is much more bewildering than outright rejection."

While people like Alyssa love to quote Muhammad Ali saying, "Service to others is the rent you pay for your room here on earth," do not forget that Ali also said, "I ain't draft dodging. I ain't burning no flag. I ain't running to Canada. I'm staying right here. You want to send me to jail? Fine, you go right ahead. I've been in jail for 400 years. I could be there for 4 or 5 more, but I ain't going no 10,000 miles to help murder and kill other poor people. If I want to die, I'll die right here, right now, fightin' you, if I want to die. You my enemy, not no Chinese, no Vietcong, no Japanese. You my opposer when I want freedom. You my opposer when I want justice. You my opposer when I want equality. Want me to go somewhere and fight for you? You won't even stand up for me right here in America, for my rights and my religious beliefs. You won't even stand up for my right here at home."

For Alyssa to conveniently highlight a part of Langston's poem that makes her feel good, that will get her some Twitter likes and then have the audacity to come back to Twitter to EXPLAIN what Langston meant in his poem, as if Black people are not the walking living personification of his words is an insult to every Black person on this earth.

Let me educate you, Alyssa beyond your performative Twitter racial justice on what Langston meant. You have failed to highlight the most important part of his poem. Langston is writing about two things in extreme juxtaposition to draw a glaring difference in what

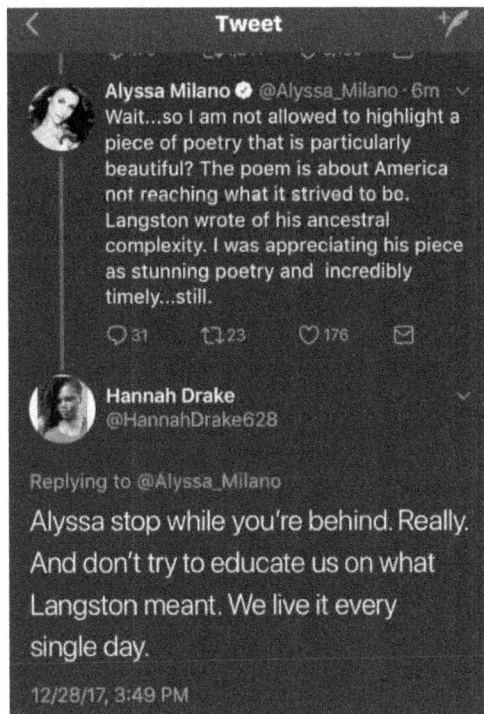

Tweet

Alyssa Milano @Alyssa_Milano · 6m
Wait...so I am not allowed to highlight a piece of poetry that is particularly beautiful? The poem is about America not reaching what it strived to be. Langston wrote of his ancestral complexity. I was appreciating his piece as stunning poetry and incredibly timely...still.

31   23   176

Hannah Drake
@HannahDrake628

Replying to @Alyssa_Milano

Alyssa stop while you're behind. Really. And don't try to educate us on what Langston meant. We live it every single day.

12/28/17, 3:49 PM

America says it is and the reality of what America actually is for Black people.

Black people were brought to this land in chains, suffered some of the worst heinous, atrocious crimes against Black humanity, worked in fields from sun up to sun down expected to pick over 200 pounds of cotton a day, and suffered the whip of the lash if they didn't meet their quota. When you tweet, "Me Too" remember that it was enslaved Black women that were raped by White men and White people turned a blind eye. It was Black women that had to look into the eyes of their husbands while a slave master stole their humanity. It was Black women that had to birth children by their slave masters. Here in Kentucky where Langston's paternal great-grandfathers were slave owners, an enslaved Black woman named Lucy was lynched for murdering her slave owner and rapist. So no, Alyssa, America has never been America to me.

Black people have suffered under the weight of racism just to have civil rights. Black people were arrested, beaten, water hosed, had dogs turned loose on them just for the right to just be. A Black boy named Emmett Till was beaten and killed because he was falsely accused of talking to a White woman. This same White woman had the convenience of admitting that she lied years later. How convenient it must be to take a stand for Black people you have harmed from the comfort of your home. Sound familiar, Alyssa? George Stinney, a 14-year-old Black boy, was sent to the electric chair for murders he did not commit. At just 90 pounds, George was so small that he had to sit on top of a Bible for the helmet of the electric chair to fit him for White America to make an example out of him. So no, Alyssa, America has never been America to me.

And here we are today with the murders of Trayvon Martin, Sandra Bland, Eric Garner and countless others. Today of all days for you to make your post, Black people are hurting as we stand in the gap for Erica Garner, the daughter of Eric Garner, a 27-year-old Black woman that fought for social justice after the murder of her father, that was declared brain dead after suffering a heart attack. Yet here you are with a misinterpreted poem from one of the most prolific writers that wrote for radical racial reform. Here we are in 2017 where the weight of racism continues to chip away at our lives daily. Here we are when a 12-year-old boy named Tamir Rice is gunned down on a playground by the police in less than 2 minutes for playing with a toy gun. Here we are where an NFL player can be vilified and blackballed for taking a knee to bring awareness to police brutality. Here we are, Alyssa, where a Black man can be wrongly murdered by the police on camera and America tries to tell us why it is justified. Here we are, Alyssa, where a Black man in Mississippi can be beheaded in 2017. Here we are, Alyssa, where Black people are STILL fighting for the right to just exist in America. So no, Alyssa, America has never been America to me.

And you come online with your Twitter post as if the world is supposed to be impressed by your performative social justice and ignorance. I am hardly impressed. It is easy to overlook Langston's meaning of his poem when you do not have to live it daily. It is easy to make a Twitter post and sit back and pat yourself on the back as people like your post and feel as if you have done something for the advancement of race relations in America. In fact, you have done nothing but show me that we still have a long road to travel.

As Langston wrote,

Who said the free? Not me?
Surely not me? The millions on relief today?
The millions shot down when we strike?
The millions who have nothing for our pay?
For all the dreams we've dreamed
And all the songs we've sung
And all the hopes we've held
And all the flags we've hung,
The millions who have nothing for our pay—
Except the dream that's almost dead today.
O, let America be America again—
The land that never has been yet—

Since you enjoy quoting Black writers, Alyssa, let me quote one for you. In the words of James Baldwin, "I love America more than any other country in this world, and, exactly for this reason, I insist on the right to criticize her perpetually."

And daily I will criticize America for what it isn't for Black people and ALL People of Color longing and screaming for JUSTICE!

Dear White People: You Can STILL Be Racist If...

Last week this issue came up on my Facebook feed, and I was going to address it, but life happens, and the point got away from me. However, scrolling through my Twitter feed, I see the, "I am not a racist because..." issue has reared its head again.

I typically like to write in-depth, thought-provoking blogs backed with facts and citations. However, there are sometimes it just is what it is. This blog is straight with no chaser.

For some (and by some I mean many) White people and ANYONE ELSE that says, "I am not racist because fill in the blank" please check the following list.

YOU CAN BE STILL BE RACIST IF...

You sleep with someone that is Black.
You fetishize and love Black dick.
You have birthed a child that is of mixed race.
You have adopted a Black child.
Your best friend is Black.
Your mother's cousin's brother's sister is married to a Black person.
You are educated.
You love Kendrick Lamar.
You voted for Obama once.
You voted for Obama twice.
You would vote for Obama a third time if you could.
You allow Black people at your dinner table.
You listen to rap music.
You Milly Rock on any block.
You can Hit Dem Folks.
You made a protest sign.
You love Beyonce and know all the moves to Single Ladies.
You marched in ANY march in 2017.
You knitted a pink pussycat hat.
Your family didn't own slaves.
You are a principal at a predominantly Black school.
You are a teacher at a predominantly Black school.
You voted for Hillary Clinton.
You supported Bernie Sanders.
You post #TrustBlackWomen.
You support Black activists online.
You did any type of missionary work in Africa.
You donate to the NAACP.
You retweet Black Lives Matter's hashtags.

You consider the White people that voted for Trump "those people" and
    not you and your friends.

You know all the words to Bodak Yellow but censor the n-word.

Your response to Black activism is, "I support your efforts I just wish you
    did it another way."

You support Colin Kaepernick protesting but wish he just didn't protest
    during the games.

You don't repeat racist jokes.

You quote Martin Luther King Jr. and Audre Lorde.

You dream about sleeping with Idris Elba.

You own black fleshtone sex toys.

You identify as someone in a marginalized group.

You are Christian.

You don't see race.

I know it may be difficult to read this list because you may have believed that
some of these things made you immune to being racist. They don't. History
is filled with White men and women that thought they were not racist when
in fact we know that not to be the case. Even today, there are many White
men and women that truly believe they stand on the side of goodness and
righteousness. However, that is not the case.

Check your actions.

Look in a mirror.

Examine your heart.

Because there is where the truth resides.

***

Author's Note: This list is not exhaustive just things that I have experienced,
read or heard and many I have experienced, read or heard in 2017. Let's try
harder.

Trump's ShitHole Comment Provides a Lesson for "Good" People

Author and poet Maya Angelou once said, "When someone shows you who they are, believe them the first time." This is a belief that I have held for years and one that often comes to mind when I read the latest racist, homophobic or sexist comments made by Donald Trump. On the near 8th year anniversary of one of the most devastating natural disasters to hit Haiti, where over 200,000 people died, in a meeting about immigration reform, Trump referred to Haiti, El Salvador, and Africa as shitholes countries.

And the media and many in the nation went into a frenzy. Thinkpieces popped up all over Twitter asking the question, "Is Donald Trump racist?" It was almost insulting after all that we have seen and read, all that Black people have stated, that we must still ask a question that we all know the answer to. Trump is going to be who Trump has shown himself to be. I am not naïve enough to believe that has a man that has been self-centered, egotistical, arrogant, racist and lacking a basic moral compass all his life will ever change. What America is getting is what White America voted for because White America supported what Trump stood for and they showed their support by voting to put him office. There is no getting around that. So, before you read any further, before you jump to "not me," before you send me a long email about how you volunteer at an inner-city community center and voted for Hillary Clinton, pause and absorb that fact. Pause and understand that is the reality. Pause and realize that is the America we are living in. Of the people that voted, White America voted for a man that was openly racist. That is a fact. Until you are willing to accept that as a fact, you need to stop reading because you are not ready to do the work that is required to fight racism.

Majority of white voters opt for Trump

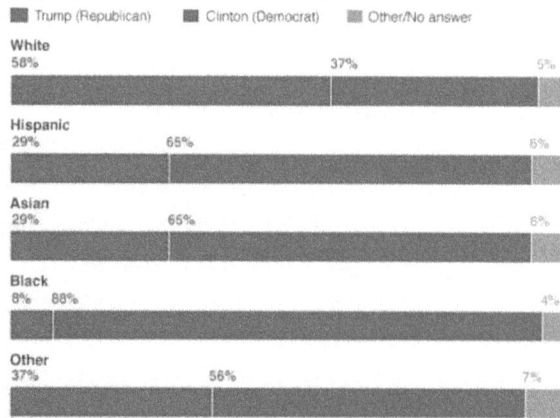

Trump (Republican) Clinton (Democrat) Other/No answer

White
58% 37% 5%

Hispanic
29% 65% 6%

Asian
29% 65% 6%

Black
8% 88% 4%

Other
37% 56% 7%

Source: Edison Research for ABC News, AP, CBS News, CNN, Fox News, NBC News   BBC

I was not shocked by Trump's comments because I have a solid understanding about race in America. My focus was not on Donald Trump, because Trump is going to be what Trump has always been. My attention immediately went to the people in the room because it is the people in the room, that will make a significant impact when it comes to fighting racism. Senator Dick Durbin was the first and only person in the room to take a public stand and confirm that Trump did indeed call Haiti, El Salvador and Africa, shithole countries. Senator Lindsay Graham came out with a statement saying what Durbin said was, "basically true." Senators Tom Cotton and David Perdue said they do not recall the statement being made. At the time of this blog, Rep. Mario Diaz Balart, House Majority Whip Kevin McCarthy, Rep. Bob Goodlatte have remained silent.

It is in that spineless silence and lukewarm admitting to the truth that racism breeds, and thrives.

When it comes to fighting racism, you must:

1. Speak Up – You have a voice so use it. All it takes is one person to speak up and say, "This is racist, and I will not tolerate this." One person speaking up can allow others to see that they can do it too.

2. Stand Up – How could the atmosphere of that room shift if everyone stood up and walked out? When it comes to fighting racism, you must take a stand. Sometimes that is in the literal sense of the word. Stand up and walk out. Do not provide an audience for someone that wants to engage in racist behavior.

3. Have Courage – Speaking truth to power is never easy. You will be afraid. I challenge you to do it afraid. You may be the only one. You may face criticism. Your heart may be beating fast, and your knees may be knocking, however, speak up even if your voice is quivering. At some point, you must decide, "Do I want to sit in my fear or stand in my courage?"

4. Understand that Silence is Compliance – Racism thrives because too many "good people" remain silent. Silence is compliance. It is too convenient to say, "not me" or "I didn't say it." I ask you, "What did you say? Did you say anything that would stop the racist comments?" While I applaud Durbin speaking up, what I am baffled by is that he said, "Trump repeatedly used the word shithole." How does that happen? I understand the first time the people in the room may have been shocked. However, how is Trump allowed to call countries with a predominately Black and Brown population shitholes more than once? There should have been no room for him to use that language a second time.

5. Be Public – Racism thrives in the shadows. Only by calling it out publicly can we start to confront it. Pretending that racism doesn't exist doesn't advance humanity. Whispering about racism to your friends doesn't help anyone. Publicly challenging racists in their statements, beliefs, and policies means they can no longer hide.

6. Prepare Yourself For the Backlash– No one likes when someone disrupts a system that benefits them, and systemic racism benefits many people. When you stand up to bigotry, be prepared for people who need it to thrive, to be upset. However, you will rest easier knowing that you did the right thing.

7. Do Not Sugarcoat Racism- Inevitably when racists get called out, their first line of defense is to lie, deny or say they were making a joke. But being racist isn't funny. Do not make excuses for their comments and do not attempt to dress them up saying, "What they really meant to say is _____." What they said, they said. Do not try to explain racism away. Racism is what it is.

Will fighting racism be easy? No. In fact, I can promise if you do the things on this list, it will be difficult. It will require you having some tough conversation with people that you respect and love. It may even require you to have some tough conversation as you stare in a mirror and confront some of your own racist beliefs and behaviors. However, it will be worth it. Because we are worth living in a world where everyone thrives. Remember, Dr. King said, "'In the end, we will remember not the words of our enemies but the silence of our friends."

America Has Selective Tragedy Support Syndrome
DISCLAIMER

Anyone that personally knows me or follows my blog knows that I believe injustice anywhere is a threat to justice everywhere. At the outset of this blog let me fully state that I support any and ALL young people that are fighting for justice. Having said that, I would not be me if I did not speak about my feelings having watched the recent protests and responses to the protests in regards to the Marjory Stoneman Douglas High School mass shooting in Parkland, Florida. This blog may make you mad. Do NOT send me ANY messages about not supporting young people. Anyone that KNOWS me knows that is a lie. However, the truth is the truth.

******

Recently in the wake of the Marjory Stoneman Douglas High School mass shooting in Parkland, Florida, where 17 people were murdered and over 15 people injured, young people have emerged strong, using their anger, outrage, and sadness to stand together in solidarity and ask for a ban on assault rifles. Their cries are being heard around the world with national media giving them the spotlight and sharing their message. Social media immediately responded with pages of support, tweets, retweets and hashtags making their message not just one that touched America, but one that is impacting the world.

Perhaps it is the writer in me, but I am always watching how a story is told, how America collectively responds and asking myself some of the following questions:

Who gets the media airtime?

How is the media framing and presenting the narrative to the public?

Who gets the frontpage coverage?

Who gets the celebrity endorsements and funding?

Who gets the sit down with the President and Vice President of the nation?

Who gets one on one time with Congressmen and Senators?

Who is allowed access and a seat at the table?

Who can stage a sit-in and protest and it is deemed a sign of leadership?

Who gets stories in Buzzfeed about the ground zero organizing of a movement?

Who gets to be the face of tragedy?

Who does American rally around and support in times of tragedy?

I sat back and watched the media coverage unfold surrounding the Marjory Stoneman Douglas High School Shooting, and a part of me is overjoyed that once again young people are leading the pack when it comes to changing the world. However, another part of me is baffled that the media is presenting this story as if this is the first time in history and even recent history that young people have responded to injustice.

In fact, we know that is not the case.

Young Black people have always been at the forefront when it comes to fighting for justice. Young Black people wrote the blueprint for protesting. Young Black people were the leaders of the Civil Rights Movement. Lara Luper was just eight years old attending an NAACP Youth Council meeting when she suggested a sit-in at the Katz Drug Store. Claudette Colvin was 15 years old when she was arrested for refusing to give up her seat on a bus. Dr. Martin Luther King Jr., Malcolm X, and Medgar Evers were all in their twenty's when they emerged as some of the most significant Civil Rights leaders this world has known. Freeman Hrabowski was just 12 years old when he was inspired to march in the Birmingham Children's Crusade of 1963, where more than a thousand students skipped school and gathered at the 16th Street Baptist Church in Birmingham, Alabama. This crusade resulted in over a thousand arrest and the use of high-pressure water hoses and police attack dogs used on the young Black people that decided to protest.

High school students are hit by a high-pressure water jet from a fire hose during a peaceful walk in Birmingham, Alabama in 1963. Charles Moore

In recent history with the 2014 murder of Mike Brown, an 18-year-old Black male, by White police officer Darren Wilson, young Black people in Ferguson, Missouri, resisted and stood in solidarity saying, "Enough is enough!" Reminiscent of leaving a Black body swaying in the hanging tree for onlookers to be discouraged about speaking up, Mike Brown's body laid in the street for a little over 4 hours, and that was 4 hours too long for many people.

Mike Brown's death was the climax moment of a community that had grown weary. The racial inequity and injustice in Ferguson was a bomb just waiting to explode, and the murder of Mike Brown lit the fuse. While the media and the many in the nation focused on the riots, they didn't look at the seeds that had been planted that produced the fruit of rage. The Black citizens of Ferguson's complaints about the police department fell on deaf ears. Complaints that were subsequently substantiated by the Justice Department which concluded the police in Ferguson practiced a "pattern of unconstitutional policing" that "exacerbate existing racial bias, including racial stereotypes." The report also cited the city's emphasis on revenue for contributing to the pattern of unlawful law enforcement.

News outlets rushed to Ferguson to tell the story of the riots, to show the fires, broken glass and mayhem but did little, if anything, to tell the backstory of what led to this moment in time. As Martin Luther King Jr said, "A riot is the language of the unheard." And when you have been unheard for centuries, you will demand to be heard by any means necessary. What starts as a whisper becomes a shout. And young Black people in Ferguson were shouting. Young Black people around the nation were screaming. In fact, this is what prompted my 18-year-old daughter to attend her first protest.

A silent protest on the campus of the University of Kentucky where she was mocked, called nigger and monkey and had things thrown at her. Similar to the Birmingham Children's Crusade police response, the young Black people in Ferguson were met with the National Guard, military-grade armored vehicles, tear gas, rubber bullets and sound cannons. When Black people protest they seem to always be met with resistance. When Black people protest there seems to be this need to shut them up. When Lebron James speaks out about the injustice in America, the media tells him to shut up and dribble a ball, however, when other people protest, they are given a national platform and a microphone. When Colin Kaepernick silently kneels to oppose injustice and police brutality, the President of the United States doesn't meet with him to hear his concerns, he calls him a son of a bitch, he is blackballed and collectively the nation calls him unpatriotic.

We didn't see positive media coverage covering Trayvon Martin or Mike Brown's death. We didn't see Buzzfeed coming to the homes of young Black activists to see how they were organizing. I don't recall glowing front-page media coverage. A multitude of politicians didn't rush to meet with young Black activists. I don't recall many politicians speaking out on their Twitter feeds to express concern and the their commitment to change the way Black people are policed in America. There was not a swell of White people standing up and saying we are going to march with you because this is an injustice. No one called these young Black people future leaders of the nation. Young Black activists are labeled Black Identity Extremists defined by the FBI as, "a movement that is deemed a violent threat, asserting that black activists' grievances about racialized police violence and inequities in the criminal justice system have spurred retaliatory violence against law enforcement officers and predicts that "perceptions of unjust treatment of African-Americans and the perceived unchallenged illegitimate actions of law enforcement will inspire premeditated attacks against law enforcement."

America seems to be suffering from a case of Selective Tragedy Support Syndrome.

How I wish when young Black people protested they were not met with resistance but the same acceptance that is being shown to the young White protestors in Parkland, Florida. I wish young Black activists didn't have to scream to be heard. I wish young Black activists didn't have to risk jail time or death to make their demands known. I wish they could have an audience with the politicians that have the power to impact policy. I wish politicians listened to young Black activists instead of proposing laws like Kentucky Representative C. Wesley Morgan suggest that makes protesting that interferes with the flow of traffic or a protest that has not been granted a permit punishable by up to a year in jail. I wish politicians like Representative C.

Wesley Morgan wouldn't propose laws where motorists "may not be held criminally or civilly liable for causing injury or death to a person" who is blocking traffic during such an event, unless it is proven that the motorist ran into the protesters deliberately."

I wish the media would be aware of how they frame the stories of young Black activists that are protesting. I wish the media would allow young Black activists to have an uninterrupted platform to voice their concerns. I wish young Black activists could garner global social media attention from celebrities and influencers to get their message across. I wish the police didn't mock young Black activists with "I Can Breathe" shirts while they protested the murder of Eric Garner whose last words were, "I Can't Breathe." I wish cities would take a look at current policies and legislation that continue to sustain and create racial inequity when young Black activists call it to their attention. I wish protesting for young Black activists wasn't such an uphill battle in America just to be heard.

How different this response has been in Parkland, Florida when you hold it up to so many young Black activists that have been screaming and continue to scream only to be met with silence and indifference.

This world will only change for the better when collectively this nation is disturbed, upset, pissed off and outraged at the senseless deaths of ALL people. DO NOT WAIT for it to be at your doorstep before you choose to become concerned. We were already screaming in Florida. We were yelling when Florida and this nation said it was acceptable for Trayvon Martin, a 17-year-old Black boy to be murdered walking home from a store in his neighborhood after buying a pack of Skittles and tea. We were shouting when the media portrayed Trayvon as a villain for wearing a hoodie. And we screamed and cried for justice when Florida allowed his murderer to walk out of a courtroom having been found not guilty, and then handed him back his gun. A gun that was used in the commission of a murder of a teenager, that he was allowed to auction off as a piece of "American History" for thousands of dollars. Perhaps you didn't hear us.

The Bell Tolls For You- Louisville Women's Rally
Women's March
Louisville, KY January 21, 2018

James Baldwin once said, "Artists are here to disturb the peace." So, today, I am just doing my job. I do not stand here to entertain you. Every time that I stand at a microphone I am speaking to shake this nation from its slumber. Consider these words the alarm.

We are at a critical point in this nation so, on this day, let's not pretend. Reality is what reality is, and the reality is 53% of White women that voted in the presidential election voted for a man that boasted about grabbing women by their genitalia. And even after all that we have been through 65% of White women that voted in the Alabama Election voted for a man that is a known racist and alleged pedophile. Today is not a day for celebration but of self-examination. Let me be transparent and honest because in 2018 #TimesUp for sugarcoating and whitewashing the truth.

And I decided, I have NO OTHER OPTION but to SPEAK THE TRUTH and ASK MY QUESTIONS that I asked months ago and allow the chips to fall where they may.

Where were you?

Where were you when we screamed for your husbands to stop raping us?

Where were you when Recy Taylor was begging for justice?

Where were you when Anita Hill was vilified for speaking up against sexual harassment?

Where were you when a former officer raped Black women?

Where were you when we buried our sons and daughters?

Where were you when Dajerria Becton had a knee on her back and was assaulted by an officer?

Where were you when a young Black girl was thrown across a classroom?

Where were you when Alesia Thomas uttered, "I Can't Breathe," after getting kicked in the throat and groin in the back of a patrol car in 2012 before it became a slogan?

Where were you when Jaquarrius, Ciara, Jojo, Keke Mesha Caldwell, Jamie Lee, and Chyna were murdered?

Where were you when we marched and shouted for Sandra, Rekia, and Aiyana?

Where were you when we demanded that Black women MATTERED in this fight against police brutality?

Where were you when this nation sterilized Black, Native American and Puerto Rican women without their consent?

Where were you when we were screaming? Your silence was deafeningly loud.

I could not stand here in good conscience in a pink pussycat hat and break my arm off to pat myself and others on the back when right now in this nation people who have lived in this country for decades are being ripped apart from their families.

Right now, the President calls countries in Africa, Haiti and El Salvador shitholes.

Right now, a man is in office that brags and boasts about sexually assaulting women.

Right now, OUR senator is using the healthcare of children as a bargaining chip.

Right now, OUR senator refuses to have the courage to call a man that has been hateful, divisive a racist.

Right now, laws are being written to allow doctors the freedom to discriminate against transgender individuals.

Right now this year 4 Black lesbians have been murdered!

Right now, a White man can kill 58 people and injure 851 people, and it's a blip on the TV screen.

Right now, the reproductive rights of women are once again being challenged.

RIGHT NOW! Here in Kentucky a former police officer of 20 years tells a recruit to shoot Black people. Right now, we have a governor that believes the cure for violence is praying it away all while instituting policies that seek to divide this state. Right now, here in Kentucky there is a proposed law for it to be legal to drive over citizens that are practicing their God-given right to protest all because they didn't have a permit. Right now, a bill is in the Kentucky Senate to allow private businesses and public institutions the right to discriminate against people if they don't align with their beliefs.

And now this swell of Women's Liberation has brought light to the Me Too Movement- a movement started by a Black woman named Tarana Burke yet commandeered by the masses. So today I stand with Ms. Burke and flip this hashtag and say #YouToo.

Because it was all good as long as it was not #YouToo.

It was okay for Black women to be raped by a police officer because it was not #YouToo.

It was okay as long as it was Indigenous women that were being raped and assaulted on their land with no recourse for justice until you realized it was happening to #YouToo.

It was okay for Black and Brown workers to be paid less because it was not #YouToo.

It was alright for Tamir Rice to be killed on a playground because it was not #YouToo.

It was just fine when it wasn't your reproductive rights because it wasn't #YouToo.

It was just fine when Sandra Bland was dead on a jailhouse floor because it wasn't #YouToo.

It was all good when it was just their jobs that were going to be lost until you realized it meant #YouToo.

It was all good that Trump was taking "their" healthcare because it was not #YouToo.

BUT NOW YOU SEE AS YOU TAKE OFF YOUR ROSE COLORED GLASSES! LOOK AROUND YOU! THE PLANE IS ON FIRE! AND THAT MEANS YOU TOO!

WE CANNOT SHOUT THIS ANY LOUDER! WE HAVE DONE OUR PART! MY SISTERS ARE TIRED!

THE ARC OF JUSTICE IS CARVED INTO THE BACKS OF BLACK AND BROWN BODIES! AND TODAY IS THE DAY FOR YOU TO TAKE A STAND! WHEN HEAR THE BELLS OF INJUSTICE RINGING, DO NOT ASK FOR WHOM THE BELL TOLLS? THE BELL IS TOLLING FOR YOU!

Black Women Do Not Exist To Save You

In a narrow win, Doug Jones has won the Senate race in Alabama. And by narrow, I mean less than 50,000 votes. So, before any of us break our arm off to pat ourselves on the back, remind yourself that this was a race between a man that prosecuted the KKK for the murder of 4 Black girls in a bombing at 16th Street Baptist Church and a man that is accused of being a pedophile. And it was still a narrow win. Let that sink in. We are that far gone in America that people considered alleged pedophile Roy Moore a viable candidate for Senate. As the rest of the nation waited for the results, articles begin to pop up online about Black people saving the Alabama election. And many people jumped on this sentiment as if this was a compliment. Then the hashtag, #TrustBlackWomen, started to make the Twitter rounds.

Admittedly, I have said Trust Black Women a million times because as a Black woman, I believe we hold the solutions to so many problems in the world. However, over time the mood and meaning of this hashtag started to shift for me. Trust Black women is now becoming synonymous with allow Black women to do the work that White people do not want to do. Trust Black women is now becoming synonymous with allow Black women to do the work for little to no pay. Trust Black women is now becoming synonymous with allow Black women to generate creative work and allow White people to take the credit. Trust Black women is now becoming synonymous with allow Black women to clean up our mess. Let me be clear, Black people, particularly Black women, do not exist to save White America from itself. Black people, particularly Black women, were not placed on this earth to rescue White people from themselves. To save yourself, you must take a long hard look in the mirror and put in the work.

Our existence, brilliance, creativity, strength, and ingenuity can never be validated by you posting a hashtag that means nothing when your actions do not support what you project online. Trust Black Women means nothing if your policies and institutions do not seek to elevate Black women and help combat issues that impact Black women.

Liking a tweet and posting #TrustBlackWomen so that you can get likes means nothing if you go to the voting booth and vote for someone that said slavery was a time when America was great. Quite frankly I feel like many of you post things that highlight Black women not because you genuinely care about Black women but because it garners you a lot of attention and likes. Your extent of concern when it comes to Black women is how many people will retweet your post because it's cool to be "down" with Black women online. However, the numbers don't lie.

Black women have warned you time and time again. And still, you do not listen. We warned you about Trump. You didn't listen. We warned you about the Governor race in Virginia. Still, you didn't listen. We warned you about Roy

Moore and once again, you didn't listen.

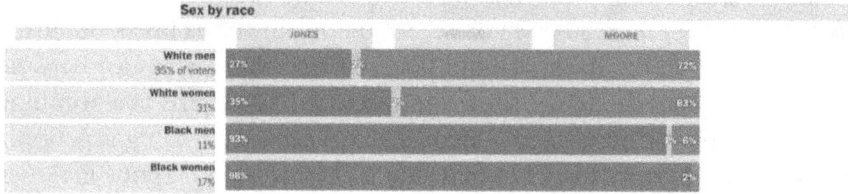

Sex by race

	JONES		MOORE
White men 35% of voters	27%		72%
White women 31%	35%		63%
Black men 11%	93%		6%
Black women 17%	98%		2%

Exit poll results in Alabama. (Results from the time this blog was written.)

At this point, I don't know what else you want. I don't want to receive one more email from a White woman that says, "Not me" or "Not All". I don't want to hear one more buzzword like intersectionality. I don't care how many Audre Lorde quotes you can recite.

Black women have done our share of the work.

Black women have carried the load until our backs have bent in agony.

Black women have smiled when all we wanted to do was cry.

Black women are tired.

Black women will no longer play wet nurse to White America.

At some point, you have to get off the breast and grow up.

We cannot nurse you through racial discord. We cannot hold your hand through fighting racism because both our hands are too busy fighting to save our lives and family's lives.

Throughout history, we have left breadcrumbs of our resistance. We have written the playbook on how to fight for liberation. From Oya to Vashti, to Harriet, to Fannie and beyond, we have drawn the blueprint.

It is time that you move from just hashtags to action. While I appreciate that you want to Trust Black Women, start learning how to trust yourself and do the work that will be required to shake a nation.

I Am NOT Writing So That You Can Feel Good

"Most anarchists believe the coming change can only come through a revolution, because the possessing class will not allow a peaceful change to take place; still we are willing to work for peace at any price, except at the price of liberty." – Lucy Parsons, orator and author once described by the Chicago Police Department as "More dangerous than a thousand rioters."

We are welcoming in 2018 with new resolutions and new possibilities. After the election results of 2016 many people who had been asleep at the wheel realized that indeed what many People of Color had been screaming for years was in fact true. The nation became consumed with thoughts of revolution, and I took it upon myself to use my voice to write my way through a year of racism, hypocrisy and outright lies. While I appreciated so many new faces and voices to the movement, I was not willing to gloss over the reasons why we found ourselves in a nation where racism was live, in color, and on display in the highest office in the land. While I appreciate that White people were joining in the conversation; I was not going to pretend as if some of the very beliefs and policies they helped uphold and benefit from, didn't get us to this place. Racism is woven into the very fabric of this nation, and I was not going to sit by and pretend as if we were all going to sing kumbayah and roast smores. There were some things that I needed to discuss with White America. In 2017, I wrote several blogs that garnered quite a bit of attention and with attention always comes criticism. And I am okay with that. Trust me; I do not write with the belief that most people will agree with me. I write with the inherent understanding that most will not. What isn't okay to me is that I switch up my message to appeal to the masses that want to feel good. That is not what I am called to do. I am tasked to speak truth to power.

Let me be clear in 2018 and beyond I am not today, tomorrow, or ever going to change my message so that you can feel good. I am not going to whitewash my message so that it is easier for you to read. I am not going to water down my message so that you can sleep better at night. I am not going to put blinders on when I write and pretend that history did not affect why we are where we are today. I refuse to remain silent so that you can rest in comfort, cognitive dissonance, and ignorance. I am not going to sugarcoat my message, so that is easier for you to swallow. Some medicine simply does not taste good going down. My job as a writer is to hold up a mirror to White America so that White America can catch of glimpse of itself in the past, the present and show a predictive future of where we are heading if we do not make some serious changes. History indeed does repeat itself, and in this slogan to Make America Great Again, some in America are merely trying to rewind time.

Not on my watch.

The argument that my style of writing turns people away from the movement doesn't shake my spirit. If reading my blog makes you decide that you no longer want to work for peace, justice, equality, and equity for all people then you were never really about that life. I am reminded of men like Andrew Goodman and Michael Schwerner who sacrificed their very lives just so that Black people could have the right to vote. I am reminded of Carl and Anne Branden a White couple that purchased a home in Louisville, Kentucky on behalf of Andrew and Charlotte Wade, a Black couple and their friends. Andrew was an electrician, however, was told that he would be denied a home in a White neighborhood. The Braden's purchased the home on behalf of him, and this kicked off a flurry of racist actions. Shootings outside the home, cross burning on the lawn and finally, a bomb planted and detonated underneath the bedroom of the Wade's two-year-old daughter. Thankfully no one was home at the time. The Braden's along with five other White people were arrested and charged with sedition another word for treason. They were accused of "hatching a Communist plot to buy the home, blow it up, touch off a race war and overthrow the Commonwealth of Kentucky." Carl Braden was convicted and spent eight months in prison before his conviction was later reversed and all other charges dropped against the remaining defendants. History is filled with White allies that have sacrificed everything even to death to fight for liberation, and you want me to change the way I write my blog because that may stop White people from joining the movement and it doesn't make you feel good?

If that is the case, I ask what are you in it for in the first place? Who told you that it would be easy? Who told you that you would always feel good? Who told you that you would not have to challenge your way of thinking? Who told you that fighting for justice meant you wouldn't have to face some hard truths? Who told you that you would not have to take a long hard look in the mirror? Who told you that you would not have to have difficult conversations with your family and friends about race? Who told you that it would not require sacrifice? If someone has told you any of those things, then they lied to you.

You want to me to change the way I write my blog because it makes you uncomfortable?

Burying your 7-year-old granddaughter shot to death by police while she slept on a couch is uncomfortable.

Having an officer toss you across a classroom like a ragdoll is uncomfortable.
Seeing your son dead in the street for over 4 hours is uncomfortable.

Having a police officer wrestle you to the ground in an illegal chokehold while you whisper, "I can't breathe" until you die is uncomfortable.

Being told your fiancé has been shot and killed by the police the morning of your wedding is uncomfortable. Your son going out for Skittles and tea and never coming home again is uncomfortable. Being raped by White men and the justice system does nothing because you are a Black woman is uncomfortable.

Walking miles to work because you are fighting for the right to sit up front on a bus is uncomfortable.

Getting a phone call that your daughter who was on her way to a new journey in her life is dead on a jailhouse floor is uncomfortable.

Being told that your son was murdered in jail because the was placed in a shower with water as hot as 180 degrees, is uncomfortable.

Being nervous every single time you get in your car to drive because you are Black is uncomfortable.

Existing in a world where your skin is your sentence, is uncomfortable.

Black people dwell in the realm of being uncomfortable every single day.

So, if you visit my blog or read any of my books, expecting to cuddle up with a steamy cup of hot cocoa and "Please-give-me-a-reward-for-doing-the-right-thing" cookies, I don't bake so I suggest you stop right here.

Replying to @HannahDrake628

Your anger is understandable & your writing has struck a chord, but please - celebrate white progress, even when it's slow and self serving, it's still progress. Let's reach those other white women who voted for Trump and Moore together.

However, if you visit my blog or read any of my books with the knowledge and understanding that you will be challenged to think and then act differently when it comes to race relations in this nation, you are in the right location. Am I infallible? No. Will I write things where I may have gotten something wrong? Possibly. Am I open to criticism? Indeed. Will we have intriguing conversations that challenge both of us? I hope so! I do not know what the future holds for Write Some Shit, but I promise to speak my truth, unfiltered and unapologetically. It may not feel good, but I believe it is good for the betterment of us and for this country.

Remember, I am not writing to entertain you. I am writing to shake a nation.

Hannah L. Drake

"No one is in control of your art, your gift, or your narrative except you.
Tell your story."

Recently selected as a 2017 Hadley Creatives, Hannah Drake is an author, speaker, poet, and activist that offers a powerful and motivational message. Hannah's blog writesomeshit.com offering commentary on politics, feminism, race, and was recently featured in Cosmo. Hannah promises that her message will be thought-provoking and at times challenging but believes it is in the uncomfortable spaces that change can take place. ***"My sole purpose in speaking and writing is not that I entertain you. I am writing to shake a nation."***

Also Available By Hannah L. Drake
Hannah's Plea-Poetry for the Soul,
Anticipation,
Life Lived In Color,
In Spite of My Chains,
For Such A Time As This
So Many Things I Want to Tell You-Life Lessons for the Journey.
Views from the Back Pew
Fragile Destiny

Website
www.hannahldrake.com

Blog
www.writesomeshit.com

Email
hld@hannahldrake.com

Follow Me
Twitter HannahDrake628
Instagram HannahDrake628
Facebook Hannah Drake

YouTube Videos
All You Had To Do Was Play The Game, Boy
https://www.youtube.com/watch?v=OjiuvLzhCrI&t=33s
Black Women Do Not Exist to Save You
https://www.youtube.com/watch?v=r8oESw6HBp4&t=13s
10 & 2
https://www.youtube.com/watch?v=WvDrrzSkLpE&t=94s

www.ingramcontent.com/pod-product-compliance
Lightning Source LLC
Chambersburg PA
CBHW081414270326
41931CB00015B/3270